Me and the
BIG BANG

Confessions of a Modern-Day Mystic

DR. RICHEY NOVAK

iUniverse, Inc.
New York   Bloomington

Me and the Big Bang
Confessions of a Modern-Day Mystic

iUniverse books may be ordered through booksellers or by contacting:

iUniverse
1663 Liberty Drive
Bloomington, IN 47403
www.iuniverse.com
1-800-Authors (1-800-288-4677)

ISBN: 978-1-4502-3411-5 (pbk)
ISBN: 978-1-4502-3412-2 (cloth)
ISBN: 978-1-4502-3413-9 (ebk)

Library of Congress Control Number: 2010907917

Printed in the United States of America

iUniverse rev. date: 6/24/2010

Preface

I am here.
The universe is here.
There is a relationship between us.
What is that relationship?
I want to understand it.

I am a product of the universe.
I consist of universal matter and energy.
Universal laws are manifested in me.
The process of producing me was complex.
Producing me took a long time.
And if me, then likely also you.

Is consciousness a product of the universe or of me?
I think it may be a product of me,
And of the many similar minds who taught me.
We are all creations of the universe.
The universe is in part a creation of us.

Articulate humans create in an intellectual world of theories and ideas,
In much the same way that the universe creates in a physical world.
The universe creates us, physically.
And we create the universe, intellectually.
This is the relationship between man and the universe.

Consciousness and self-awareness are things which the universe produces,
But only through man.
Alone, the universe cannot produce articulate consciousness.
Just as man cannot produce the physical universe.
Consciousness is man's and the universe's crowning achievement.

Exploring this man-universe relationship,
Is what *Me and the Big Bang* is all about.

Setting the scene

It was July, 1952, and I was in Paris.
I was very serious about life and angry with America.
The month before I had been discharged after five years active duty in the Navy.
The previous year and a half were in Japan and Korea where our light cruiser
had routinely bombed the mountainous shoreline of the Inchon peninsula,
For reasons I could not understand, something about containing communism.

When I joined right out of high school in 1945, I thought I knew why: To
defend America from tyranny.
I served three and a half years in the Atlantic and Mediterranean occupation
fleets.
Then with the G.I. Bill I started college, studying philosophy and languages.
After two years they recalled me to participate in the "Police Action" in Korea.
I didn't want to go.
I was preparing to become a pastor in the Presbyterian church.

So there I was in Paris, 25 years old, healthy, G.I. Bill, energetic, interested in
French, German, Europe, philosophy, war and peace, civilization, women,
And super serious about most everything.
I lost my Christianity in Japan when I saw Christian creches populated by
Japanese Marys, Josephs, and Jesuses.
And I knew all along that Mary should look like a clean-cut Texas—or at
least an American—girl.
And little baby Jesus surely did not have slant eyes.

Paris, the Sorbonne, and a beautiful German fellow-student, helped me
outgrow my native Texas, country-bumpkin naiveté.
But she did not quite succeed in changing my serious approach to most things.
Especially things like meaning, purpose, and what the hell life is all about.
She encourages me to write children's books!
She thinks I'm funny!
She laughs a lot, at and with me.
She's my greatest teacher.

I'm glad I did not stay in Japan and become a Zen Buddhist.
Or in America and become a Christian minister.
I became a professor of humanities instead.

Setting the scene #2

The following is a long, somewhat rambling internal monologue,
About the most interesting topics I know: life, thinking, meaning, purpose,
And trying to make sense of the human situation.
It is designed as a friendly conversation and sharing of ideas,
It makes no pretense of being an academic study or a scientific inquiry.
It is an intimate talk with myself and an imaginary friend,
Who is also a searcher and a seeker.
It is not filled with footnotes or scholarly references,
But a sympathetic reader will find the factual material essentially correct.

The famous German poet Goethe wrote, read, and reviewed a lot of books.
He said there are only three questions to ask about a book:
What does the author plan to do?
Is that a meaningful, worthwhile project to undertake?
How well does he accomplish what he set out to do?

I have taken his advice to heart while writing this book.
I respond to Goethe's questions in the following way:
First, I want to grasp as well as I can modern science's story of the universe,
And then my place as a typical human within that story.
Second, given my background, experience, and interests,
The project strikes me as vast but quite feasible and legitimate,
And probably of interest to many other curious modern people.
Third, the reader will have to decide how well or poorly I have done.
My ambition has been to be as clear, honest, and straightforward as possible,
With two complex topics: me and the Big Bang..

The book will strike some as too personal and therefore limited,
But that is the only way I know how to write.
There is a flesh-and-blood person behind every book,
And that person is necessarily part of the book,
Whether it shows or not.

Contents

Introduction

My formative high school years, age 13 through 17, were exactly the years of World War II in America, and I spent them in Amarillo, Texas. Immediately after graduation in 1945 I joined the US Navy and spent five years traveling around the world. As a naive youngster from a small town I was curious but poorly informed about the make-up of the world and its peoples. The major distinction in my mind concerning my fellow human beings was who had accepted Jesus as his personal savior, was saved and going to heaven, and who was lost and on his way to hell and eternal damnation. My view of the physical world and the universe was that God had created them and all living creatures in 4004 B.C. as depicted in the first chapters of Genesis and calculated by Bishop Ussher about 1650.

This world view stayed with me until my early twenties, and I was troubled by what I was experiencing personally and directly and its clash with the fundamentalist religious story that I had been indoctrinated with early in life. Three books helped me out of my muddle by offering a more comprehensive and realistic view of reality. The first one, *The Story of Mankind,* written by Henrik Willem Van Loon in 1921, offered the reader a simple, almost childlike story of creation, the galaxies and stars, including evolution, the dinosaurs, the rise and fall of civilizations, etc. I found it shocking but very exciting. The second book was H.G. Wells' *Outline of History,* written in 1920, which told essentially the same story but more persuasively and in greater detail. Still later, after my Navy travels had taken me all over America, plus parts of Europe, Japan, and Korea, I discovered Will and Ariel Durant's monumental *Story of Civilization* in eleven volumes, written in 1945-1975. I have read and re-read these splendid Durant books over the years.

These three works came at the right time in my life and, together with my travels, studies, and personal experiences, they helped me greatly to have a broader, more informed, and more realistic world view. I would like in this essay to present in outline form what I have learned about the make-up of the universe, plus my own answer to the question, "What's it all about?" I have outlined in broad strokes the stages in the path that I have taken in my quest for meaning and purpose in life. My hope is that my ideas and experiences may help other searchers along the way, particularly in terms of encouraging them to discover their own thoughts and to determine their own path in life.

My explanations are interspersed from time to time with brief essays, reflections, and short items of insight that seem to fit well into one chapter or the other. It will be obvious from the outset that this little book is a purely personal investigation, with all the limitations and shortcomings which that entails, but it's the kind of intimate, honest communication from an older, experienced person that I would have greatly welcomed as a youngster.

Getting started

During the academic year 1952-53, after military service and two years of college, I attended a special, year-long course in French language and culture at the Sorbonne at the University of Paris. It was called *Cours de Civilization Française pour les Étrangers* and was given by some of the top professors of the university. There were perhaps 400 foreign students from around the world taking part in the large general lectures given every morning from 8:00 until 12:00, Monday through Saturday. In the afternoon we attended language classes according to our level of proficiency in French as determined by an entrance exam given at the beginning of the year. It was a splendid course and is, as far as I know, still being given every year.

The designers of the course had a clear objective in mind: to have people understand France. They reached that goal by giving interested students a good general introduction to France by presenting different approaches or perspectives to the complex subject of French civilization. This meant one-hour lectures three times a week for a year on diverse topics such as French history, geography, literature, art, philosophy, history and structure of the language. The lectures were well organized and delivered in 45 minute sessions by excellent professors without interruption or discussion. Discussion of the material was relegated to the afternoons in two-hour sessions in the language classes with other staff members. All in all, this was some of the best teaching and organization of courses that I have ever experienced in my long academic life. The result of the year's course was that I feel even now, many years later, that I have a good general grasp of France and its civilization.

I had just come from the "police action" that America was undertaking

2

in Korea and had been discharged from the US Navy only a couple of months before arriving in Paris. The Korean War had left me confused about American politics and values, and I was ready to experience some new cultural and philosophical perspectives. I found a place to live in a student boarding house with a dozen French students, and we had many lively discussions during our communal lunch and supper meetings around a huge table. The French had just been expelled from Vietnam and Cambodia, so my French colleagues were quite sensitive to what was happening in that part of the world and were curious about what I thought about the American involvement in Asia, and about General Eisenhower's bid for the White House. I found that life in this French pension was a perfect supplement, both linguistically and culturally, to my formal academic studies at the Sorbonne. The G.I. Bill was paying my tuition, plus books, and giving me $75 a month in addition, which was quite enough to cover my basic expenses, so I was all set to settle in for an exciting life-altering experience. And it turned out to be exactly that, especially after I started dreaming in French my third or fourth month in Paris.

Schematically, the course at the university would look something like this: an oval-shaped sketch with various topics focusing on a central goal:

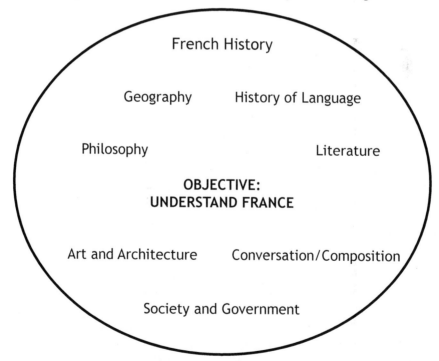

In the following academic year, thanks again to the G.I. Bill, I had a similar year-long course in Heidelberg on German language and culture, but this second course, although interesting and well done, was far less successful than the one in Paris. Years later, a similar course in Mexico City gave me a good introduction to Mexican life and culture, but again, not on the excellent level of the French program.

My point in all this personal information is to say that I found it is possible to learn a great deal of fundamental information about complex subjects in a short time if the material is well-organized and kept general, stressing the major points and giving the important results without confusing the learner with excessive details, interpretations, and commentary, provided, of course, that the learner is truly interested in the subject matter. This is the plan that I want to carry out here in this book.

My subject matter in this essay is vast, and some readers may think that the book itself is an impossible and useless undertaking. There are indeed many negative things to say about a book with the ambitious title and sub-subtitle, *Me and the Big Bang: Confessions of a modern-day mystic*, but the importance and the universal nature of the subject matter override such reservations. I think virtually all human beings, under various circumstance in their lives, sometimes truly wonder, "What is my life all about? Is this all there is?" This essay proposes to give my answers to those questions in a broad, general way.

Some 200 years ago the great German poet Goethe, one of the most intelligent and well-informed men of his time, and perhaps indeed of any time, said, "He who cannot give an historical account of some 3000 years, is a poor devil who must live from day to day,"(*Wer sich nicht von 3000 Jahren Rechenschaft kann geben, ist ein armer Tor und muss von Tag zu Tage leben*). I think this was Goethe's way of saying that the person curious about the meaning of his life must have a larger general perspective or framework in which to see his own personal existence. Otherwise, he is buffeted and tossed about by daily circumstances and forces which he can scarcely grasp at all. All of us are only parts of a larger whole, and it is imperative to have some idea of what that larger whole might look like, but getting such a perspective takes a lot of doing. It doesn't just happen by itself.

I think Goethe was obviously referring to the origin and development of civilization over the last 3000 years, and the need to have some general idea about that development and the individual's place in it. In terms of what modern scientists tell us about the origin of life and its terrestrial background, Goethe was a few billion years short of the mark. That is to say that today a person truly curious about his own life needs to, and is able to, have a far vaster backdrop against which to see his own personal existence. We are now in a position—as far as I have been able to understand modern scientific developments—to see ourselves as being directly and physically related to the origins of the universe some 13-14 billion years ago. If the American astronomer Carl Sagan is to be believed, we are all "star stuff" and able to see ourselves in such a light.

But I am getting ahead of my story and need to go back to clarity and simplicity. On the following page I have reduced my basic ideas to a simple scheme similar to that of my Sorbonne studies. There I show the entire structure of my book, going from the origin of the universe through many stages and developments to arrive at a clear crisp awareness of my existence as I sit here writing and thinking about all this, and about my attempt to explain my ideas to you, an unknown fellow human who may be thinking through these words long after I am gone.

This is obviously heavy stuff, and many, perhaps even most, people will have absolutely no taste for it. That is perfectly okay with me, since I am not writing for them. But the person who is more than just casually curious about the fact that he is conscious and alive may find my one-page outline and my book interesting and enlightening, perhaps even fun, just as I have. The book is aimed essentially at seekers and searchers, and there are probably more of these than we are aware of.

I have spent a lifetime working out a meaningful answer to my question, "What is it all about?" I want to show in this essay the path I have taken in coming to an answer which for me is both comprehensive and satisfying. But this is my answer and can be helpful only as a guide or stimulus for others. You will have to work out for yourself your own answers if you seriously ask yourself the question. There are a thousand reasons why my answers cannot be your answers: age, gender, body build, nationality, natal family, conjugal family, experience, sexual orientation, education, profession, work experience, travel, health, wealth, etc.

The serious question, properly framed or focused, has to be, I think, "What is MY life all about?" But since you and I are both closely tied in to a lot of other humans, many aspects of our answers will have close overtones with the answers of other people, but I believe that the deeper we go into a serious attempt to give a meaningful answer, the more personal and idiosyncratic our answer will be. I think it may ultimately come down to me and the universe: I am here, the universe is here, and what is our relationship to one another? I believe in the final analysis it may become a sort of mystical solution for each individual seriously searching for more than superficial answers. Here is my answer in a nutshell: The cosmos has created me and others to answer the universal call to wake up out of our half-sleep and become alertly aware of the miracle of existence. On its extreme outer fringes, I think the universe is becoming conscious of itself through humans, who, in their own way and over the millennia, have developed an increasing sense of general awareness through art, poetry, religion, philosophy, science, and mysticism.

In the following chart, imagine a large oval of topics focusing on the central theme of understanding human life, the Socratic admonition: "Know thyself!" Imagine also that there are two arrows at the top of the page curving downwards, one to the left and one to the right. One arrow suggests that we start with the Big Bang, the very beginning of everything, and make our way through a circle of many developmental stages to arrive finally at personal awareness. The other arrow starts with our intense personal awareness here and now and moves backwards through an equal number of stages explaining how we became so aware, all the way back to the origins of the universe. One arrow therefore goes theoretically from the very big picture to the individual person, while the other arrow goes from specific individual awareness back to the beginning general picture and largest context. In practice, of course, we bounce around all over the place with ease and facility, and it doesn't really matter where we start and stop. We end up at the same point: me and the universe, and the relationship between us.

START AND END HERE

I. Creation of Universe
Time, space, matter, the Big Bang

X. Mystical Insights

II. Evolution of Life
Life as a struggle

IX. Psychology, Awareness

III. Human Evolution

**OBJECTIVE:
UNDERSTANDING HUMAN LIFE**

VIII. Art, Music, Literature

IV. Society, Economy,
Political Systems, War

VII. Science and Technology V. Myths and Religions

VI. Philosophy

Heavy thoughts

How can there be meaning and personal significance in the vast impersonal picture of the cosmos which modern science draws for us? For most people, meaning and significance come from the merely human context, but humanity and the earth are local and provincial in terms of the larger reality of what's out there. I think the meaning and significance of my life will lie ultimately in my participation in the unrolling of the universe, in my attempt to see myself and my fellow humans as active participants in the evolution of the total reality of what's there.

From what I have been able to understand thus far about the creation of the universe, the constituent elements or building blocks of my physical body (energy, matter, chemicals) came into being soon after the Big Bang. My spiritual, intellectual, and emotional parts have come into being only much later on the more local, provincial level of the earth and its life forms many billions of years after the Big Bang. Consciousness, man's crowning glory, has been formed only recently through the universal elements of speech and social living, plus the history and development of language in general and the English language in particular through millions of former users. My American heritage, and my good fortune of having been able to study many of the great poets, mystics, philosophers, and thinkers of humanity have also played a crucial role in my coming into consciousness, my awakening. All of this has culminated in a lively, keen awareness of being the heir of a colorful human heritage and history.

But all this is still local and provincial in terms of the totality of things that exist. I try to break this provincial barrier by relating my own consciousness to the Big Bang and by seeing humanity as being involved in the construction of an expanding, evolving reality which has shifted from a physical and material level to one of awareness, ideas, and knowledge. The Big Bang created the physical universe, and now the human mind—and perhaps other forms of intelligence in other parts of the universe—creates intellectual and emotional order through language and awareness. In this way, humans become co-creators of the universe just as Adam became God's co-creator in the Garden of Eden by naming the animals and telling them what they were.

There are in my view two fundamental and co-equal aspects of the universe: the physical and the intellectual or rational. By "physical" I mean material things such as water, stones, mountains, living creatures, suns, stars, galaxies, etc. and the physical laws which hold them all together and cause them to act and react as they do. The creation of this physical aspect of reality and the forces holding everything together was done by powers and entities that are still largely unknown. By "intellectual or rational" aspects of the universe, I mean an awareness or knowledge of these material objects and their underlying laws. The intellect obviously does not create in the physical realm; its job is to create and describe in the realm of understanding and knowledge. Conversely, the physical universe obviously does not produce theories, knowledge, and awareness; this is done by minds and intellects.

Modern astronomers and astrophysicists have done a tremendous amount of creative work by trying to explain the origin and size of the cosmos, in much the same way as Newton who fleshed out parts of the general plan of the universe by explaining universal gravity and the laws of motion. In this way, scientists, poets, and mystics help the universe become aware of itself by doing things which the physical universe itself cannot do: create words and explanations. In doing so, they also give additional meaning to their own lives above and beyond the local, provincial scheme of the solar system. Man can save himself from being a helpless creature imprisoned in a vast mechanical and chemical universe by participating in the total creative process. We save ourselves, create ourselves, and create the universe at the same time.

What is it all about?

We wake up running. This is to say that we become conscious of our existence only after we have been living quite a few years and have already become so programmed that we are no longer able to ask big questions in an unbiased, unencumbered sense. We are so locked into our specific language and cultural mores that we are in some meaningful sense in a deep hypnotic cultural trance. I think the purpose of life is to wake up and come out of this hypnotic trance in which we are imprisoned and thereby to experience our existence in this world as vibrantly and directly as possible. Escaping the trance is difficult for many reasons, one of the main ones being that you have to do it yourself, since virtually no one else knows what you are talking about. The trance varies a little from culture to culture, but in broad outline form it is always the same: Be like everyone else, think the same thoughts, hold the same values, believe the same things, live the way all your fellows are living, fit into the mold. This is the human part of our nature; the divine part whispers a quite different song: Know yourself, be yourself, follow your own inner calling, whatever it may be and whatever it may cost. Get as close to reality as possible. It seems to me that this divine call is what human life in a higher sense is about, and our purpose in life is to discover and fulfill our highest nature.

Doing so is an intense activity. It usually brings us into close interaction with our fellow humans, and we have to learn how to deal with them easily and productively; otherwise they can block our development or even terminate our existence. Our patron saints Socrates, Jesus, Gandhi, and Martin Luther King taught us that at the cost of their life. We need to listen to them carefully and learn from their example.

A few words about perhaps the most important element in our life: our fellow humans. We humans are strange creatures and combine within ourselves so many opposites and self-contradictions that only a human could even imagine them: love and hate, gods and demons, spirituality and sensuality, childlike play and wisdom of the ages, male and female, war and peace, living and dying. Many things tie us all together: joy, laughter, love of family and friends, apprehension and fear of the unknown, the strength of emotions, the love of ideals and universals, the excitement of dynamic activity and group enterprises. Many of these same tendencies also drive us into cliques and groups which can readily and ruthlessly destroy one another. War is probably the best example and brings out both the best and the worst in us.

People believe essentially what they want and need to believe to make sense of their lives. To fulfill the human desire to know, we make up the most unbelievable stories, myths, and legends to explain things to ourselves and one another. Such creations usually go by the name of religion and find willing ears in many quarters. Among those people who want a more detailed explanation, philosophy, and from it, the various sciences, originated. Science now satisfies our desire to know by telling us a fascinating story so complex that most of us soon lose interest and settle for a shorthand answer. This short answer concerns the Big Bang some 14 billion years ago, the formation of our local solar system and the earth some 5 billion years ago, the creation of one-celled organisms some 3 to 4 billion years ago, the gradual development and evolution of innumerable species of life, and eventually humans and civilizations, including you and me today.

Big Bang language

At the end of each section of this book I want to make some personal remarks on how the content of that particular discussion affects me. For example, I'm a product of the Big Bang, as is everything and everyone else in the world, but what is the significance of that for me personally? I sometimes wonder if there might be some sort of mark or scar or residual memory built into me and all other things of that experience of the Big Bang. I remember reading a book many years ago by Timothy Leary, the inventor of LSD, entitled *The Politics of Ecstasy*. In it, he presented the idea that in all our cells we have a kind of residual memory which comes to the fore from time to time under certain circumstances and conditions, usually fostered by LSD. He had an unusual but persuasive argument which impressed me at the time, similar to Carl Gustav Jung's notion of a collective unconsciousness. I didn't try Leary's LSD, but I have talked to people who did, and they tell of strange ideas and pictures passing through their minds and emotions under the influence of this drug. I want to do my experiments without drugs, with just my mind, and thereby remain as sober as possible.

I sometimes have the feeling that 14 billion years of existence must have left some trace of itself in all of us, traces of which we are largely unaware but can become conscious of under the proper conditions of attention and concentration. By proper conditions and concentration I do not mean some drug induced alteration of the mind; I mean simply a clear awareness of what we can know and can attend to concerning our human past. We know, for example, that the hair on our body relates us to all mammals, and that the heart pumping blood through our system relates us to virtually all animals with a similar pump. We also know that the chemical make-up of our body relates us to all chemical structures in the universe, since they also have the same chemicals, by and large, as we do. We don't need LSD, marijuana, alcohol, or any other stimulant to make us aware of our chemical connection to everything in the cosmos. Knowledge and quiet reflection can suffice to induce the appropriate state of awareness. The universality of energy, matter, time, space, and motion also await our sensitive and critical investigation as to how we are related to them and they to us.

It seems to me that there is a great deal that we can know about ourselves and the universe simply by sitting in our rocking chair and thinking about being here on earth. We have, of course, no direct memory of a great noise, flash of blinding light, intense heat, or sensation of being hurtled through space at a tremendous speed—all the things which scientists say were associated with the Big Bang—and yet in some strange sense that was the beginning of everything, including you and me. Trying to understand our origin and history will lead us through many stages, and at every step our sense of awareness and inter-connectedness will increase as we become more and more cognizant of what makes us the way we are. The discovery of DNA, for example, tells us that all living creatures are in some sense closely associated and share the same beginnings, and that our closest animal relative, the chimpanzee, is genetically less than 2% different from us. Just this one bit of knowledge is enough to boggle the mind, at least mine.

Our normal daily languages is an example of what I'm trying to explain here. We all speak our native language easily and without problem: English, German, Farsi, or Japanese. Normally we are completely unaware of what a complex and fascinating thing we are doing when we say a simple sentence to one another. Grammar, phonetics, vocabulary, and ideas come flowing out of us effortlessly, and we understand each other so easily that we are puzzled to hear that using our commonplace language borders on the miraculous. We are amazed to learn that physiologically and neurologically our daily speech is an on-going and universal human miracle which has evolved over millions of years and relates us back to our earliest primate ancestors struggling to make themselves understood linguistically through grunts, groans, gestures, flashes of emotion, etc. Language is so universal and so commonplace among all humans that we have to make a conscious effort to recognize its miraculous nature. Language makes us human. Learning a foreign language as an adult soon makes us aware, sometimes painfully so, of its complexity.

On a closer level, the story of the English language takes us back over the centuries to Middle English and Chaucer's *Canterbury Tales*, Old English or Anglo-Saxon and the legend of *Beowulf*, then to a larger group of languages called the Germanic family, itself the offspring of a still-larger Indo-European group five to ten thousand years ago. The story becomes vaguer and more uncertain as we go back further still to the big questions of when and where human language originated, how and why our distant ancestors started communicating with one another many thousands of years ago, and what profound effect this tool of articulate language had on their way of life. We don't know the answers to these questions, but we do know that language is an essential characteristic of being human, and that our daily speech links us historically with our very distant past. The science of etymology—the origin of words—makes it clear that each word in every language has a special history and must have been created or invented by some individual or group in the nebulous past. Our English vocabulary didn't just happen by itself, and by using it we are deeply indebted to our ancestors who created it long ago.

What's my point in all this? The point is that with little or no formal study, a conscious look at normal human activity today can teach us a great deal about our history and evolution. With a little imagination we can relate to and understand to some extent our distant forbearers living under trying circumstances and struggling to survive and flourish. They must have been energetic, intelligent, and creative individuals of whom we can be justly proud. As speakers of a modern language today, we are inheritors of their struggles and successes. Language is only one of the many such threads that, with a little thoughtful reflection, can lead us back to our early origins and developments. Others include upright posture, loss of body hair, bipedal locomotion, stereoscopic vision, the prehensile thumb, hand-eye coordination, and so forth, all of which are essential human characteristics and near-miracles once we see them in the proper light. But they are all so commonplace among all societies that we easily fail to recognize their unique contribution to making us human. To help see them in the proper light is one of the major goals of this essay.

Book synopsis

I want to become as aware as possible of who and what I am, where and with whom I am living, the country and the times in which I live, what I have spent my life doing, what my relationship to the earth and the cosmos is, and similar things. I have worked out a helpful method for allowing me to concentrate more sharply and become more aware. My method is to practice focusing closely on a specific thing, situation, or person. I do this daily, for example, by watching my wife and thinking about her, talking to her about the many things we have done together, the many years we have had together, specific happy trips and occasions, telling her how much I appreciate her and am thankful for all the things she has done for me. I find that this helps me closely focus on her, her great attributes, and our life together. This method especially increases and enhances my awareness of her, of me, of our personal relationship, and of human relationships in general. It turns out to be very worthwhile for her as well.

With this method I have gained an important insight through this first-hand experience with Ziggy: namely, that by conscious concentration and awareness on something clear-cut and specific I can learn a great deal and enormously enrich my life. Having practiced on innumerable smaller items (e.g., the stomach as a miraculous chemical factory, the shape of the ear, the distinction between vowels and consonants, the mind-body relationship), I want now to apply this technique to the big questions which I have been working on practically all my life: What is my life all about? Does it have any larger meaning? What is my role in the overall drama of existence? Where did I (and all these other people, animals, things) come from, and where am I (and they) going? In this book I am obviously regarding myself as a spokesman for all mankind and not as some special person.

One of the big lessons to be learned in philosophy and in life is the importance of seeing the part in its relationship to the whole. It is an important lesson, but one hard to learn, especially in matters relating to us personally. We experience ourselves and our problems vibrantly and acutely; we concentrate on them closely with great intensity, but usually without paying proper attention to the larger context into which they fit and in terms of which they must be understood. Without that larger context, we are essentially trapped in our own often incomprehensible and insoluble situation, trapped in the prison of our own personality.

Parts must be understood in terms of the whole. I think this is absolutely essential in trying to come to terms with anything. Text without context is misleading and incomplete. I am quite aware of being only one part of a larger society, a nation, mankind, life forms on earth, just as I am aware that my home planet is only one small part of the solar system, the Milky Way, and of the total universe. And I am also quite aware that, while seeming to be an independent, more-or-less self-contained entity, I and all these other people and things are interrelated and have a complex history of origin, development, and evolution. If I am to follow the Socratic maxim to "Know thyself," I must try to see the larger whole of which I am but a part, the great drama in which I and the rest of us have only minuscule roles. In this essay I want to note some of the major stations in the universe's creation of my body and mind.

So, "What is our human life all about?" is my question, studying parts and wholes is my method, and developing an ever-increasing sense of awareness while trying to answer my question is my goal. That's what this little book is about.

Chapter 1.
The Big Bang

Reading instructions

The following pages contain many really unusual ideas, many from the astrophysicists and a number from me. The ideas of the scientists and theorists about the origin of the universe are readily available in books, magazines, T.V. films, and the internet, and I have freely borrowed from all of them to instruct myself concerning the Big Bang. It is tough going. The ideas are often difficult to grasp, and much I simply have not understood. The other ideas in the text are my reactions and comments on these mind-boggling notions on the origins of *everything,* including you and me. To comprehend the scientists as well as me, I suggest we take an idea from the American psychotherapist Carl Rogers and apply it to this text.

Rogers asked himself, "How is it that one imperfect human can understand and help another imperfect human solve his problems?" He came up with the notion of an "unconditional positive regard." This is the notion that if the therapist can put aside his own prejudices and agenda unconditionally for the short 50-minute therapy session and take what the client says in the most positive way possible, while at the same time regarding the client as a serious human being trying to explain himself, some sort of human and psychological magic takes place and progress can be made. My suggestion here is similar: that the reader put aside his own thoughts and reservations as far as possible, try to read and think through a few pages at a time, and regard the writer as a serious thinker struggling to explain some admittedly complicated thoughts. This will be especially helpful towards the end of the book when I try to summarize the whole enterprise and apply it to life in general.

How it all started.

In 1927, the Belgian scientist George Lemâitre was doing pioneering work in applying Einstein's theory of general relativity to cosmology. He published an article that preceded Hubble's landmark article on the redshift of galaxies (i.e. they are moving away from one another) by two years. He derived what later became known as Hubble's law and proposed it as a generic phenomenon in relativistic cosmology. In doing so, he developed a revolutionary theory on the origin of the universe. He called his theory a 'hypothesis of the primeval atom,' and described his idea as the cosmic egg exploding at the moment of creation. It became better known later as the 'Big Bang.' Lemâitre discussed the theory with Einstein at an international conference in Brussels in 1927, but Einstein dismissed it out of hand, saying that the calculations were correct but Lemâitre's physics was 'abominable,' adding that not all good mathematics leads to correct theories. Nevertheless, in 1931 Lemâitre published his expanded theory of the 'primitive atom' and with it changed the course of cosmology.

Two years later, working at the Mount Wilson Observatory in California, Edwin Hubble was studying a curious phenomenon caused by the Doppler effect called the redshift of galaxies. He observed that the galaxies were all moving away from each other at great speed and theorized that they must at one time have been close together. His conclusion: The universe is expanding, as suggested by Lemâitre. However, Lemâitre was the first to propose that the expansion explains the redshift of galaxies and to conclude that an initial creation-like event must have occurred in the distant past.

As used by cosmologists, the term 'Big Bang,' generally refers to the idea that the universe has expanded from a primordial hot and dense initial condition called a singularity at some finite time in the past, and that space itself has been expanding ever since, carrying the galaxies with it. It is pleasant to note that after Hubble's discovery with its substantiating data was published, Einstein quickly and publicly endorsed Lemâitre's theory, helping both the theory and its proposer get fast recognition. In January 1933, Lemâitre and Einstein traveled to California for a series of seminars. After the Belgian detailed his theory at the conference, Einstein stood up, applauded, and is supposed to have said, "This is the most beautiful and satisfactory explanation of creation to which I have ever listened."

Now, as we look into this theory, we discover that scientists are telling us a fantastic story about how *everything* started: time, space, matter, motion, the stars and galaxies, the chemical elements, the earth, all life forms, and eventually you and me. It is such an amazing story that it is hard indeed to get one's mind around it. And yet virtually all the leading thinkers in science give us essentially the same explanation, and it seems to me that any serious searcher must have at least a nodding acquaintance with these wondrous ideas. These theorists, of course, catch a lot of flak from religious leaders, conservatives, the naive, and the uninformed. But they stick to their guns and assert that the universe is about 14 billion years old and started with a mighty explosion called "The Big Bang." According to this story, in the beginning all matter and energy of the universe, all the future galaxies, stars, planets, oceans, mountains—*the essential building material of everything* was tightly compressed into an extremely small bundle, perhaps the size of a bowling ball, an orange, or even smaller. I find this virtually impossible to conceive of, but that is what we must accept if we are to grasp the theory.

Where this hot, highly packed ball of material and energy came from, what was there before it exploded, who or what was responsible for the whole thing, etc., are questions still unresolved. But somehow, say the theorists, the whole thing was inexplicably so densely packed that it could no longer contained itself and exploded with a mighty bang—a big, big bang. It then started expanding, cooling, and evolving in every possible direction, with the energy and matter morphing in time into galaxies, nebulae, stars, eventually planets and moons, and finally life forms, at least here on earth. Time, space, and all the chemical elements eventually got created during the course of this still-continuing expansion. According to the theory, all matter is composed of essentially the same chemical elements throughout the universe, and all the elements evolved from the same original substance contained in the Big Bang. This theory allows us to know, through the amazing science of spectroscopy, the chemical composition and relative location of the galaxies and stars out on the very fringes of the universe. Thanks to the Doppler effect, we can also know in which direction and at what speed they are moving.

The Big Bang theory, in so far as I have been able to comprehend it, strikes me as an attempt to understand and explain everything with one unified theory. The chief motivation behind it seems to be modern man's desire to see reality—all reality—as one complex continuum rather than having separate, independent parts of reality existing side by side and explained by competing theories from different perspectives. I find that this theory—proposed in my birth-year—expresses contemporary man's wish and need to see his existence on earth as an integral part of one coherent whole—complex, opaque, and confusing though that whole may be. Such a view provides him the possibility of finding some meaning and coherence in life rather than seeing himself as an alien creature in an incomprehensible, materialistic cosmos driven by impersonal laws of physics and chemistry. I find the theory an admirable attempt of man to be at one with himself and with the universe. Of course, no self-respecting cosmologist would ever be caught expressing or embracing such non-scientific thoughts as these. Hence the need for mystics who are not afraid of speculation and far-out ideas.

Problems of understanding

As a non-scientist looking in from the outside and trying to grasp the big picture of what modern cosmologists are telling us, there are so many difficulties that one is easily tempted to simply give up and renounce the whole enterprise. But as concerned crew members of Buckminster Fuller's "spaceship earth," we all have a vital interest in knowing where we came from and where we might be going, despite the almost insurmountable complexities. Fortunately, there are scientists who can explain complicated scientific matters for the laymen, and I am much indebted to them, even if my naive questions of when? and where? and how? concerning the Big Bang often receive almost nonsensical answers which I cannot really understand. As it turns out, many of my questions seem to be similar to the query, "What is north of the North Pole?" That is, they are not properly framed and can therefore not be answered or even discussed meaningfully. Nevertheless, it is almost impossible to give them up.

Time-space and evolution

Two concepts need to be emphasized here at the outset: the idea of time-space and the idea of evolving. Evolving or evolution is perhaps the easier to grasp. It means that over time, things change and develop or morph into new shapes, forms, entities, and structures, usually for reasons that are not altogether clear. Take hydrogen, for example, apparently the first and most basic chemical element in the universe. It was instrumental and indispensable in giving rise to the second element, helium, then to lithium and deuterium. Eventually all the other chemical elements were created through a sort of evolutionary process, an unfolding of something intrinsic to hydrogen itself, an unpacking of possibilities. An acorn is perhaps a clearer illustration of the inherent power within things, and it's closer to home in terms of our ability to understand it. An acorn is a small seed that you can hold in your hand. It can mean a morsel of food for a squirrel or a projectile for a boy's slingshot. But on a far more profound level it is a tiny item which under proper circumstances can become a mighty oak tree producing thousands of copies of itself, because it—like so many other things—has within itself far more possibilities than meet the eye. Countless additional entities follow this analogy, and we learn that most things—virtually *all* things—are far more complex than they appear on the surface.

Another example of change, closer to the question of the Big Bang, is the relationship between energy and matter. Einstein's famous formula, $E=MC2$, means that energy and matter are two different aspects or manifestations of one thing—two sides of the same coin, so to speak— and that under proper conditions one can change into the other. This is the only way I can make sense of the idea that all the material in the universe was contained in an extremely dense, hot ball just prior to the great explosion. As the energy was released at the moment of the Big Bang, it started expanding, cooling, and being transformed into gases, chemical elements. cosmic dust, and more substantial matter. While expanding, these particles of material under the force of gravity began attracting one another and started forming larger entities which became so dense that they started glowing as stars. Large groups of these stars became countless swirling galaxies creating and filling the space of the universe.

Since there is no dramatic action or explosion involved in dealing with time-space, it is a far more difficult concept to grasp, even apart from the Big Bang theory. Time, like space, is quiet, invisible, imperceptible in and of itself, and therefore hard to comprehend. It is used to measure change, motion, development, and evolution over periods which we arbitrarily call minutes, hours, days, years, centuries, millennia, eons. We can grasp the changes and developments which have happened over the past few centuries in the history of the United States, for example, or in the ten thousand or so years in the history of civilization, but that is already stretching and almost exceeding our imagination. Imagining the hundreds of thousands of years in man's evolution is a real mental workout, at least for me. When it comes then to the thousands of millions of years in the evolution of life on earth or the millions and billions of years in the history of the universe, however, I, for one, simply shake my head and try to imagine that those are meaningful concepts, despite the fact that I have absolutely no clear idea what they mean. Time, like the concept of deep space, is simply beyond my grasp. This is in large part due to my intuitive belief that both time and space must have limits, i.e. they must have a beginning and an end, a starting and a stopping point. But my belief is apparently far more a reflection of my naiveté than of reality. According to modern cosmology, it is not meaningful to talk about the beginning or ending of time and space in any absolute sense, as we will see.

The Big Bang, some questions

It is also hard to talk meaningfully about the Big Bang because some of the ideas strike me as being similar to a dog chasing its tail: they go round and round in circles and simply make us all the more confused. We ask what seem to be simple, straightforward questions and get complex, incomprehensible answers. Questions of where, when, how, why, and what was there before the Big Bang, seem to get us precisely nowhere, in large part because we are forced to examine our preconceived notions about what we thought we knew all our life about time and space. Common sense and our daily experience tell us that time and space must have a beginning and an end, or limits of some sort, but modern cosmology tells us something quite different. It turns out that time, space, and motion are relative concepts used to define each other. I guess we are in a situation similar to people who had to learn from Copernicus that our earth is up in the sky spinning around on its own axis at a thousand miles an hour and orbiting the sun yearly at a fantastic speed, things that seem on the face of it absolutely absurd and definitely go completely against all common sense and our daily experience.

We have to re-orient our way of thinking in order to grasp the basic ideas of modern cosmology, and we find that changing our long-standing concepts of such basic notions as time and space is difficult indeed. This can perhaps best be illustrated with a few questions which occurred to me in my attempt to grasp the Big Bang, along with the answers which I found in various sources. Just posing them meaningfully and trying to give a clear answer can take us deeper into the mystery of the Big Bang. See what you make of them.

Where did the Big Bang occur in the universe? There is a common assumption that the Big Bang was an explosion that occurred in the pre-existing empty space of the universe, and that the explosion expanded out into that empty nothingness. This idea is wrong, say the specialists, because their theory says that there was no universe and hence no space prior to the Big Bang. Space and time and the universe were created with one and the same primordial explosion. At the beginning of the universe, the infinitely small, existing space, or non-space, was completely filled with incredibly compacted matter. The matter was originally extremely hot and dense, and then it exploded, and started expanding and changing into various configurations. It created time and space and the universe as it went. Wow! How are we supposed to conceive of that? This exploding, expanding matter gradually cooled over some billions of years to eventually produce the stars and galaxies we see in the nightly sky. Although space had been concentrated into a single point at the Big Bang, it is equally possible, say other theorists, that space was infinite at the Big Bang. In both scenarios, the space was completely filled with matter which began to expand in all directions.

The concept of expansion has to be re-thought, as well as those of time, space, motion, and the universe. There was no center of the expansion. The universe simply started expanding at all points. Observers in any galaxy would theoretically see most of the other galaxies in the universe moving away from them. The only answer to the question, "Where did the Big Bang happen?" is that it occurred everywhere in the universe and expanded in all directions.

Is the earth expanding with the universe? This seems like a legitimate question, and gets the following answer: The earth is not expanding and neither is our solar system nor the Milky Way galaxy. These objects formed under the influence of gravity and stopped moving away from each other. Gravity also holds the galaxies together in groups and clusters. And it is mainly these groups and clusters of galaxies that are still moving apart in the universe.

What exists outside the universe? Space was created in the Big Bang, but cosmic or galactic space is something quite different from our normal concept of local, three-dimensional space. Our universe has no edge or boundary and no center, and there is therefore no "outside" of our universe. Again, our question turns out to be a sort of non-question.

What existed before the Big Bang? Another obviously reasonable question which again gets a sort of non-answer which leaves us all the more confused, as though the question itself is silly. Time was created in the Big Bang, so we cannot know what existed before the Big Bang. There was no "before," so the question is meaningless, again. Some theories suggest that our universe is part of an infinity of universes called a "multi-verse" which are being continuously created. This theory is possible but hard to prove, so it seems there is only one universe.

The Big Bang thrust out matter and energy in all directions, but a few scientists today question whether the universe is still expanding or if it has begun to contract through the force of gravity and will eventually start the whole process all over again. Most cosmologists agree, however, that for now it is still expanding. Theorists wonder if, after the final expansion, there will be a contraction of all matter again into one dense entity, called the Big Crunch, which will in turn engender another Big Bang and a new universe will be formed. A few theorists believe that the universe will continue to expand indefinitely, with the result that the energy of the stars and galaxies will eventually burn out, and the whole cosmos will go into a terminal Big Freeze.

How and why did the Big Bang happen? These again seem like reasonable questions, but the only answers I could find are as enigmatic and self-contradictory as the other answers. The answer is that prior to the Big Bang, the existing (??) matter, energy, and space were so densely packed that the whole situation became extremely unstable, could no longer be contained, and exploded.

It takes a great deal of imagination and creative intelligence to even think such mind-wrenching thoughts, but a great many very intelligent and well informed scientists seem to be in essential agreement that something like a Big Bang got the entire creative process of the universe started. Just listening to them and trying to follow their theories is exhausting, but at the same time stimulating and exciting. Such theories stretch the human mind out to the fringes of an inconceivably large universe and then down to the equally inconceivably smallest particle or atomic energy packet in what is called the string theory. Despite the difficulty of grasping these ideas at first encounter, the Big Bang concept may over time become as commonplace and as acceptable among the informed public as the heliocentric idea of Copernicus or the evolutionary theory of Darwin. I, for one, have confidence that the human mind has almost limitless possibilities to evolve and expand along with our expanding universe and our rapidly growing store of knowledge.

Creationism or Science

For the normal, workaday person this Big Bang creation story is simply too much to grasp, and many of us will prefer to embrace instead a far more manageable myth called Creationism or Creation by Intelligent Design. This theory posits an intelligent creator behind it all, some power which most thinkers simply call God, and this Supreme Being created everything more or less as told in the creation story in the first few chapters of Genesis, sometimes with a few ideas about evolution thrown in to lend it more credence. This more sophisticated version of the traditional Biblical story satisfies a great many people, probably in large part because the Big Bang theory is so difficult to get one's mind wrapped around.

In the history and philosophy of science, the Big Bang theory is all the more credible due to the lack of supernatural forces or elements needed in the explanation. Logic, reason, cause-and-effect thinking have made such a powerful impact on modern intellectual life that they are far more persuasive than mythological, theological, or metaphysical explanations. Using the scientific method of clear rational thinking, plus experimentation and trial-and-error testing, man has travelled to the moon and back, done heart-and-lung transplants, developed atomic energy, and vastly improved the lives of billions of humans. Any sensitive person who has ever flown across the country or across the ocean in a jumbo-jet with hundreds of other travelers can hardly fail to be impressed by the intelligence and credibility of modern scientists. Such successes encourage us to take the scientific Big Bang theory seriously despite the difficulties involved in grasping it. I strongly suspect that if science had not made such an enormous impact on modern life through the technological implementation of many of its theories, we humans in general would be far less prone to accept such fantastic concepts as the Big Bang.

Our local galaxy and the earth

But on with the story. After the Big Bang explosion some fourteen billion years ago, time, space, matter, and the early elements were leisurely created. The Big Bang has been supported by numerous observations and remains the key element in our understanding of the past. It is known that galaxies formed from large clouds of gas in the early universe. Gravity caused the gas to collect into large clusters, and star formation began. Drawings and graphic representations of these early events show swirling masses of clouds and dust, spinning pinwheels of stars and galaxies, more spirals whirling off the larger constellations and forming planets and moons, and all of this in vast oceans of space and emptiness.

So out of this swirling, hot, expanding mass came the galaxies, nebulae, stars, planets and moons over the next several billion years. Our local, more interesting neighborhood of the Milky Way galaxy with its billions of stars came into existence after a few billion years of expanding and cooling, and then, some five or so billion years ago, our home planet and its moon came onto the scene. After a couple of billion years and long periods of rain, our red hot planet cooled off enough for some primitive forms of life to develop and evolve into a myriad of forms over the next three billion years. What these earliest life forms were and how and why they first came into being is still a matter of conflicting theories, but they did. The most primitive forms of life were not solid enough to leave much of a fossil record, so they are hard to track and verify. The God-story of creation is easier to understand and makes explanations far simpler and superficially more satisfying, but it has its own problems as well.

Me and the Big Bang

A look at the starry heavens at night, even without any idea of the Big Bang or specific concepts of the origin of the universe, can easily fill almost everyone with awe and admiration. A brief introduction to the Big Bang theory, however, can greatly excite our creative imagination and fill us with wonder and appreciation of the scientists who spend their time and energy trying to explain such things. The great English philosopher Francis Bacon said some four centuries ago, "Knowledge is power!" An unstated corollary is that ignorance means bondage and servitude. Dedicated scientists around the world are helping greatly to free the human mind from ignorance and helplessness and to increase man's power and control over his life. They do this by investigating and explaining as best they can, things which will perhaps remain forever inexplicable but which can be approached little by little, often with fantasy-like theories such as the Big Bang or the Copernican theory just a few centuries ago.

I have great confidence in the power of the human mind to grow, develop, and become increasingly capable of finding answers to the great questions which mankind has been asking from the beginning. In the last two and a half thousand years since the burst of intelligent curiosity among the Greeks, tremendous progress has been made in virtually every branch of human inquiry. The last hundred years has seen almost unbelievable advances in the development of theories, facts, creations, and demonstrations in countless fields of intellectual activity. If we can just avoid killing ourselves, I believe that an exciting and rewarding future is in store for humanity. To be here knowingly in the middle of this great adventure, even merely as an interested spectator, is indeed a special privilege.

Chapter 2.
Evolution of life on earth

Life in Berlin, March 2008

Living on the 14th floor of this high-rise apartment in downtown Berlin has generated a number of complex thoughts about me and the four million other humans in this part of Germany, a country heavily laden with an unusual, historical burden concerning people and their interactions. In trying to come up with a large-enough framework in which to place myself at this moment in my life, I conceived of the following very broad perspective.

Against a backdrop of time, space, and change, there exists a world governed and explainable by the laws of physics, chemistry, causality, gravity, evolution and probably other agents of which I am not aware. We know that rocks roll downhill, objects fall if unsupported, salt and water have a certain affinity to one another, flames and smoke tend to rise, and many other common-day occurrences and phenomena. Against this background of a mechanistic setting, life occurs. How, when, why, etc. we don't really know, but life is here and has manifested itself in an almost unbelievable multiplicity of forms: plant, animal, human, and all the spaces in between. All these forms are related to one another in a broad sense and often share amazingly similar attributes.

We don't really know exactly how or when life began, but once started, it took on innumerable forms and variations, and today we can find creatures living in virtually every conceivable location in the world: in the sky, in the water, under the ground, in the guts of animals, and almost every imaginable place on earth. On the earth's surface and in its oceans, life has taken on a vast, almost incomprehensible variety of shapes and forms. We humans are simply one of those countless forms. I recently read that there are perhaps four million different species of life on earth. That's hard for me to imagine, but it may turn out to be actually short of the mark.

As far as I have understood it, virtually all life forms seem to follow a very similar pattern: The individual member of whatever species comes into being, grows and develops towards its mature form by taking from the environment whatever it needs to survive and flourish. It reproduces and creates more of its own species, then the individual ages, dies, and goes out of existence, while the species continues. The underlying mechanism or motor behind all this activity seems to be the simple desire or instinct to live, the struggle for survival and reproduction, and then aging and dying.

Each life form handles these stages in its own way. We don't know what degree of awareness the various species and individuals within that species attain during their life tenure. We humans like to believe that we are quite special in regard to our awareness of existence, and that we stand apart from all other creatures in this regard. But this may in the long run simply turn out to be wishful thinking and fanciful illusion on man's part, as so many of his other favorite thoughts and prejudices have turned out to be.

Where does this leave the concerned individual contemplating his or her place among the six or more billion fellow humans now inhabiting our home, the earth? Getting to the point of asking the question is in itself an arduous task; answering or resolving it may be even more arduous and futile than asking it. Perhaps the only recompense is in knowing that through individual and general human experience we have arrived at a solid, factual basis on which to pose such questions and to undertake such a tantalizing inquiry. Modern man now knows a great deal about life in general and what it means to be a human being in particular, and today we build on that knowledge.

It seems that in some sense it is perhaps the larger life force itself which is using individual life forms like you and me to become aware of itself, just as it has used poets, prophets, preachers, philosophers, artists, scientists, and countless other sensitive people to ponder and struggle with what seems on the surface to be foolish and hopeless questions: What is it all about? What does it all mean? Does our existence here in this complex, fascinating world have any deeper meaning or significance at all? If so, what is it? How can we find out? Does the only real answer lie simply in the doing and asking and struggling? Is the goal of the journey simply the journey itself and not the arrival at some final destination? Is that the searcher's main reward for all his struggles and efforts?

I have been wrestling with such queries all my life, from my early teenage years to living now for a while in Berlin. I think I have made some progress, although I would be hard-pressed to say briefly what that progress has been. Perhaps it is simply that I am less naive now and more realistic than I was before.

Getting started

Somehow, life on earth began, and with it the fascinating story of evolution. In trying to investigate and understand big topics like the origins of the universe, the creation of the earth, the beginning of life on earth, and the origin and development of man, questions and problems abound at every turn, especially in light of the speculative nature of the investigation and the paucity of hard evidence. In Heidelberg, for example, I once saw the famous jawbone fossil on the basis of which paleontologists created a whole new species of man, *Homo heidelbergensis,* and I remember wondering how they could do that with so little evidence and how valid such ideas really are. How they can do such things turns out, in fact, to be a long, complicated story.

One also wonders what was happening prior to the Big Bang, and where all that densely packed energy and matter ready to explode came from. One wonders if the currently expanding universe will one day stop its expansion when the original explosive power dissipates and universal gravity starts pulling all the parts back together again into a Big Crunch. Will the whole process then repeat itself over additional billions of years, like breathing out and breathing in? Will the Big Bang-Big Crunch cycle continue forever? Will the ultimate definition of reality be Big Bang-Big Crunch, Big Bang-Big Crunch, forever, *ad infinitum*? Is this all simply too much for the human mind to grasp, or does the mind's capacity to understand somehow expand with our expanding knowledge and interest? I hope and trust this latter idea is the case. The widely accepted ideas of Copernicus, Newton, Darwin, and countless others give me confidence that our mind does in fact become increasingly capable as our knowledge grows. It seems that the human mind and consciousness, like life itself, are flexible and capable of tremendous stages of development and adaptation,

A recent example of the mind-wrenching nature of such investigations is the story of scientists with some very special equipment who claim to have heard echoes or seen some sort of indication or afterglow of the Big Bang explosion which happened some 14 billion years ago! How can that be possible? This makes for fascinating reading, but one wonders how substantial such research really is and how much we can rely on things which, at least on the surface, seem utterly impossible to believe. Nevertheless, the inquisitive mind continues to ask the big questions and to be intrigued by the perennial inquiries of Who? What? When? Where? How? and Why? We seem to make progress, but some of it is strange indeed.

Most scientists today seem to agree that the universe as we know it started some 14 billion years ago with a gigantic explosion sending all existing energy-matter in every direction. I try to visualize this as a great burst of fireworks such as we see on the Fourth of July creating a huge ball of colorful specks of light and movement expanding in all directions. Each dot of light represents, in the Big Bang theory, millions or billions of galaxies and stars, which over vast expanses of time and space give rise to solar systems and suns with orbiting planets. One such system is our own Milky Way galaxy which gave rise to our local solar system and its planets. One recent humorous television program has appropriately named our planet 'The Third Rock.'

Origins of the earth and moon

The theory is that our earth was formed as part of the solar system, which was a large rotating cloud of dust, matter, and gases like hydrogen and helium produced in the Big Bang. Most of the mass of the cloud concentrated in the middle and began to heat up, started to glow, and eventually became our sun. Lesser whirlpool concentrations of debris circling the sun formed into the various solar planets, one of which was our own early, molten earth. The fiery earth gradually solidified, cooled off for a billion or so years, releasing gases and slowly creating its own atmosphere. Our planet is roughly five billion years old and its general shape was largely completed within the first ten to twenty million years of its existence.

The earth was a hot molten ball whose surface gradually cooled off and formed a solid crust. The earth was bombarded by planetoids and other material left over from the formation of the solar system; it had no oceans and there was no oxygen in the atmosphere. Volcanic activity was intense, steam and gases escaped as the crusted parts shifted around forming the continents, and eventually an atmosphere that was formed and held in place by the earth's gravitational pull. For millions of years the planet continued cooling, clouds formed, and it began to rain, giving rise to the oceans about four billion years ago. As I vacation here on the edge of the Pacific Ocean at my son's home in Hawaii and look at this massive expanse of water, I am forced to think that it must have indeed rained long and hard to produce the vast oceans which now cover three-fifths of the earth's surface and are in many places miles and miles deep. Again, one stands in awe and wonder at where all this water came from, how much salt and minerals were washed from the land, and how long all this took. A few moments of quiet observation and questioning can result in an almost overwhelming sense of awe and wonder.

The origin of our moon is still uncertain, but there is much evidence to support the idea of a giant impact by some large object—perhaps an asteroid or a smaller planet—rotating near the earth and eventually colliding with it, probably somewhere in the area of the Pacific Ocean, and knocking a large portion of the earth's hot crust out into space. The impact is also thought to have changed the earth's axis to produce the large 23 degree tilt that is responsible for our seasons. The flying debris circling around the earth became a solid mass held in its orbit by the gravitational pull of the earth; under the influence of its own gravity, the moon formed into a spherical body and continued orbiting the earth while keeping the same side always facing the earth. It is still unclear to me why the moon does not rotate on its own axis. It is thought that the moon is almost as old as the earth.

Origin of life on earth

Now for the really big question which directly touches every living creature on earth: How did the vibrant, pulsating miracle called organic life emerge from dead, inorganic materials and lifeless molecules? This is a great mystery which has exercised many highly informed minds and about which there is as yet no generally agreed upon answer, only theories and speculations. This is in part because of the uncertainty about the conditions on the young earth some four billion years ago. It is believed, for example, that there was very little oxygen at that time, and the range and fluctuation of temperature is uncertain; also, what chemicals, acids, minerals, and elements were available to be components of the chemical soup reputed to have been the substratum of life? Scientists working in modern clean laboratories have produced amino acids, one of the key ingredients for the origin of life, but other theorists point out that life surely originated in the gutter, not in a sterile laboratory.

Despite the many problems and uncertainties, however, there is some agreement on a number of key points, perhaps chief among which is the idea that life must have originated in water, as a very simple organism, and that the earliest simple forms of one-celled life happened a very, very, long time ago. Another central idea is that the evolution of life proceeded very slowly, and took two to three billion years to arrive at a point where the life forms could leave some trace of themselves in the fossil record. The concept of life slowly evolving over billions of years leaves the mind, at least mine, spinning and unable to form any clear picture of what might have happened.

Scientific research theorizes that the early beginning of life occurred sometime between four and a half to three and a half billion years ago, relatively soon after the formation of our planet, perhaps only a few hundred million years later. Scientists think that the first couple of billion years of life's development consisted of primitive, single-celled organisms, but since these simple forms of life could leave virtually no fossil record at all, there is no trace of their existence. Multi-cellular forms appearing in soft-bodied animals less than a billion years ago were finally able to leave somewhat more of a fossil trail, although often very slight, perhaps trails or tracks of worms in the mud. Then hard-bodied forms of animals developed about half a billion years ago, and with them the fossil record becomes clearer, richer, and more diverse.

Only a fossil record, of course, can provide actual evidence of the history of life, and small, soft-bodied creatures were unable to leave much in the way of fossils. Much of the theory of life's early development on earth during several billion years is therefore based solely on inference, extrapolation, and speculation. After the arrival of hard-bodied life forms, however, the fossil record began to provides detailed evidence concerning the evolution of hard-shelled and vertebrate sea forms such as trilobites, clams, shell fish, conches, vertebrate fish, and reptiles, and then later came the origin of birds and mammals from reptilian ancestors.

Photosynthesis, necessary for aquatic plant life, occurred on earth about two and half billion years ago and caused an increase in the oxygen concentration in the earth's atmosphere, plus an increased food supply for many creatures living in the water. Photosynthesis on land occurred much later and greatly increased the possibilities of terrestrial life forms. Photosynthesis made possible an immense larder in the water and on land, and on the basis of this enormous food supply life exploded into countless aquatic and terrestrial forms, all of which, in as far as I have been able to understand it, are fundamentally related and point back to simple, one-celled creatures in the primordial seas. All life is one and comes from the same beginning,

Aquatic plants and animals colonize the land

The scientific consensus is that life seems surely to have originated in the water, and water remains essential for practically all life forms. Then somehow, after a long period of aquatic development, life emerged from the water and began spreading over the land in various plant and animal forms, becoming continuously more complex and sophisticated. Living creatures, probably in the form of mosses or simple plants, slowly came out of the water onto land to begin their own many-sided evolution. Primitive lung-fish were not far behind and slowly developed into a vast number of reptiles, then into birds and mammals. Early forms of vertebrate fish, for example, began to be able to gasp air and use their fins as a means of locomotion over the mud flats in search of food or new pools of water as their own ponds began to dry up. Some animals, like today's sea turtles and grunion, came out of water to lay their eggs in the sand, but then returned to live in the sea. Others came out and stayed out of the water permanently, evolving and populating the land

and sky. All forms of life adapted to exploit available food sources, climatic conditions, and a particular habitat, and the number of variations of life turned out to be just phenomenal. The time involved, however, the millions and billions of years that it took for all this to happen, just boggles the mind and is simply beyond my ability to grasp.

Despite our inability to explain how and why and when, the fact is that life on our planet did begin very, very long ago, almost certainly in the water, and began to change and evolve into millions of different forms.. Theorists believe that life on earth first evolved in the seas over 3.5 billion years ago, and even today the majority of living things are aquatic. For most of earth's history, all life forms were in the water and there were no multicellular organisms on land. Some cells in the water, early on, developed photosynthesis, the ability to use sunlight as a source of energy. Later on, the terrestrial realm of land and air offered many challenges as well as opportunities to creatures originally adapted to aquatic life.

However, for over 3 billion years, life was essentially limited to the water in the form of soft-bodied organisms basically incapable of leaving any trace of their existence. The marine realm eventually became as crowded with living things—including eventually crustaceans and vertebrate fish—as the modern oceans, but the land was still barren.

The first organisms that spent at least some time out of water were algae mats along the edges of seas and lakes. These colored spots of land left by collections of primitive algae or moss at the water's edge are among the oldest fossils known. The oldest fossils of land fungi and plants came later and date to 480–460 million years ago, although molecular evidence suggests the fungi may have colonized the land as early as 1000 million years ago and the plants 700 million years ago. Initially remaining close to the water's edge, mutations and variations resulted in further colonization of this new terrestrial environment.

The first fully terrestrial organisms were primitive plants that colonized the land by about 450-500 millions years ago. The terrestrial world offered these primitive plants additional mineral resources and more space to collect sunlight than could be found in the crowded seas. This most likely happened at the water's edge with something similar to algae and moss-like creatures. So the earliest forms of terrestrial life happened at the water's edge, but then slowly this primitive beginning of terrestrial life developed into more recognizable plants, like ferns and early trees. Later still, invertebrate and vertebrate animals started coming onto land and developed eventually into reptiles, insects, birds, and mammals.

Early life on land

The timing of the first animals to leave the oceans is not clearly known. The first terrestrial animals were various types of arthropods (jointed, segmented creatures like crabs and insects); the oldest clear evidence of land animals is around 450 million years ago. These early creatures began to thrive and became better adapted due to the vast food source provided by the terrestrial plants. They were the ancestors of millipedes and centipedes, the earliest spiders, and the ancestors of insects. They ate the early plants, and each other. In time, they became very successful and developed into many new species.

Then, around 380 to 375 million years ago, the first four-legged animals (tetrapods) evolved from fish. It is thought that probably their fins evolved to become limbs which allowed the first tetrapods to lift their heads out of the water to breathe air. This ability to breathe air would let them survive in oxygen-poor water or pursue small prey in shallow water. They may have later ventured onto land for brief periods. Eventually, some of them became so well adapted to terrestrial life that they spent their adult lives on land, although they hatched in the water and returned there to lay their eggs. This was the origin of the amphibians.

Life continued evolving through great changes in climate and environmental conditions, and around 230 million years ago dinosaurs split off from their reptilian ancestors. By about 200 million years ago, dinosaurs had become the dominant land animals among the vertebrates and ruled the earth for almost 200 thousand years. The very early mammalian lines began to develop during the late reign of the dinosaurs. Our earliest mammalian ancestors were small, mouse-like animals resembling shrews, but they developed essential traits (warm blood, live birth, nursing their young, body hair) which helped them exist when the environmental conditions changed. More about them later on.

Theories of the origin of life

I have come across several theories of the origin of life on earth. One popular idea goes back to Charles Darwin himself, who suggested that perhaps a sort of chemical cocktail could have formed in shallow ponds. This murky mixture was then struck by lightning strong enough to start a vital reaction, thereby creating some form of amino acid which then started doing remarkable things: growing, dividing, and making copies of itself. Another idea is the same basic story but far down in the ocean depths where hot lava flowing into the water from a fissure in the earth's crust created ideal conditions and gave the necessary impetus to start the life process going. Still another theory says that life on earth might have come originally from some other star or planet by means of asteroids landing on the earth and bringing the seeds of life with them. This theory, however, just pushes the origin of life in the universe back one step and is not particularly helpful. All modern theories seem to presuppose the essential element of water in order for life to begin and to be maintained.

Another, much older theory of the origin of life is based on the old idea of spontaneous generation. This theory held that complex, living organisms are generated by decaying organic substances. It goes back at least as far as Aristotle, who observed maggots forming in decaying meat. This belief reminds us that the field of optics was not developed until the 17th century, with the Italian physicist Galileo improving the telescope and the Dutch lens grinder Anthony van Leeuwenhoek making improvements in the microscope. People were not aware of the egg-laying activity of flies and other insects on meat and other organic materials. Already in the mid-17th century, however, it was shown that no maggots appeared in meat when flies were prevented from laying eggs. Nevertheless, until the early 19th century people generally believed in the on-going spontaneous generation of life from non-living matter. Then, due to the work of Louis Pasteur and others, the general scientific opinion gradually became that every living thing comes from a pre-existing living thing.

Scientific research has advanced a great deal since Darwin and Pasteur, but the answer to the question of the ultimate origins of life on earth is still unknown, and the question remains under intense investigation. One of the key aspects of the question is how a living thing such as a cell can replicate or make a copy of itself. Another key aspect of the subject is that all life forms are intimately related and go back eventually to the same origin. This is the concept of the unity of all life.

For decades, those studying the origin of life have imagined that it emerged in balmy conditions from primordial chemical soups, tropical ponds, even boiling volcanic vents. A few scientists began to suspect that life may not have begun in warmth but in ice—at temperatures that few living things can now survive—and they have carried out experiments along theses lines. They filled a container with a mixture of ammonia and cyanide, chemicals that scientists believe existed on the early earth and may have contributed to the rise of life. The mixture was cooled to a very low temperature for several years and then re-examined with surprising results that showed some of the earliest stages of life. This gives rise to yet another possible theory about life's origins.

Divine origin?

Despite our ignorance of How? When? and Why?, life did appear on earth and started undergoing a fascinating evolution into a myriad of forms. There are many ideas about the early origins of life on earth, but probably the most widespread belief and the easiest to understand among the general population is that God created all life forms, and that we should be content with that as an answer. This is not, however, a particularly informative statement, and does little to satisfy our native curiosity.

Inquisitive minds prefer a more detailed explanation, vague and uncertain though it may be. Such minds assume that tiny, one-celled organisms somehow originated, then developed cilia or tails which allowed them to move about in the water in their search for food. Some cells may have joined together into multicellular organisms or developed additional internal cells to be used for mobility, digestion, defense, etc. Given the fragile nature of the material itself, little or no fossil evidence remains for demonstrating such speculation at the earliest levels, but there are ample fossil remains at a more advanced level, things such as trilobites, ferns, shellfish, clams, etc. The fossils tend to show an increasingly complicated story of the evolution of life, from simple to more complex forms. Fish, the earliest vertebrates, evolved in the oceans around 530 million years ago and began leaving numerous fossils documenting the story of life on earth.

The struggle for survival and the survival of the fittest

The concept of life leads us more-or-less automatically to the idea that life often involves a battle for limited resources, a struggle for survival, since all living organisms need food, space, and other necessities and often have to compete intensely for them. Charles Darwin wrote that in the struggle for survival, the fittest win out at the expense of their rivals because they succeed in adapting themselves better to their environment. Herbert Spencer, one of Darwin's early admirers and defenders, coined the phrase, "survival of the fittest," soon after the publication in 1859 of Darwin's revolutionary work, *The Origin of Species*. The phrase became popular and a kind of shorthand for a concept relating to competition for survival or predominance. Darwin preferred the phrase "natural selection," explaining that the prevailing conditions of nature are the selecting element. In the fifth edition of his work, in 1869, Darwin uses the phrase "natural selection, or the survival of the fittest."

Nature seems to have been trying all possibilities at all times, and there were hundreds of millions of years to try out all the various combinations for getting food, defending oneself, finding a mate, and reproducing additional copies of oneself. Over the millennia and eons, life took to the land, the water, and the sky in innumerable forms and variations. The basic mechanism of sexual reproduction of almost all forms of life assured that the offspring would be more or less carbon copies of the parent forms, but with the possibility of slight variations. These slight variations, over time, gave rise to countless new species. Offspring that could best find food, defend themselves, and make themselves attractive to the opposite sex flourished, while less able forms left no offspring and died out. This is the famous struggle for survival and the theory of natural selection, in which those species best suited to meet the local conditions survived and flourished, while species less well suited perished and left no offspring. Nature, or natural conditions, is the great selector.

Some thoughts on evolution

In trying to grasp these ideas of variation and development, I must constantly remind myself of the vast expanse of time in which these things could happen. The earliest forms of life on earth happened, say, three to four billion years ago. This provides almost endless stretches of time to experiment with every possible and impossible combination of life elements under numerous changing conditions. We know from the fossil record of dinosaurs, for example, that nature did experiment with a great many forms of dinosaur life and created many variations of this life form on land, in the water, and in the sky. We can only imagine how many thousands of different forms and countless other species of life have existed without leaving a single trace. Some theorists say that there are perhaps four to six million different species of life existing on earth at present, but that many species have not yet been identified. How many different species must have existed in the three or four billion years in the history of life? The number of possible species and individual creatures which have theoretically come into being and then gone out of existence without leaving a single trace during the course of billions of years of history simply stuns and confounds the mind.

The basic pattern of life

The underlying mechanism or pattern of life seems essentially to be more or less the same everywhere: the search for food, the need to defend oneself through flight or fight, and the need to reproduce and thereby create more specimens or copies of oneself. When conditions change, in terms of temperature, food and water supply, new predators, over-crowding, etc., competition can become very intense. Variations occur, and new life forms come into being. We can only vaguely imagine the geologic and climatic changes during the millions and billions of years since life appeared on earth.

The fossil study of dinosaurs, mammals, or insects, for example, shows that such changes must have happened innumerable times during the course of history. Darwin's study of finches in the Galapagos Islands is a striking early demonstration of how variations in the food supply in the Islands gave rise to a number of different species of finches with beaks capable of eating different kinds of food. The detailed fossil records of the evolution of the horse, for example, also show how the tiny eohippus has changed over the millennia into the mighty Clydesdales pulling the huge Budweiser beer wagon.

We humans are of course especially interested in our own evolution, and this has been documented in considerable detail with numerous fossil remains of our ancestors. One wonders how any thoughtful, open-minded person surveying the fossil remains of dinosaurs, horses, finches, or humans could fail to be persuaded by the theory of evolution. My own explanation is that we humans tend to ask simple, profound questions about our origins, for example, but we want quick, simple, straightforward answers and have neither the time, patience, nor interest to hear involved, complex answers. But virtually all matters touching on evolution, however, tend to be complex and involved.

Species of life

There are tens of thousands, if not tens of millions, of different kinds of life, from eagles to ants, whales, and orchids. But we humans are of course chiefly interested in ourselves, not in birds or bugs or plants. It seems to me that in general we tend to regard ourselves primarily as unique individuals, and only later—if at all—as members of the larger human species. We pay only scant attention to the thousands of other life forms around us, but to understand ourselves properly we need to see ourselves as parts of a larger whole, i.e. as specific, specialized creatures within the vastly larger panorama of life. We need to recognize that basically we are animals living among millions of other kinds of animals. It is important, at least in my view, to realize as fully as possible that our species is only one of millions of species of life presently living on earth. A brief glance at the history of life on earth shows us that countless other species—including a dozen or so other species of humans—have lived before us. And just as individual creatures come and go, so it is also with species. It is estimated that 99% of all species of life that have ever lived are now extinct. As we will see in the next chapter, our species of *Homo sapiens* is only one of several human species that have walked the earth before us and then gone out of existence. So, let us spend a few moments with the concept of the various species of life, where our *homo* species fits in, and then with the extinction of species.

A species is generally defined as a group of interbreeding organisms capable of producing fertile offspring. Horses and donkeys, for example, are two closely related groups of equine animals and can interbreed to produce a mule. But the mule itself is not fertile, and this means that horses and donkeys are two separate but different species of a larger horse-like family which also includes the zebra, the wild ass, and others. For me, the concept of species emphasizes the notion of fundamental differences between groups of otherwise very similar creatures. For example, the range of superficial differences within the present human family is enormous (body build, skin color, hair texture, etc.), and yet we can all interbreed and are therefore all closely related in a biological sense because we belong to the same species.

Species, genera, and families

There are so many different kinds of life that they have to be put in larger groupings or categories which can show that they are related and yet different, such as the equine family of which the horse and the donkey are species. This is the Linnaeus system of all living things and was started by the Swedish botanist and medical doctor Karl von Linné about 1750. His classification system has been greatly expanded and elaborated by scientists around the world and allows them to know in great detail what they and their colleagues are talking about when referring to specific plants and animals. This desire for classification—and thereby clarity—goes back at least as far as Aristotle and has reached its highest form with the international system of Linnaeus and his followers. It greatly advances knowledge through precision and ease of communication by using a system of nine interrelated groupings to clearly classify all living things, with "species" as the lowest broad category, then come classes called "genus, family, phylum", etc., all the way up to the highest, broadest category of all: "life."

The Linnaeus system of labeling creatures has two parts in each definition: the first part relates the individual creature to a larger category, and the second part of the definition sets that creature off from the larger category by adding a distinctive element peculiar only to that group. Modern humans, for example, are classified as *homo sapiens*, with *homo* meaning 'man' or 'human' and *sapiens* meaning 'wise' or 'modern,' an attribute which sets us off from other *homo* groups such as *heidelbergensis* or *neanderthalensis*. This has proved to be a very useful and convenient classifying system.

If we divide all animals into two groups, invertebrates and vertebrates, an estimated 97% of all species would be invertebrates. Invertebrates are, of course, those animals with no backbone such as sponges, mollusks, octopi, and insects. Most invertebrates are small, but others, like the giant clam and some species of octopus, can grow quite large. We know most about large plants and animals because they are easily visible from the land or sea. It is humbling for us to realize that humans, elephants, and other large animals are freakishly rare life forms, since 99% of all known animal species are smaller than bumble bees. This comes as somewhat of a shock to most of us who are accustomed to seeing huge herds of wildebeests and zebras on the many nature programs on television.

Man, our primary interest, belongs to a rather small group of animal species called mammals, and this grouping has only about 5,400 members. Mammals stand in stark contrast to the largest group of species, insects, which has millions of different groupings. In some senses, insects are the most successful animals on earth: Their species are very old, very widespread, greatly diversified, and highly organized. Insects are by far the most numerous creatures on earth, and will, according to many experts, eventually inherit the earth.

How many species are there?

In trying to determine how many species of life there are presently living in the world, a clear distinction must be made between species that have been studied, classified, and named on the one hand, and estimates on the other hand of how many other species are waiting to be investigated, labeled, and placed into the larger international Linnaeus classification system. According to the most recent counts, scientists have described somewhat less than two million species of plants, animals, and algae. Researchers estimate, however, that there may be as many as ten to one hundred million more undiscovered species, primarily fish, fungi, insects, and microbes. The greatest diversity exists among the insects, which account for nearly a million of the earth's known species. Mammals—the group to which we humans belong—make up one of the smallest groups, with scarcely more than five thousand species.

Even the known level of almost two million species of life on earth is an enormous number and must impress any sensitive observer. New species are being classified at the rate of about 15,000 a year, but scientists feel that this is not nearly enough to close the knowledge gap. There are still millions upon millions of forms of life waiting to be studied, labeled, and put into perspective in the overall system of life. Major scientific institutions around the world are working together to create an online database to make all the known information readily available to the international community and to facilitate new knowledge. It is expected that most of the new species awaiting discovery will be among insects and microscopic life forms in tropical regions.

So, less than 2 million species have been formally described and given names, and most estimates of the total number of living species seem to fall between five and thirty million. But other estimates range then on upwards to one hundred or more million different species of life. Most of these are microorganisms or tiny invertebrates. These include viruses, bacteria, algae, fungi, etc. as well as more recognizable ones such as sponges, insects (estimates of 2 to 30 million species of insects!!), plus worms, birds, reptiles. etc. However, for most groups of organisms other than vertebrates, these estimates are little more than educated guesses.

Finding and labeling species

A great many living species are microorganisms and tiny invertebrates, elusive and hard to find. The larger the creatures, of course, the easier they are to locate, describe, count, and classify. It is estimated that the earth's oceans and continents support about 300,000 species of plants and 60,000 species of vertebrate animals. On the other hand, it is estimated that perhaps as much as 97% of all species on earth are invertebrates, and of these invertebrates, the insects are the most numerous and in many ways the most successful group of animals on earth.

Why the wide discrepancies in determining the number of species on earth? In addition to the inherent difficulties in defining a species, there are perhaps the two chief reasons for the uncertainty in determining how many species there are: size of the organisms and the biased interests of the investigators. Generally speaking, the smaller the species and its organisms, the more difficult it is to find, classify, and count them. General interest and economic considerations on the other hand encourage people to study birds, bees, and mammals more thoroughly rather than digging around for grubs, earthworms and microscopic creatures.

Some of the information about the number, diversity, and fertility of life forms is simply amazing. A couple of dramatic examples will illustrate the explosive power of life. It has been estimated that the descendants of one pair of common house flies, provided that they all survived during a five month season, would total 190 quintillion individuals! Recent figures indicate that there are more than 200 million insects for each human on the planet! A recent article in The New York Times claimed that the world holds 300 pounds of insects for every pound of humans! Can you imagine that there are 5000 species of lizards! Such staggering figures leave me simply dizzy and incredulous.

In trying to establish a manageable human context, I narrowed my focus to the closest biological group to which our species belongs: mammals. This is something of which most of us have a more-or-less clear-cut idea. A mammal is generally defined as a warm-blooded vertebrate having skin more-or-less covered with hair. Its young are born alive and nourished with milk from the mammary glands of the female. The authorities estimate that at the present time there are approximately 5,400 species of mammals, ranging in size from the tiny bumblebee bat measuring less than two inches long to the 110 foot blue whale, and including some six and a half billion human creatures like you and me. The more limited class of mammals to which we belong are the primates, and there are estimates of 230 to 270 species of these. The narrowest group of primates to which we belong are the five great apes: orangutang, gibbon, gorilla, chimpanzee, and humans. With our very closest animal relatives, the common chimp and the bonobo chimp, we are genetically 98.5% identical. Our own human grouping is called *Homo*, and has had a dozen or more exemplars over the last 200 thousand years. We are simply the latest.

Extinction events

Like individuals, species come and go. An extinction event is described as a sharp decrease in the number of species in a relatively short period of time, and numerous extinction events have happened during the billions of years of life on earth. They affect most major groups present at the time: plants, birds, mammals, reptiles, amphibians, fish, invertebrates and other simpler life forms. Extinctions may be caused by drastic climate changes resulting in ice ages or droughts, intense volcanic activity sending ashes into the high atmosphere and blocking out the sunlight for extended periods of time, rise and fall of sea levels, meteors striking the earth, and the shifting of tectonic plates. Right now, the human species is driving many other species out of existence through exploitation and encroachment on their habitats. Many scientists think we may even be rapidly driving ourselves to extinction by exploitation of our natural resources and by fouling the land, water, air, and the entire ecosystem.

Major volcanic explosions and meteors striking the earth can produce dust and gases which inhibit photosynthesis and thus cause food chains to collapse, both on land and at sea. Sometimes great amounts of sulfur oxides are emitted during such events and can precipitate as acid rain and thereby poison many organisms, contributing further to the collapse of food chains. Carbon dioxide is also emitted and can possibly cause sustained global warming once the dust and volcanic gases have dissipated.

Since life began on earth, several major mass extinctions have significantly altered the earth's environment, and therefore the life forms on the planet. Scientists estimate that in the past 540 million years there have been five major events when over 50% of the animal species died out. There were probably mass extinctions in former eons, but prior to half a billion years ago there were no animals with body parts hard enough to leave a significant fossil record. The most recent mass extinction occurred some 65 million years ago, and has attracted more attention than all others because it killed off the dinosaurs and opened the way for the rise of mammals.

Some 65 million years ago, a 10-kilometer wide meteorite likely struck the earth just off the Yucatan Peninsula, ejecting vast quantities of volcanic dust and vapor into the air that blocked out sunlight and inhibited photosynthesis for a long period of time. Most large animals, including the giant dinosaurs, became extinct in a quite short period of time. The small existing mammals rapidly diversified, grew larger, filled the void left by the dinosaurs, and became the dominant vertebrates, spreading over the earth in a great variety of forms. Perhaps a couple of million years later (around 63 million years ago), the last common ancestor of primates lived, and the primates began their own ascent. By about 34 million years ago, some terrestrial mammals returned to the oceans to become the ancestors of whales, dolphins, and other marine mammals.

Over the last half-billion years, there have been a number of mass extinctions, and they have sometimes accelerated the evolution of life by making room for new forms. The specialists tell us that when dominance of particular ecological niches passes from one group of organisms to another, it is rarely because the new dominant group is "superior" in any way to the old, it is usually because an extinction event simply eliminates the old dominant group and makes way for the new one.

Early mammal-like forms, for example, existed throughout the reign of the dinosaurs, but they could not compete for the food and territorial niches which the dominant dinosaurs monopolized. The evolution of mammals from reptiles is an example of adaptive evolution and the fossil record reveals that it proceeded in a series of stages, through various groups of mammal-like reptiles. The mass extinction of 65 million years ago removed virtually all dinosaurs and made it possible for mammals to expand into the large terrestrial vertebrate niches. It is estimated that perhaps 75% of all species were destroyed at that time, but the way was opened for mammals and birds to become the dominant land vertebrates.

Mammals, the group out of which we developed, are a distinct group of vertebrates in many respects: They have warm blood and a constant body temperature, bodies generally covered with hair, comparatively large brains, live births and milk for their offspring, plus an extended period of dependency of the offspring on the adults. This period of the young mammals living with the parents allows the offspring to learn vital lessons and skills from the parents. Many television programs have shown how young lions, elephants, monkeys, etc. learn essential hunting, social, and survival skills from their parents during this period of extended childhood. This period has proved to be of especially crucial importance in the development of human civilization and the advancement of knowledge. Young humans learn directly and indirectly many cultural skills plus a huge store of ideas and knowledge from their parents and are not compelled to "reinvent the wheel." In highly developed cultures with formal educational systems, this special state of "childhood" lasts until the early '20s or even longer.

What have I learned?

From this short excursion into the origins of life on earth, I have learned that life is tenacious, tough, vibrant, highly adaptable, almost unbelievably diverse, and worthy of our utmost attention and admiration. Life will always find a way to continue, and when one door is closed, life will come in by another door or window or through the roof, usually in a new form or variation. Life is not in a hurry, and time is of little consequence in the three or four billion year history of living things on earth. Individual creatures and specific species come and go, changing and evolving along the way, coming into or going out of existence altogether, but life itself continues and flourishes in ever new species and individuals. The Buddha and Albert Schweitzer talked about a certain "reverence for life," and we contemporary exemplars of life would do well to listen and learn.

It appears that life in its more profound aspects has been shrouded in a certain mystery from the very beginning, and it may be that man, despite all his modern science and technology, will never fully understand or grasp the very essence of the miracle of life. Even if scientists are eventually able to clarify the chemistry, physics, and biology of life down to the last iota, will anyone ever be able to explain consciousness and self-consciousness, the fact that we are acutely aware of being alive and asking questions about life? It may be that in the last analysis we may have to content ourselves with the somewhat nebulous notion that life could simply be a kind of divine or cosmological principle manifesting itself in countless, inexplicable, but fascinating ways.

This exercise into the origins and multiplicity of life has made me all the more aware that my very existence is intimately linked to a fascinating chain of being that stretches back almost four billion years. We are part and parcel of that dynamic force that has been around for a very long time and has tremendous possibilities and potential, one of the greatest being awareness, self-awareness, and self-discovery. The more aware we become of who and what we are, and of the long and fascinating process of how we got to be here, the more we can appreciate the miracle of being alive at this particular time in the earth's history.

What I have also learned is that the whole Big Bang story can be seen fundamentally as a sort of evolution, a unique development or movement from simplicity to complexity. Galaxies and stars are in many ways far more complex phenomena than the original big explosion which contained only hydrogen and helium. Planets are physically and chemically more complex still. With life on earth we make a quantum jump in complexity. The progression continues by increasingly huge jumps to the self-aware brain of modern man, probably the most highly developed and complex piece of matter in the universe.

Chapter 3.
Human evolution

We present-day humans have a long, colorful history behind us, so long and so colorful in fact that it is often difficult to grasp. It centers on the process of evolution and the explosion of life into a great multiplicity of forms during hundreds of millions of years, an explanation which many people refuse to accept despite the overwhelming amount of evidence supporting it. They prefer the simpler Biblical story of a special creation of man. Indeed, it is hard to believe that the distant ancestors of the pilot flying a 747 jet non-stop half-way around the earth or the astronaut walking on the moon could have been ape-like creatures not all that many generations ago. Nonetheless, something like that seems clearly to be the case. The biological and cultural evolution of man is accepted by the scientific community today as factual and undeniable. The inquisitive person need only to look at the hair on his arm to be reminded that we humans have evolved from hairy ancestors who have lost almost all their hair over the course of a few million years. *The Naked Ape*, by the British anthropologist Desmond Morris, inquires into the curious locations where our remaining tufts of hair have remained.

Time and space

The concept of time is one of the key concepts in the story of evolution and one of the most difficult to grasp. Let me explain. As a native Texan, I always thought of America as an old, established nation with a venerable history, but living in Europe taught me that as a country we Americans are in fact cultural and political youngsters, still wet behind the ears. Virtually every larger European community (Rome, Vienna, Paris, London, Istanbul) is five or ten times older than the first settlements in America. It takes a real stretch of the imagination—at least for me—to imagine that civilization started in the Fertile Crescent in the Middle East ten thousand years ago, and that people like you and me wandered about as hunters and gatherers for hundreds of thousands of years before that. Then they discovered how to domesticate plants and animals, which marks the beginnings of "civilized" or "city life."

As we push our story back farther and farther into human and animal history, the concept of time becomes more and more blurred. Thousands of years become tens and hundreds of thousands of years, and then the numbers slip easily into the millions. However, long before we get into the hundreds of thousands of years, human history becomes a purely intellectual exercise and difficult to relate to in any sort of personal, emotional way. Occasionally a good film such as "Quest for Fire" or the recent television series on Neanderthal Man helps us relate to our ancestors on a more than purely intellectual or academic manner.

A world map showing the paths our forefathers took on their journey from South Africa to Australia, Europe, Asia, Siberia, the Americas, and all the way down to the tip of South America always makes a powerful impression on me. Especially striking is the fact that they went all that way on foot, step by step, over thousands of years. Paleontologists and anthropologists tell us that we are all Africans by origin, and that our ancestors walked over countless millennia from South Africa into every corner of the globe. Pictures and dioramas, for example, showing how during the ice ages they followed herds of animals through Mongolia and Siberia over the Bering Straits into Alaska are always instructive and impressive. Having followed the animals into the New World, they spread during the course of many centuries throughout Canada and North America, and then all the way down to Tierra del Fuego. Our ancestors must surely have been intelligent, resourceful, energetic, rugged individuals of whom we can be proud indeed. Thinking about their exploits and struggles can, in my view, help us establish much more than a purely intellectual connection with them.

For centuries they wandered about during all kinds of weather and climate as opportunistic hunters and gatherers, living off the fruits, nuts, roots, berries they could find and whatever wild animals they could kill. They had to adjust constantly to rugged conditions and to protect themselves from being killed and eaten by other animals. Their only defensive weapons and hunting instruments were at first clubs and pointed sticks, and their only cutting tools at the beginning of their development were the jagged edges of broken stones or parts of broken animal bones. Simply staying alive in a hostile world full of other wild and hungry creatures must have been a full-time job for our forbearers. The fact that they flourished, multiplied, and spread out to all parts of the globe is for me simply astounding. Their physique and skin color adapted to local climatic and geographical conditions. In this way, various types or races of humans within the one surviving species developed in terms of their skin color, body-build, types of hair, culture, language, etc.

The naked ape

All today's humans are of one species (*homo sapiens*, or sometimes called *homo sapiens sapiens*) and can interbreed with all other humans, everywhere. An Eskimo child raised from birth in New York City would become a typical New Yorker in terms of language and cultural habits and would manifest virtually nothing of its Eskimo heritage other than skin color, body build, and facial characteristics. Today's species of *homo sapiens* is the result of a long and involved evolution involving numerous forms, species, and variations of early humans over millions of years, as we will see.

The earliest ancestral forms are all called primates ("man-like") and closely resemble us in terms of basic anatomy, physiology, and nervous system. All our primate ancestors, except man and the four species of great apes (gorilla, chimpanzee, orangutan, gibbon), retained their tails. British anthropologist Desmond Morris points out that there are some 200 species of primates today, and they would all look rather similar if one exemplar of each species were lined up in a row, with one exception. And that is man. All the other primates are completely covered with hair. Man would stand out like a sore thumb in this line-up of his 200 closest animal relatives because he has virtually no body hair. Man is the great naked ape.

The great chain of life

Going back even further in our animal history, the primates are closely related to all mammals in the sense of having warm blood, body hair, live births, and feeding the newborn by means of the female mammary glands. Further back, mammals are related to the dinosaurs, birds, fish, snakes, lizards, etc. Deeper still in the ancient past, all these rather advanced manifestations of life are related still to worms, slugs, sponges and other extremely old and primitive forms of life. The further back we go, the more fascinating and complex it all becomes, until we finally arrive at the big questions of how and why, when and where, did it all begin? We find ourselves in some nebulous realm of time and space as the earth cooled off and the oceans formed some three or four billion years ago. Then, somehow, life began and started its dynamic career of mutation and evolution.

Virtually all life forms seem to follow a broad general pattern: they come into existence, grow and develop by taking from the environment whatever they need, they mature and reach full form, then reproduce, grow old, and finally go out of existence. As we learn from Charles Darwin, life is a struggle to survive, and only those forms which can best adapt to their local conditions of food, climate, competitors, etc. will live, reproduce, and pass on their characteristics to their offspring.

Life in the family

In addition to the physical evolution and changes in life forms in general, there has been among humans a similar cultural evolution or development in the way our ancestors lived their lives. One of the basic characteristics of humans is that we live in groups, probably at first small family groups and extended families. This emphasis on family is determined in part by the fact that human babies are completely helpless at birth and would quickly die without a great deal of help and support from their parents for the first ten or more years of life. Thus the central role of the family and the extended family in all societies. A larger group with a number of adult men providing food and defense has a much better chance of survival than isolated parents and children.

For tens of thousands of years, small groups of perhaps 20 to 50 members wandered about, learned to make and control fire, developed stone cutting edges and tools, created language, and stayed alive by eating whatever wild foods and animals that could find. Then roughly ten or so thousand years ago, they learned how to domesticate plants and animals. They discovered some particularly fertile area near a lake or river where grains such as wild wheat, rye, and rice were growing in abundance; they spent longer periods of time there rather than constantly moving about. Some hunters killed wolves and sheep and brought the baby animals home to be eaten later. The children played with the infant wolves and learned that wolves are also very social animals who like to be in a family environment. The small sheep were kept in a pen or tied up, but they also became accustomed to men and parts of the human family. Excess seeds from the wild grasses were stored and planted along the river banks the following year. To "domesticate" means to bring something into your house and cultivate it. This is what our ancestors did with plants and animals roughly ten thousand years ago.

An assured food supply

The domestication of plants and animals thus provided an assured food supply and is generally thought of as being the beginning of human civilization. Human groups could now grow substantially in size, and various individuals could begin to specialize in doing one job very well: creating pottery for containers, developing bows, arrows, and spears for hunting and defense, making better flint cutting edges, etc. They learned eventually to work metals, develop weaving, tame horses, keep records and even to write out their experiences for the next generation. Out of the extended and greatly enlarged family grouping developed a *civis* or "city" of people dwelling permanently in one location, generally on the edge of a river or lake. The size of the group and the degree of specialization grew as people discovered and developed their many latent human abilities.

The word "civilization" comes from the Latin word *civis* meaning community or city, and means "life in the city" in contrast to constantly wandering about hither and yon over the land. Most authorities agree that civilization began some 10,000 or more years ago along the river banks of the Middle East in an area called the "Fertile Crescent," in Iraq, Iran, Babylonia, and Egypt. The major rivers are the Tigris, Euphrates, and the Nile. Other more or less contemporaneous but independent creations of civilization include the Chinese forms along the Yangtze and Yellow rivers, and in India in the area called the Punjab ("five rivers"), and much later in the distant Maya-Aztec regions in Mexico and the Incas in the mountains of Peru.

In this chapter I want to briefly outline the path our ancestors took by listing some of the major development stages in our evolutionary development and then some of the early major cultural accomplishments. The purpose of this review is to deepen my appreciation of our ancestral heritage, both animal and human. The evolutionary stages are *australopithecus africanus* (southern African ape), *homo habilis* (handy man), *homo erectus* (upright man), *homo heidelbergensis* (Heidelberg man), *homo neanderthalensis*, (Neanderthal man), and finally *homo sapiens* (modern man). The major physical and cultural accomplishments in this long development are upright posture, increased brain size, loss of body hair, development of language, control of fire, use of stone tools, domestication of the dog, domestication of plants and other animals marking the beginning of civilization.

The major stages in man's physical evolution

The evolutionary history of the primates (a group of animals which includes lemurs, monkeys, apes, and man) can be traced back for some 85 million years, and is one of the oldest of all surviving placental mammal groups. Paleontologists call our more recent animal ancestors hominids, meaning the family of great apes and humans. Recent discoveries suggest that the early ancestors of the hominids migrated from Africa to Eurasia about 17 million years ago, just before these two continents were cut off from each other by an expansion of the Mediterranean Sea. The 99 species of lemurs are all limited to the island of Madagascar and form a special chapter in primatology.

The fossil record demonstrating man's early development over several million years is sketchy and far from complete, but enough fossils have been found to draw a fairly good general picture of his evolution. In addition to the vast stretches of time involved, other important elements to keep in mind during the following discussion include great changes in climate and temperature causing droughts and ice ages, raising and lowering of the sea level, major changes in habitats and animals used for food by early man.

Australopithecus africanus and *Australopithecus afarensis*

The use of the words "man" and "human" must be taken here in a rather loose sense, with the meaning of early primate forms which eventually developed into *homo sapiens* (modern humans) some 150,000 to 200,000 years ago. It is easy and tempting to assume that there is a straight linear progression of early hominids in which each successive species looks more and more like modern humans, but the path is much more complicated, and many species were dead ends, dying out without leaving any descendants.

It is estimated that the last common ancestor of chimps and humans died out about seven million years ago. Today there is only one species of hominids, and that's us, modern *homo sapiens*, but for most of man's evolutionary history a variety of early humans inhabited the earth at the same time. It is believed that between 3.5 and 1.5 millions years ago, at least eleven hominid species lived in Africa, many of them members of the genus *Australopithecus*. By the time the entire *Australopithecus* group went extinct about 1.4 million years ago, the earliest members of our genus, *homo*, had come on the scene. The precise origins and development of our genus are still unknown, but most scientists think we evolved from *Australopithecus*.

One of the earliest of the hominids or "man-like" ancestors in our history was a small African ape living about six million years ago, *Australopithecus africanus* (southern African ape, also known as australopithecine: "australo" = "southern", "pithecus" = "ape"), whose descendants include both us humans and our closest relatives, chimpanzees and bonobos (pigmy chimpanzees). These relatives are in fact so close to us that there is only about one and a half percent difference in our genetic structure or DNA. For reasons that are still debated, some apes in one branch that split off from the australopithecines developed the ability to walk upright. These early ancestors spent much of their time in the trees, but unlike other primates, they also walked readily on two feet when on the ground. This upright posture is a trait which scientists often use to designate the human family. Upright posture allowed these early primates a better range of vision and the freedom to use their other two limbs and hands for other purposes, chiefly grasping and manipulating objects, and this is associated with a rapid increase in brain size and development.

The most famous of our very early ancestors is a young woman called "Lucy," named after the Beatle's song, "Lucy in the sky with diamonds" which was being played repeatedly in the camp when paleontologist/anthropologist Donald Johanson and his student Tom Gray discovered the first fossils of a 40% complete skeleton in Ethiopia in 1974. Lucy is estimated to have lived 3.2 million years ago. Her discovery was significant because the skeleton shows evidence of small skull capacity akin to that of apes, but the structure of her knee and pelvis showed that she routinely walked upright on two legs, like us. This form of bipedal locomotion is the earliest and single most important difference between humans and apes.

Homo habilis and homo ergaster

By about 2 million years ago, the very first animals to be classified in the genus *homo* ("man") had appeared. "Handy man" (or "skillful person") is the earliest known species of the genus *homo* and lived from approximately 2.5 million to at least 1.6 million years ago. The definition of this species as *homo habilis* is credited to the famous paleontologist team of Mary and Louis Leakey, who found his fossils in Tanzania, East Africa, between 1962 and 1964. In its appearance and morphology, "Handy man" was the least similar to modern humans of all species to be placed in the genus *homo*. He was short and had disproportionately long arms compared to modern humans. It is thought he descended from a species of australopithecine hominid. He had a cranial capacity of about 650 cc, slightly less than half the size of modern man's 1400 cc. Despite the ape-like morphology of the body, his fossilized remains are often accompanied by primitive stone tools, for example at Olduvai Gorge in Tanzania and Lake Turkana in Kenya, indicating that he used cutting edges made of stone.

Homo habilis spent time both in the trees and on the ground. He evolved in South and East Africa in the late Pliocene or early Pleistocene (three to two million year ago), had smaller molars and a larger brain than the australopithecines, and made tools from stone and perhaps animal bones. He was nicknamed "handy man" by Louis Leakey due to the association with many stone tools.

Homo habilis has often been thought to be the ancestor of the lankier and more sophisticated *homo ergaster* (*"working man,"* due to his tool-making ability), a species more advanced than *habilis* but more primitive than *homo erectus*. Slight morphological differences in anatomy gave rise to the more human-appearing species, *homo erectus* or "upright man." Debates continue over whether or not *homo habilis* is a direct human ancestor of *homo erectus*. However, in 2007, new findings suggest that the two species co-existed and may be separate lineages from an unknown common ancestor instead of *homo erectus* being descended directly from *homo habilis*.

Some two million years ago, several different species of the genus *homo* lived in Africa, and *homo ergaster* is the most plausible ancestors of modern humans. He had a body essentially like that of modern man: long legs, short arms, and a moderately large brain. Some of our relatives began leaving Africa at least 1.8 million years ago, long before *homo sapiens* evolved. Who were they, and here did they go? It seems they left through Egypt towards the Middle East and northern Eurasia. *Homo ergaster* with his long legs designed for walking over long distances in the sun was perhaps the first. His slender body build and probable loss of body hair allowed for more efficient cooling.

Homo erectus

In the Early Pleistocene (1.5 to 1.0 million years ago in Africa, Asia, and Europe, presumably), some populations of *Homo habilis* evolved larger brains and made more elaborate stone tools; these and other differences are sufficient for anthropologists to classify them as a new species, *homo erectus*. In addition, it is believed that *homo erectus* was the first human ancestor to walk truly upright. He may have also used fire to cook his meat.

"Upright man" is an extinct species of the genus *homo* believed to have been the first hominid to leave Africa. For unknown reasons, he originally migrated from Africa during the Early Pleistocene, perhaps as early as 2.0 million years ago, and dispersed throughout most of the Old World. His fossilized remains, dated as 1.8 and 1.0 million years old, have been found in Africa, Europe, Indonesia, Vietnam, and China.

The first fossils of *Homo erectus* were discovered in 1891 on the Indonesian island of Java and later near Peking, China; he was originally given the name *Pithecanthropus erectus*, "upright ape man." He was often referred to as the "Java ape man" or "Peking man," and was considered an intermediate step between humans and apes. *Homo erectus* lived from about 1.8 million to 70,000 years ago.

Once hominids set out from Africa some two million years ago, they first moved into Asia. One Asian species, *Homo erectus*, seems to have enjoyed an extraordinarily long existence, surviving well over 1.5 million years. He had a large range, extending from northern China through Indonesia. Fossils of

"Peking Man" from a cave near Beijing show some 40 members of the species that lived in China for at least several hundred thousand years.

Homo erectus was one of the world's most successful hominids, having evolved in eastern Asia and living there perhaps as long as 1.5 million years, perhaps ten times as long as modern man has been around. (*Homo sapiens* have lived for only 200,000 years at the most.) Recent fossils of *Homo erectus* may be no more that 40,000 years old, indicating that several hominid species were probably living at the same time.

Throughout much of the 20th century anthropologists debated the role of *homo erectus* in human evolution. Early in the century, due to discoveries on Java and in China, it was believed that modern humans first evolved in Asia. This contradicted Charles Darwin's idea of the African origin of man. However, during the 1950s and 1970s, numerous fossil finds from Kenya yielded evidence that the oldest hominids originated there. It is now believed that *homo erectus* is a descendant of earlier hominids such as *australopithecus* and early *homo* species (e.g., *homo habilis),* although new findings in 2007 suggest that *homo habilis* and *homo erectus* coexisted and may be separate lineages from a common ancestor. One wonders if various species of man existing at the same time and in the same area battled and killed off one another, or if they were able to mate and merge in that way. That might be the case here with these two groups and later with the Neanderthals and modern man. There is simply a great deal about human history that we do not know.

Homo heidelbergensis

This species of man was one of a number of hominid species living in Europe between 500,000 and 40,000 years ago. It seems clear that a variety of hominids existed in Europe before the arrival of the Neanderthals. The Heidelberg man is one of them; he seems to be closely related to Neanderthal, but different.

"Heidelberg Man" is another extinct species of the genus *homo* and is likely the direct ancestor of *homo neanderthalensis* in Europe. The best evidence found for these hominids dates between 600,000 and 400,000 years ago. The *Homo heidelbergensis* stone tool technology was considerably close to the advanced tool kit used by *homo erectus*. It is believed that Heidelberg Man was a robust group with a primitive form of language, and his fossils have been found in Germany, Italy, Spain, Greece, France, and Great Britain. The fossil remains show that he is closely similar to *homo ergaster,* "working man," from Africa, but has a larger brain—almost the size of modern man's—and more advanced tools. He was six feet tall and more muscular than man today.

His may have been the first species of the *homo* genus to bury their dead, but no forms of art or sophisticated artifacts other than stone tools have been uncovered, and it is therefore difficult to say much about his life style. This species likely gave rise to the Neanderthals but not to modern man, who is believed to have originated in Africa and spread northward to Europe.

His name comes from the university town of Heidelberg, Germany, near which a workman in 1907 found a fossil jawbone while digging and gave it to a professor at the university who identified it as an important fossil and made it known to the scholarly world.

Homo Neanderthalensis

The Neanderthals were a remarkable group of ancestors. They had brains as large as ours and were outstanding toolmakers. First appearing about 200,000 years ago, they dominated Europe and parts of Western Asia until their lineage died out less than 30,000 years ago, which is historically not all that far in the past. Today, scientists think Neanderthals lived in complex social groups, controlled fire, and were proficient hunters. As far as we know, they did not create art and probably did not possess complex language as we know it. They did bury their dead, however, but probably not with an elaborate ritual as modern humans do.

Neanderthal Man is an extinct member of the *homo* genus that is known from Pleistocene specimens found in Europe and parts of western and central Asia. In the beginning, paleo-anthropologists believed Neanderthals were dim-witted brutes with clubs and beast-like features, who walked with bent knees and shambling gaits, with heads slung forward on their big squat necks. Later research has shown, however, that this first assessment had to be drastically revised; they are the most interesting hominids because they are closest to us, and in many ways much like us. Neanderthals, named after the Neander Valley in Germany near which the first fossils were found, are either classified as a subspecies of modern humans (*Homo sapiens neanderthalensis*) or as a separate species (*Homo neanderthalensis*). This illustrates some of the problems and uncertainty associated with the classification of fossils.

These early men built permanent homes to shelter them from the long, harsh winter of the Ice Age. In the summer they followed the herds, and lived in tents and caves. Winter homes were solid huts, built teepee style, from branches and mammoth bones, covered with animal skins. These primitive dwellings were often used for many years, so they built them carefully. It is now believed that their lives were not a constant struggle for sheer survival, because they were very good hunters. They learned to organize hunts and to cure and store food for the long winter. Hunting was done individually and in-groups. Their most important aids in survival were their tools and weapons. They had learned to be very skilled toolmakers, and their weapons included stone axes, knives, spears, harpoons, wooden bows and sharp, stone-tipped arrows. There is also clear evidence that they had control of fire, often lived in caves or open-air structures of stone and vegetation, hunted large game from which they made clothing, cared for their sick or weak, and even buried their dead with some religious ceremonies.

The Neanderthals died out around 30,000 B.C. Why? One theory is that they were killed off by some groups of *Homo sapiens* man, but there is no evidence of this. Another theory is that they married into other groups, and that over time they ceased to exist as a separate species. But these are just theories and hard to prove one way or the other. However, it has been suggested that they disappeared because they are our direct ancestors, i.e., they perhaps evolved into modern humans.

The first proto-Neanderthal traits (large cranial capacity, prominent brow ridge, no chin, heavy bone structure) appeared in Europe as early as 600,000–350,000 years ago. By 130,000 years ago, complete Neanderthal characteristics had appeared. These characteristics then disappeared in Asia by 50,000 years ago and in Europe by 30,000 years ago. The most recent Neanderthal finds include those in Great Britain, considered older than 30,000 years ago, while the fossils from the Croatian Neanderthals have been re-dated to between 32,000 and 33,000 years ago. No definite specimens younger than 30,000 years ago have been found. Modern human skeletal remains with 'Neanderthal traits' found in Portugal, date to 24,500 years ago and are interpreted as indications of extensively mixed populations.

Neanderthal stone tools provide further evidence for their presence where skeletal remains have not been found. This can serve as another example of the complex detective work involved in telling a story which has so few concrete facts. The last traces of Mousterian culture, a type of advanced stone tools closely associated with Neanderthals, were found in a cave on the remote south-facing coast of Gibraltar.

The belief persists that Neanderthal cranial capacity was much larger than modern human's, but a 1993 analysis of 118 hominid crania showed that the two brains were almost the same size, with just a slight edge to *homo sapiens*. Since they lived in the Ice Age when much of the earth was frozen, it is believed that the diet of Neanderthals consisted almost entirely of meat, fish, seeds, roots, and nuts. They became well adjusted to cold conditions, and their low, squat body-build helped preserve their heat. On average, the height of Neanderthals was comparable to contemporaneous *homo sapiens*. Neanderthal males were about 5'5" tall and were heavily built with robust bone structure. They were skilled makers of tools and weapons. They made warm clothes of animal skins, sewn together with string made from animal guts They were much stronger than modern man, having particularly strong arms and hands. Females stood about 5'1".

The Neanderthals seem to be the first of our ancestors who buried their dead, and this has led to the idea that they were socially and spiritually quite advanced, perhaps even with a religion. However, only a few burial sites have been discovered, and on just one were grains of pollen discovered, which led researchers to believe that the body had been covered with flowers. The Neanderthals seem to have died out or merged completely about 35,000 years ago.

Homo sapiens: Origins of modern man

When and where did our species, *Homo sapiens,* evolve? Scientists are confident that we emerged in Africa, perhaps 150,000 years ago, but they cannot pinpoint exactly when, or who our immediate ancestors were. Hominid fossils from the crucial period between 200,000 and 100,000 years ago are rare, and researchers have to rely on isolated fossils from across Africa to piece together the origins of our species. By about 100,000 years ago, *Homo sapiens* had already spread out of Africa and reached the Middle East, then on to Australia by 60,000 years ago, and the Americas by perhaps 25,000 years ago.

In 1868, workers digging at Cro-Magnon, a rock shelter at Les Eyzies-de-Tayac, France, uncovered several skeletons of ancient *Homo sapiens*, and since that discovery the first modern human residents of Europe have been known as Cro-Magnons.

These early modern humans displayed a wide range of cultural and technological abilities that had not been seen among our earlier hominid relatives. They had a highly developed language and could make sophisticated tools; they created elaborate cave art and practiced complex rituals. These hominids exhibited virtually the entire array of behaviors that characterize people today.

Our species evolved not much more than 150,000 years ago, making us young compared to other hominid species, some of which survived for more than a million years. But in the short time we have existed, we have populated the entire globe. Language, creative expression, and sophisticated tools helped modern humans to gain an advantage over other hominids and eventually drive them out of existence. Today, *Homo sapiens* is the only living species of hominids in the world and is to be found in every continent except Antarctica.

Homo sapiens have a characteristic look: their faces are small and tucked under a high, domed brain case. They have small eyebrow ridges and their lower jaw ends in a prominent chin. On average, their bodies are less muscular than those of earlier hominids. The appearance of modern humans coincides with the appearance of highly crafted tools, efficient food-gathering strategies, and a complex social organization facilitated by a highly developed language.

Early modern humans lived in mobile groups and established extensive social networks to trade goods and exchange gifts. These networks probably developed for the purpose of securing future favors when times were hard. And it seems that times were indeed hard for many of the first modern humans. During the last Ice Age, for example, humans were pushed to the edge of extinction, perhaps by famine and drought caused by a sharp drop in global temperatures. For these early modern humans, an increased reliance on social alliances and creativity was key to their survival.

Later, ancestral humans developed a much larger brain—typically 1,400 cc in modern humans, well over twice the size of that of a chimpanzee or gorilla. The pattern of human postnatal brain growth differs from that of other apes and allows for extended periods of social learning and language acquisition in juvenile humans.

Human beings, humans, or man

Humans have a highly developed brain capable of abstract reasoning, language, introspection, and problem solving. This mental capability, combined with an erect body carriage that frees the arms for manipulating objects, has allowed humans to make far greater use of tools than any other species. Humans are distributed worldwide, with large populations inhabiting every continent on earth except the South Pole, and even there we have a large colony of international research scientists. Like most higher primates, humans are very social by nature. Humans are particularly adept at utilizing systems of communication—primarily spoken and written language—for self-expression, the exchange of ideas, and organizational needs. Humans create complex social structures composed of many cooperating and competing groups, from families to tribes to states and nations. We humans have a marked appreciation for beauty and aesthetics, which, combined with our strong desire for self-expression, has led to highly sophisticated cultural innovations such as art, architecture, writing, literature, comedy and drama, plus music and dance.

Humans are the only animal species known to build fires, cook their food, and clothe themselves, along also manipulating and developing numerous other technologies. The unusually long period of juvenile dependence on the parents allows humans to pass on their acquired skills and knowledge to the next generation, at first informally within the family circle as well as later on through formal educational institutions. After the invention of writing, a large store of collected wisdom from many generations became available for later generations to use and profit from.

Transition to civilization

The rise of agriculture and domestication of animals led to stable human settlements. Until ca. 10,000 years ago, virtually all humans survived as hunters-gatherers. They generally lived in small nomadic groups and wandered over large areas, foraging and living off the land. The advent of an assured food surplus led to the formation of permanent human settlements, the domestication of animals, and eventually to the use of metal tools. Agriculture encouraged trade and cooperation, and led to specialization and a complex society.

About 6,000 years ago, the first proto-states developed in Mesopotamia, in the Sahara/Nile and the Indus Valleys, and along the rivers in China. Military forces were formed for protection, and government bureaucracies for administration. States cooperated and competed for resources, in some cases waging wars with their neighbors. Around 2,000–3,000 years ago, some states, such as Persia, India, China, Rome, and Greece, developed through conquest into the first expansive empires. Influential religions also rose to prominence at this time and were fundamental instruments in forming large numbers of people into a social entity and cohesive force.

Close relationships between human groups have encouraged the growth of science, art, discussion, and technology, but it has also led to major culture clashes and wars. The more highly developed the cultures and technologies became, the more vicious and destructive became also their wars. The development and use of weapons of mass destruction has occurred in more recent years, and today increased environmental destruction and pollution threaten to affect not only all human groups but also most other life forms on the planet as well.

Early man's major achievements

Here is a brief discussion of what strikes me as some of the most important accomplishments of early man. Some are anatomical and physiological, others are social and cultural; all are difficult to explain in detail and uncertain as to the time and mechanisms by which they were accomplished. But they all contributed greatly to making humans what we are today.

Upright posture and loss of body hair

Man's upright posture is one of the two most obvious physical characteristics distinguishing him from his primate relatives. The other is his loss of body hair and his essentially "naked" appearance as an animal. Questions of when, where, and why these two things happened are primarily a matter of conjecture and informed guessing, in the one case more than in the other. The fossil records show us, for example, that the knee and leg bones of Lucy pretty clearly indicate that she could walk upright more or less as we do, when she wanted to. So there is some hard evidence for when man-like creatures stood upright and walked, but what kind of evidence could possibly demonstrate that our ancestors started losing their body hair? So the specialists try to reconstruct temperature charts of bygone eons and then theorize that since naked skin can dissipate body heat better than hair-covered skin, man must have begun losing his body hair during such and such a geologic period in areas with hot climates. But why then did he not regain it back during the long ice ages?

Man develops language

It is even more difficult to find answers to questions concerning the origin and development of human language, however, because in the production of articulate speech, much depends on the delicate position of the larynx higher or lower in the throat. And what fossilized evidence could exist to show us that? The use of language is one of the most conspicuous and important diagnostic traits that distinguish *Homo sapiens* from other species. Unlike writing, spoken language of course consists of just sound and leaves no trace of any kind. Hence linguists have to resort to indirect methods in trying to decipher the origins of language.

The question of language origin significantly depends on the view taken of the communication skills of *Homo neanderthalensis*, our closest hominid relative, who died out perhaps only 30,000 years ago. Earlier evaluations suggested that he was a muscular brute with only a primitive language, but this was later revised upward. In view of the paucity of real evidence, theories about the origin of language have become a guessing game of inference and speculation. The basic idea is that a complex society such as ours requires a highly sophisticated language, so anthropologists try to determine the complexity of Neanderthal's language and social structure by his way of life. In any case, a lengthy stage of continuous pre-language development, intermediate between great ape language and full-blown human language, needs to be assumed for each stage of hominid evolution. Much work has been done on the language skills of chimpanzees in particular, including their rather limited ability to acquire and produce some sounds and elements of human language, but much concerning the complex subject of the origins of language is still open and subject to many questions.

Man conquers fire

Another vital step forward in human evolution was man's controlled use of fire, but again, questions of when, where, how remain open because of an almost total lack of hard evidence. What evidence of fire could remain after hundreds of thousands of years? Theorists speculate that the ability to control fire likely began with *Homo erectus* or *Homo ergaster* probably at least 790,000 years ago, but perhaps as early as 1.5 million years ago. In addition, it has sometimes been suggested that the use and discovery of controlled fire may even predate *Homo erectus*. Fire was possibly used by the early hominid *Homo habilis* and perhaps even by robust australopithecines. It seems to me that early possession of both fire and a fairly good ability to communicate would be indispensable for the survival of our hominid ancestors in the harsh world they inhabited.

The control of fire was a turning point in human evolution in that it allowed humans to proliferate due to the incorporation of cooked proteins and carbohydrates, expansion of human activity into the night hours, protection from predators, and keeping warm during extreme weather. When we consider the dangerous environment and rugged weather in which early man often lived, it seems that he must have had some powerful tools or methods of defending himself, of avoiding being eaten, and of not freezing to death. Since no stone tools have been found for very early man, it seems that fire may have been his most helpful instrument for staying alive and flourishing. Since there is no fossil or factual evidence concerning early man and fire, these are the kinds of theoretical considerations used in trying to construct a theory about our ancestors' controlled use of fire.

Stone tools and technology

Around 2.5 million years ago, something new appears in the record of man: stone tools. Here, finally, is hard evidence, at least something that can last for millennia. They are at first glance not much to look at, just sharp-edged flakes of rock, but their appearance makes a major advance in our story of human evolution. They mark man's basic insights and intelligence into which stones make better tools and how best to knock off and shape cutting edges. Having tools to cut meat from animal bones opened up new possibilities into man's struggle for survival, especially combined with fire for cooking the meat and making it thereby more easily digestible. The invention of stone tools represents a significant advance in human evolution because it shows that our ancestors had developed mental capacities far beyond those of modern apes. For many years researchers linked the first stone tools with the relatively large-brained species *Homo habilis,* or "handy man."

Stone tools are first attested around 2.6 million years ago, when Habilis in Eastern Africa used so-called pebble tools, choppers made out of round pebbles that had been split by simple strikes. These were followed later by large stone hand-axes made from flint, then flint flakes and fragments of obsidian (volcanic glass) used as carving and cutting tools; then scrapers, slicers, needles, and flattened needles were made. Ever more refined and specialized flint tools were made by the Neanderthals and the Cro-Magnons. These often remarkable knives, blades, arrow heads, and spear points show the increasing technical skill and mental acuity of our forbearers. Most paleontology and anthropology museums have examples of the early cutting edges used by our ancestors. Specialists estimate that stone tools were used by proto-humans at least 2.5 million years ago and the controlled use of fire began around 1.5 million years ago.

Archaeology attempts to tell the story of past or lost cultures in part by close examination of the artifacts they produced. Early humans first left stone tools, then pottery, jewelry, and other artifacts that are particular to various regions and times. Precisely when early humans started to use tools is difficult to determine, because the more primitive these tools are (for example, sharp-edged stones) the more difficult it is to decide whether they are natural objects or human artifacts. There is some evidence that the australopithecines (4 million years ago) may have used broken bones as tools, but this is debated.

Using tools has been interpreted as a key sign of intelligence, and it has been theorized that tool use may have stimulated certain aspects of human evolution—most notably the continued expansion of the human brain. Paleontology has yet to explain in any detail the expansion and development of this crucial organ over millions of years. We know, for example, that the brain is very demanding in terms of energy consumption. It has been estimated that the brain of a modern human consumes one fifth of the energy consumption of his body. Making and using tools is brain work—like playing chess—but increased and improved tool use also allows for better hunting and therefore an increased consumption of meat, which is more energy-rich than plants. Researchers have suggested that early hominids were thus under a kind of evolutionary pressure to increase their capacity to create and use tools.

Man and the dog

Dated as 400,000 thousand years ago in England, 300,000 years ago in China, and 150,000 in southern France, wolf bones have been discovered in association with those of early hominids. These mixed human and wolf fossils indicate that hominid populations of the time must have overlapped wolf territories. Humans probably killed wolves as a food source and also used the wolf skin as clothing. And wolves must surely have also killed and eaten many humans, as the fairy tale of Little Red Riding Hood leads us to believe. How did these two large, meat-eating predators, man and wolf, become so closely associated? Most theorists agree that the first animal man domesticated was the wolf. We speculate in the following way.

Let us say early hunters killed a mother wolf with a litter of pups. They take the pups home for later consumption. Their own children play with the pups and adopt them as pets. Little by little, one of the litter becomes somewhat tamed and is not eaten. The adults discover that wolves, like humans, are very social creatures and have a strong sense of belonging to a group, even a human family. Could such a "tamed" wolf have indeed been the precursor of the dog and could this have been the means by which the modern domesticated dog first evolved?

Food and shelter were the biggest problems of life for both man and wild wolf/dog in those difficult days long ago. The only way both man and wolf could keep alive was to hunt animals for food, kill them with their stone hatchets or teeth, and bring some of the flesh back for their families to eat. Man and his family lived in a cave; wild wolf/dog and his family lived either in a cave or in a hollow tree trunk. When winter came and food was harder to find, maybe the wild dog became so hungry that he grew bold and crept close to man's campfire. Maybe he found some bones there that man had thrown away as useless since he could not chew them. But the wild dog could chew them, and did! And then one bitter, snowy night, maybe the dog brought his family to the campfire, too, so they could also get warm and gnaw on the bones.

Man noticed when he was out hunting that the wild wolf/dog, with its very keen sense of smell and fast feet, caught its animal prey more easily than man could. He watched the wild dog run, nose close to the ground, right to the hiding place of a fat rabbit. And somehow, through some mutual need and combined abilities, man and dog became hunting partners living either together or in close proximity to one another. The dog soon learned that all he had to do to be warm and well-fed was to help man catch his food. Such scenarios could help explain the man-wolf association which became so beneficial to both.

Other animals domesticated by man

The first animal to be domesticated many thousands of years ago and in some unknown manner, appears to have been the dog/wolf. This preceded the domestication of other species by several millennia or more. Later, a number of important species (such as the goat, sheep, pig and cow, all about 10,000 BC) were domesticated. The goat, sheep and pig in particular were domesticated independently in the Near East and Asia. There is even early evidence of beekeeping, in the form of rock paintings, dating to 13,000 BC. The cat, chicken, donkey, water buffalo, camel, llama, silkworm, reindeer, goose, duck, and other animals were domesticated in various parts of the world between 7500 BC and 3000 BC. The earliest secure evidence of horse domestication, bit wear on horse molars in the Ukraine, dates to around 4000 BC. The domestication of these animals signified a major step forward in man's way of life and caused significant changes in his development.

Plants

The earliest attempts at plant domestication seems to have occurred along the river areas in the Middle East and Asia about 10,000 to 12,000 years ago. The central item was variations of wild grass seeds: rye, wheat, barley, and others. It is believed that cereal crops were first domesticated around 9000 BC in the Fertile Crescent in the Middle East. The first domesticated crops were generally annuals with large seeds or fruits. These included pod fruits such as peas and beans, along with wild grains such as wheat.

The Middle East was especially suited to these species; the dry-summer climate was conducive to the evolution of large-seeded annual plants, and the variety of elevations led to a great variety of species. As the domestication of plants took place, humans began to move from a hunter-gatherer way of life to a settled agricultural society. This change would eventually lead, some 4000 to 5000 years later, to the first city states and eventually the rise of civilization itself as we know it.

All these domestications were surely gradual and involved a process of trial and error that occurred slowly. Over time, perennial plants and small trees began to be domesticated, including apples and olives. Gourd-type plants were important because the dried gourds were useful as containers prior to the development of pottery. In different parts of the world, quite different species were domesticated. In the Americas, for example, squash, maize, and beans formed the core of the diet, while in East Asia, millets, rice, and soy were the most important crops.

Metal cutting edges

For most of mankind's history, man's only cutting edges were made of stone. Only in the last few thousand years has man learned how to work metal as cutting edges. The first metals known to man were gold, silver, and copper, about 6000-8000 years ago. The use of copper in antiquity is of more significance than gold because the first tools, implements, and weapons were made from copper, since it could hold a much better cutting edge than either gold or silver. Since this occurred during prehistoric times, it's hard to know details about how all this happened. These three metals are widespread from natural outcroppings over the earth in more or less pure form and are often found near the surface. Later they were of course all mined. Gold and silver were used for decorations, but are not hard enough to make tools or be of much practical use. Copper is hard enough for some tools but still quite soft. Eventually man learned to melt and mix copper with tin to make bronze, which is a much harder metal than pure copper, and thus much better for tools, weapons, and armor. The development of bronze marks the end of the Stone Age in human history and the beginning of the Bronze Age. This took place some 5500 years ago in Mesopotamia and Egypt; bronze artifacts in China are dated at about the same time.

The Iron Age began when man learned how to to use bellows to create very hot furnaces, hot enough to forge iron out of iron ore. Iron does not occur on earth naturally as a metal (except in meteors); it is always in the form of iron ore, which is why it took so long for people to recognize it as a metal. The ore had to be heated very hot, until it turned soft, then the impurities had to be beaten out of it, because at first they could not make fires hot enough to melt the iron and let it run off in a pure state. But the superior strength and hardness of iron made it worth all the hard work. The Hittites of Asia Minor were the first iron workers, around 1500 BC in Asia Minor (modern Turkey), and managed to conquer quite a bit of the Middle East because of their superior weapons.

Iron was available to the ancients in small amounts from meteors. There is some indication that man-made iron was available perhaps as early as 2500 B.C.; however, iron making did not become an everyday process until about 1200 BC. In the early days, iron was five times more expensive than gold, and its first uses were merely as ornaments. Iron weapons revolutionized warfare and iron implements did the same for farming. Iron and steel were soon to become the building blocks for civilization.

The start of modern man

The first humans to show evidence of spirituality which we can infer from tangible evidence were the Neanderthals; they buried their dead, often apparently with food or tools for an afterlife. However, evidence of more sophisticated beliefs, such as the early Cro-Magnon cave paintings in France (probably with magical or religious significance) did not appear until some 32,000 years ago. Cro-Magnons also left behind stone figurines such as the fertility symbol of the Venus of Willendorf, probably also signifying religious belief. By 11,000 years ago, *Homo sapiens* had spread worldwide, reaching even to the southern tip of South America, the last of the uninhabited continents (except for Antarctica, which remained undiscovered until 1820 AD). Tool use and language continued to improve, interpersonal relationships became more complex, and man was well on his way to becoming the highly complex and versatile creature we know and are today.

Modern human behavior is observed in cultural universals which are the key elements shared by all groups of people throughout the history of man. Examples of elements that may be considered cultural universals are language, religion, art, music, the incest taboo, myth-making, cooking, games, laughter, and jokes. Since cultural universals are found in all cultures, including some of the most isolated indigenous groups still living today, scientists believe that these traits must have evolved or have been invented in Africa prior to the exodus of *Homo sapiens*. This points once again to the African origins of all humans today.

Origins of civilization

Throughout more than 90% of their history, *Homo sapiens* lived in small bands as nomadic hunter-gatherers. Cultural evolution quickly outpaced biological evolution, and history proper began. Somewhere between 8500 and 7000 BC, humans in the Fertile Crescent in the Middle East, as well as in India and China at about the same time, began the systematic husbandry of plants and animals, marking the growth of large social groups, and therewith the beginning of civilization. This phenomenon spread to neighboring regions, and also developed independently elsewhere (Central and South America), until most *Homo sapiens* lived sedentary lives in permanent settlements as farmers and herdsmen.

Not all societies abandoned nomadism, especially those in isolated areas of the globe poor in plant and animal species which could easily be domesticated, such as Australia. However, among those civilizations that did adopt agriculture, the relative security and increased productivity provided by farming allowed the population to greatly expand and develop many kinds of specialists. Agriculture had a major impact on man's way of life, and humans also began to have a decided effect on the environment as never before. Surplus food allowed a priestly or governing class to arise, followed by increasing divisions of labor. This led to earth's first full-blown civilization at Sumer in the Middle East, between 4000 and 3000 BC. Additional civilizations quickly arose in Ancient Egypt, at the Indus Valley, and in China.

Origins of writing

The creation of writing is surely one of man's greatest achievements and allowed societies to preserve their own historical and religious traditions. These greatly strengthened the cohesive and spiritual nature of the group. Reading and writing were probably invented by merchants for the mundane sake of record keeping, but soon these special skills of retaining exact information were taken over by priests and jealously guarded by selected members of the religious hierarchy. The priests created and controlled the history of the people, including early myths of the earth's origins, its people, and the divine creative powers.

Starting around 3000 BC, Hinduism, one of the oldest religions still practiced today, began to take form in India. Others soon followed among the Jews, Persians, and Egyptians. The invention of writing enabled complex societies to arise: Record-keeping and libraries served as a storehouse of knowledge and increased the cultural transmission of information. Favored humans no longer had to all spend their time working for survival—curiosity and education encouraged the pursuit of knowledge and wisdom among a select class. Various disciplines, such as religion, philosophy, and science (in a primitive form), arose. New civilizations sprang up, traded with one another, and engaged in war for territory and resources. Powerful city-states and empires began to form. By around 1000 BC, there were city-states and empires in the Middle East, Iran, India, China, and Greece, approximately on equal footing; at times one empire expanded, only to decline or be driven back later. War and preparations for war began to be one of man's major occupations.

Models of human evolution

Today all humans are classified as belonging to the species *Homo sapiens sapiens*. However, as we have seen, this is not the first species of hominids: the first species of genus *Homo*, *Homo habilis*, evolved in East Africa at least 2 million years ago, and members of this species populated different parts of Africa in a relatively short time. *Homo erectus* evolved more than 1.8 million years ago, and by 1.5 million years ago had spread throughout the Old World.

Virtually all physical anthropologists agree that *Homo sapiens* likely evolved out of *Homo erectus*. Has human evolution reached an end with us, or are there other human species yet to come?

Some scientists now believe that the physical evolution of humans has ceased, and that we are as advanced physically as we are ever going to be. We have become so clever at adapting our environment and creating tools to suit our needs that we no longer need to evolve physically; we simply invent tools to do new tasks for us.

But it seems to me there are other kinds of evolution, especially cultural and intellectual, which are especially important in the story of man. Cultural evolution would include modern man's ability to live harmoniously in increasingly larger social groupings, fundamentally different from the family and extended family environment in which he has lived almost his entire existence. Today there are vast masses of people in cities with millions of inhabitants who are both cooperating as fellow citizens and yet remaining complete strangers at the same time. Driving a car through downtown Los Angeles, New York, Tokyo, or Berlin dramatically illustrates how far man has evolved from his traditional small group mentality. International trade and financial transactions, plus massive global travel and internet communications on the part of millions of people, are additional examples of man's cultural evolution.

Intellectually and emotionally, great numbers of modern people are beginning to regard all human beings as fellow human beings and are concerned with their well being. Many believe that all people are our brothers and sisters, and all children are our children. This is far removed from the traditional concern only for members of one's own group. Millions of people are becoming less provincial and more cosmopolitan, as we see when there are tsunamis, earthquakes, or mass starvation as in present day Haiti or Africa. The recent Olympic Games in China helped us all rejoice in the sheer fact of being a human among other fellow humans.

The upshot of this chapter for me is simply that I become increasingly aware that we are complex creatures with a complex and fascinating history. And that we are deeply indebted to countless hundreds of thousands and millions of fellow humans more or less identical to us who over many, many generations have struggled to survive and flourish under difficult conditions. They have left us an amazing legacy of artistic and cultural values, health, intelligence, physical and spiritual strength, linguistic skills, energy, tenacity, enterprise, and self-confidence without which they and we would not and could not exist. My hat is off to them.

Chapter 4.
Society, economy, political systems, war

Opening remarks

Anyone who can read these pages is by that very fact a civilized person and simply takes civilization for granted, as do all of us. We are so civilized that it is usually difficult even to recognize what the distinctive features of civilization are. Practically everything we do is closely related to or is some aspect of our being civilized. In this chapter I want to briefly outline some of the main features of civilization, how they came into being, and how they form us and our view of the world. The purpose is to underline and enhance our own awareness of what it means to be the inheritors of ten or more millennia of civilized humanity.

A number of intertwined elements or factors are involved here: civilization, culture, being social. The simplest perhaps is being social; man by nature is a social animal and loves to be surrounded by fellow humans, as seen in the fact that one of the worst tortures society can impose upon criminals is solitary confinement. (Aristotle says that a completely isolated creature would be either a beast or a god.) The second element is culture, by which I mean here simply the general way things are done in our larger group. This starts above all with our language, the foods we eat, the way we dress, our value system, etc. The broad term 'enculturation' encompasses all of this and is with us from birth until we die. There are as many cultures and subcultures as there are groups and subgroups. Civilization is the idea of living in a group of fellow humans who more or less share the same culture (especially the language) and the general value system of the group. There have been many civilizations in the past, but many observers say that today there is only one world civilization, meaning that—apart from the language factor—most of the world's people share essentially one large set of values. All three of these terms—being social, culture, civilization—will figure in important ways in the following discussion.

Civilization is based on an assured food supply and stands in sharp contrast to the hunting-gathering period of human existence, a period which comprises almost the entire time of man's life on earth; it also stands in contrast to the nomadic way of life which some groups of modern humans still follow. In comparison to those two ways of life, civilization is distinguished in part by the following traits: size of the community, permanent residence, division of labor, distinct social classes, trade and commerce, money or some medium of exchange, ownership of land and property, a structured government, writing and history, etc. We all know and have experienced a great deal about the civilized way of life, so the discussion here will be primarily on how I think these things started and will necessarily stay on a broad, general level. Civilization is of course a huge, complex topic, but I want to stress only some of the highlights in order to make clear its impact on our life,

Basis of civilization

The indispensable basis of any large group of humans permanently living together is an assured food supply. This happened historically about ten thousand years ago more or less simultaneously in several parts of the world as man learned to domesticate plants and animals. We don't really know how all this happened and can only speculate. Our wandering ancestors found some very fertile areas between the Tigris and Euphrates rivers where wild cereals grew in abundance, and they made camp. They were able to harvest an excess of grain which could last them until the next crop came in; so they stayed longer than usual, built more permanent dwellings, and settled in for a longer period. Most authorities agree that many sites in Mesopotamia, Egypt, China, and India seemed to have developed roughly along these lines nine or ten thousand years ago. About some of these sites we know more than about others and we tend to emphasize them, but there is a great deal of course about other sites that we still don't know.

All human civilizations have depended on agriculture for subsistence, and we can only speculate about exactly how our wandering ancestors came upon the idea of just staying where they were until the local natural cereals were depleted. Since the soil in that area of Mesopotamia was rich and fertile, the people were able to harvest and store enough grain to last until the next growing season. The ability to keep food in reserve was crucial and the key to success. Growing food on farms resulted in a surplus, particularly when people began using intensive agricultural techniques such as irrigation and crop rotation. Grains have been especially important from the beginning because they can be easily preserved for long periods of time. The large majority of the people were active in agriculture, but a surplus of food permitted some people to do things besides producing food for a living, e.g. to make containers to store the excess grain or tools needed in farming. So these early civilizations soon included artisans, guards and social leaders, priests, and other people with specialized skills. Eventually, a surplus of food led to social classes, a division of labor, and a more diverse range of human activity, all of which are defining traits of civilizations.

While the majority of people in the early "cities" were preoccupied with the task of raising and distributing food, others were dealing with the many specialized aspects of a large group of people living permanently together in one locale: artisans making food and wine containers, houses, clothes, utensils, weapons; merchants buying, selling, trading, locally and with neighboring cities; government officials organizing civic functions and activities, keeping order within the group, preparing for the common defense against outsiders; and many others. Such activity engendered concepts of property, ownership of land and possessions, the need for some sort of money, trade and commerce, a need for formalized government with leaders and law-givers, a police force to see that the laws are observed, distinctions in social classes, etc. Again, these are all defining traits of civilization in general.

Origin of civilization

When a group of people living together permanently in a fixed place reaches a certain mass, "civilization" begins. Since the word itself means life in the *civis* or city, civilization begins when the group living together is big enough to be called a city, and this seems to have happened first some ten thousand years ago in the Fertile Cresent in the Middle East. Due to the constant need for water, civilizations developed by necessity on the banks of rivers or lakes. One of the first civilizations to arise was Sumer in the Middle East's "land between the rivers", Mesopotamia. Other civilizations soon developed on the banks of the Nile River in Ancient Egypt, in the Indus River valley and along the great rivers of China. Several millennia later and tens of thousands of miles away, civilizations again developed independently in Meso-America and South America.

"Civilized" stands in contrast to life outside the city, living off the land in loosely organized groups, such as the nomadic way of life which still exists today in scattered parts of the world. Nomads tend to live in areas where there is poor soil and only sparse vegetation, usually only enough to sustain wandering flocks of grazing animals like sheep, goats, or cattle. The nomadic way of life tends to remain on a rather primitive level because of the scarcity of people and the lack of an intense social life.

Origin of social classes

As human communities grew in number and complexity, all sorts of interesting developments took place, chiefly in terms of specialization and division of labor, or who should do what. Some of these distinctions are determined by the physical differences in men and women. Women, for example, are generally confined at home with childbirth and the nurturing of small children, whereas the stronger and usually larger men easily take on problems of communal defense, the struggle with wild animals, and the risks of the hunt. The man's contribution to procreation is minimal in contrast to the life-altering changes caused by pregnancy of the female.

For any community to exist and thrive, two things are essential: protection from outside dangers such as wild animals and other human groups, and an assured food supply. But who should decide how the necessary roles should be assigned to the various members of the group? Some roles would be automatically filled: for example, childbearing and rearing for most women, with fighting and hunting for the majority of the men. But who will make the major decisions about when and where to fight, who should lead in battle, how to train the young adult men, etc? Probably the older father figures with experience would automatically assume the leading roles in most decision-making situations, whereas older women experienced in childbirth and child-rearing plus knowledge of medicinal herbs and procedures would assume leading roles in other kinds of decisions.

A leading role early on would very likely be that of the story-teller who creates myths and explanatory tales, someone who can explain things to the general satisfaction of the group. This gives rise to the seer, shaman, or religious leader who creates myths to bind together the members of the community and is able to create a tribal religion. Successful leaders of the society would surely combine features of strength, experience, personal persuasive power, speaking skills, and so on, much like today's political and religious leaders. These positions can easily become hereditary, and the leaders do less and less of the daily work of providing their own food and housing; instead, they spend more and more time settling disputes and leading the activities of the community. As long as the leaders are successful in providing protection and ensuring the food supply, the majority of the people in the group willingly go along with the system. A major defeat in battle, however, internal unrest, or a drastic shortage of food will cause a major shake-up in the government of the community. Other ambitious people will gladly try to take over the leadership positions.

Origin of government

Government arises out of the very real need for authority, leadership, and decision making; otherwise there would be chaos and mayhem in a large group of people living together. But as the community grows in size and complexity, the leaders will naturally need assistants and advisors. A council of the older, experienced members—primarily men—will form and eat from the communal food supply without doing much manual labor themselves to grow or harvest food. With more respect and responsibility comes also more wealth, prestige, and power. The leaders' sense of authority and dominance will easily lead them to demand more obedience and more personal attention, plus the desire to maintain their positions as long as possible and then to pass it on to their children, probably the firstborn male.

The leader needs an astute helper who can explain and justify the leader's actions to the general population, regardless of whatever action the leader may take. This helper creates myths and legends explaining the early origin of the people; he has answers to their questions, and explains how the divine powers have put this leader in charge of everything in the society. This religious priest, along with his assistants, becomes the leader's right-hand man and shares in most of the benefits of leadership. The leader also needs a military man who trains the warriors and keeps them in fighting trim. This military chief and his helpers also become special assistants to the leader and share in the leader's benefits and privileges. The leader also needs administrative helpers who ensure that all citizens contribute the proper amount of food and supplies to the common good. These contributions will first be in kind, and then later in the form of military duty, community work, and taxes.

It doesn't take much imagination to envision the growth and development of an increasingly complex society in which most people work and a privileged few direct the total activity of the group. Supported by spiritual and military assistants, the rulers become increasingly powerful and end up assuming—and then believing—that they are fundamentally different from the common laboring masses. Encouraged by their priests, they are easily led to believe that they rule not by intrigue and exploitation, but by a sort of divine right, having been set on the throne by the divine powers of the universe itself. Over time, the people themselves become thoroughly indoctrinated by their spiritual mentors and come to believe in such fables. Even today, after centuries and millennia of such political myths, there are many modern nations still with a king, queen, and royal families who live off the labors and beliefs of the masses of people. In Japan, for example, there is still the doctrine that their emperor is a direct descendent of the ancient Sun God himself. In such societies, a revolt against the head of state and his government is at the same time a revolt against the divine powers as well.

Origin of writing and history

Writing probably arose out of merchants' need to keep records, perhaps something as mundane as wine or oil merchants having their logo or symbol formed into their clay jugs so that they could be returned to the proper wine or oil shop, similar to Texas ranchers branding their young calves for easy identification. As trade became more complex, additional reminders of transactions and accounts were needed. Trade and commerce would be impossible without some detailed method of keeping records and numerical accounts. Later, the government needed to specify exactly what the laws were, to spell out the penalties for transgressions, to know who had and had not paid their taxes, the history of the royal families, records of important battles and heroes, etc. And the religious leaders, of course, needed a unified account of the gods' creation of the world and all its creatures in order to keep the general populace intellectually satisfied.

Writing of some sort seems to have developed rather soon in the history of civilization, since there was a need to keep records of business transactions, important events, stories of the leaders, creations myths, etc. These records were written down on clay tablets, the bark of trees, hides of animals, cloth, and mats made of reeds. Soft clay tablets were a favorite medium because clay was cheap, abundant, and durable when baked in the sun; this system of writing was with a reed making wedge-shaped marks called cuneiform, and was commonly used throughout Mesopotamia. Ancient Egyptians wrote on ivory, bone, papyrus (a paper-like material made from tough reed fibers), leather, and linen, on which they formed hieroglyphics with ink made of ochre and carbon. For ceremonial occasions the ancient Egyptians carved stone or monuments. Hammurabi's code setting out laws and punishments was carved in cuneiform letters on a basalt slab stele about 1760 BC in Ancient Babylon.

Writing is a system of representing language graphically and evolved differently in several early civilizations. True writing is thought to have developed independently in only four different cultures in the world, namely Mesopotamia, China, Egypt, and Meso-America. The Chinese and Mesopotamian writing systems have especially been influential in the development of the various systems of writing in use in the world today.

Except for the Meso-American writing systems, which developed considerably later than the rest (possibly around 900 BC), all writing systems are thought to have originated and developed starting about six thousand years ago.

There are essentially two ways of writing things down: draw a picture of the thing itself, or draw a picture or symbol of the sounds for the word standing for that thing. The Chinese word for 'house,' for example, would be a simplified picture of a house; the alphabetic word for 'house' will be a picture of the letters representing h, o, u, s. There are hundreds of thousands of things in the world, and the system of drawing pictures of specific things is a cumbersome method and requires hundreds and thousand of pictures or pictographs. On the other hand, since most languages have only 35 to 45 different sounds which, when put together in various combinations, can name all the things in a people's vocabulary, drawing a picture of the sounds in the word for that thing is far simpler and more manageable. Both systems have been used in the history of writing and still exist today. Drawing pictures or symbols of things is called pictographs and is best illustrated in Chinese writing used today; the other method is phonetic, and uses an alphabet standing for sounds. This method is used in most of the world's languages today.

Apart from commercial uses, writing in general was done by a leisure class anxious to guard this special way of retaining precise information and to keep it in their own hands as a source of power and influence. Reading, i.e, the perfect recall of information, must have struck the great masses of illiterate people as a sort of magic and mystery. Only in recent times have reading and writing become a necessity for life in the city and engaged in by the majority of people in advanced societies.

As symbols became associated with sounds and syllables (word parts) standing for things, written language began to require fewer and fewer symbols. Little by little, people learned to draw picture of sounds rather than of things. Symbols began to represent individual sounds rather than syllables: for example, one symbol for 'B' and one for 'A', rather than one symbol for 'BA.' This was a great advance in simplicity and efficiency. These so-called "alphabets" are extremely flexible: the half-million or so words in English, for example, require only 26 symbols, or letters, while classical Chinese required up to 50,000 "logograms" — symbols representing whole words — to write an equal number of words. This difference causes Chinese to be a far more difficult linguistic tool than the alphabet system; the great advantage of the Chinese system is that everyone who knows the symbols can read and understand messages written in a number of different languages. The one symbol for 'house,' for example can be read as "casa" in Spanish, "Haus" in German, "maison" in French.

The history of our alphabet began in Ancient Egypt, more than a millennium into the history of writing. The first pure alphabet emerged around 4000 years ago to represent the language of Semitic workers in Egypt, and was derived from the alphabetic principles of the Egyptian hieroglyphs, which were primarily consonants. The Greeks added letters for the vowels, thereby making pronunciation and meaning clearer. Most alphabets in the world today either descended directly from this development, for example the Greek and Latin alphabets, or were inspired by its design. The word "alphabet" comes from the first two letters of the Greek alphabet, "alpha" meaning the vowel 'A' and "beta," meaning the consonant 'B.'

The Code of Hammurabi

This famous text is the best-preserved ancient law code and was created ca. 1760 BC in ancient Babylon. We can use it here to illustrate or exemplify two fundamental aspects of civilization: writing and the rules of social living as shown in the laws of the group. This code was enacted by the sixth Babylonian king, Hammurabi, and was inscribed in cuneiform script on a seven foot tall stone slab or stele placed in the market square for all to see. Even though the masses could not read it, they knew that the rules of social living were fixed. There are 282 laws in the Code of Hammurabi, each no more than a sentence or two long. These short laws spell out the rules of social interaction and the usually harsh penalties for infractions. Here are a few examples:

#6. If any one steal the property of a temple or of the court, he shall be put to death, and also the one who receives the stolen thing from him shall be put to death.

#25. If fire break out in a house, and some one who comes to put it out cast his eye upon the property of the owner of the house, and take the property of the master of the house, he shall be thrown into that self-same fire.

#109. If conspirators meet in the house of a tavern-keeper, and these conspirators are not captured and delivered to the court, the tavern-keeper shall be put to death.

#129. If a man's wife be surprised (in flagrante delicto) with another man, both shall be tied and thrown into the water, but the husband may pardon his wife and the king his slaves.

#154. If a man be guilty of incest with his daughter, he shall be driven from the place (exiled).

#195. If a son strike his father, his hands shall be hewn off.

#202. If any one strike the body of a man higher in rank than he, he shall receive sixty blows with an ox-whip in public.

There is a prologue in which Hammurabi introduces himself, and an epilogue in which he affirms his authority and sets forth his hopes and prayers for his code of laws. This stele is important as an excellent example of cuneiform writing as well as an early attempt to clearly set out what is to be expected of the citizens and of the administrative authorities. The laws are said to have come from God.

Economic systems

In the small hunting and gathering societies of early mankind, everyone was a general jack-of-all-trades and master of none, but in a large permanent society in one locale various forms of specialization developed. One person was simply better than others at making clay pots and containers, for example, and found that he could trade directly his products with other people for food or for things they were good at making: flint cutting edges, bows and arrows, clothing, help in the fields, etc. An early economic system of trade and barter arose through personal contact, but as the community grew larger and more impersonal, a mechanism called the market evolved in which many people offered their products, usually at the community gathering place and on specified days. All of this evolved gradually, of course, and over centuries.

As the trading and exchanging became more and more complex, a more or less standardized medium of exchange became necessary, and money was invented to replace the barter system. This greatly simplified and promoted trade, but we don't know exactly how money was developed or if it was developed in each community separately. There are surely a number of ways money and pricing evolved, but it seems rather certain that the idea of supply and demand emerged rather soon. At first, many things were used as money: beads, shells, amber, flint cutting edges and tools, almost anything of general value and convenient to count and carry. Later, metal coins evolved; later still, paper money and credit emerged and began to play an important role in business transactions.

All of this developed over hundreds or thousands of years, of course, and the economic systems of societies became more and more complicated in step with the increasing complexity of life. Today's varied civilizations offer a bedazzling number and types of general economic systems, made all the more complex by the degree to which a people's government becomes involved in the business activities of its citizens. Here are some variations and highlights of these different types:

An open market or free enterprise economy such as capitalism, where the government generally takes a "hands off" attitude and lets the economy do whatever it wants. In "rampant" capitalism, however, the government has to step in when one group of businessmen becomes too rich, powerful, and a law unto themselves.

A planned economy such as socialism, where the government has a "hands on" approach and generally tries to control and direct the economy. Socialism tries to avoid rampant capitalism by setting up legal mechanisms and taxes to keep the economy in control.

A command economy such as communism, where the government has a complete "hands on" approach and tries to plan for everything. In large complex societies, however, communism has a bad track record because people's needs and desires become too complex for the authorities to oversee and control.

A mixed economy is a compromise system incorporating some aspects of the market economy with aspects of the planned approach. Modern life and commerce have become so complicated that it is probably safe to say that most of the major economies in the world today are of this mixed type. In America, and elsewhere, we are still trying to develop the proper harmonious balance between free enterprise and governmental control of the economy.

Forms of government and political systems

Aristotle said long ago that there are only three possible forms of government: rule by one (monarch, dictator), rule by a few (aristocracy, oligarchy) or role by the masses (democracy). Here are a few illustrations and a brief review of some historical highlights. Each example turns out in practice to be far more complicated than this simple presentation, but it is the overview and basic principles of each that I find fundamental and important, not the details.

Throughout history, many kinds of political systems developed in different areas of the world depending on the needs of the people, and the economic resources available. Monarchy, a political system in which the government is under the control of one powerful leader, is one of the oldest forms of government and has had a long history in Europe, China, India, Africa, and South America. Rule by one has the great advantage of getting things done quickly and without a great deal of debate. Its great shortcoming, however, is that it generally favors the rich and powerful at the expense of the great masses of people, and this eventually leads to problems, including revolutions and overthrow of the government.

Democracy had its beginnings in Ancient Greece but dissolved into mob rule in Athens; historically, it has been rather short-lived as a form of government until recently. A viable democracy requires educated and informed citizens who take their political responsibilities seriously. Otherwise, democracy can easily change into an oligarchy or plutocracy, rule by the wealthy and powerful. Modern democracy has existed since the American Revolution in 1776 and the French Revolution in 1789. Despite its high-flown ideals of freedom and human rights, democracy continues to be an on-going struggle between the rich and powerful few and the masses of the lower and middle classes.

In both Europe and Japan during the Middle Ages, a complex system of relationships and obligations called feudalism developed between the land-owning nobility and the peasants or serfs who worked the land. This often came close to being a virtual form of slavery in which the serfs were bound to the land and to the land owner. Feudalism came to an end in Russia only a few years after Lincoln freed the slaves in the United States. Millions of people worldwide continue to exist today in economic bondage, however, which is only a step or two removed from feudalism.

Absolutism or rule by divine right existed in Europe and elsewhere for centuries and led to excesses that are hard for us to understand today. The "right of first night" and the selling of soldiers to other countries are two flagrant examples of the absolute power of ruling monarchs. The philosophical movement during the 17th and 18th centuries called the Enlightenment was a rejection of absolutism and forced massive political changes in Europe, North America and Western Asia.

Communism in the late 19th and early 20th centuries was an often violent reaction to the spreading of the capitalist economic and political system. A pure communist system is one in which all resources are publicly owned with the intent of minimizing inequalities of wealth, among other social objectives. This powerful, idealistic system caught the imagination of millions of people, especially in countries like Russia and China which were economically lagging behind the capitalist powerhouses of Europe and America. Perhaps beautiful in theory, communism turned out to be dismal in practice for many reasons, chief of which was the suppression of individual initiative and the unwillingness to allow private property.

The spread of civilization

Civilization has been spread by a number of methods: invasion and conquest, religious conversion, the extension of bureaucratic control and trade, technological superiority, and by introducing agriculture and writing to non-literate peoples. Some non-civilized people may willingly adapt to civilized behavior if it is attractively presented, particularly when they have no real choice. But civilization is also spread by sheer force: if a non-literate group does not wish to embrace agriculture or accept a certain religion, it is often forced to do so by the civilized people, who generally succeed due to their more advanced technology and higher population densities. Civilizations often use religion to justify their actions, claiming, for example, that the uncivilized people are primitive savages, barbarians, godless sinners, or the like, who should be subjugated and enlightened by civilization for their own sake!

Many theorists regard civilization as being similar to an organism which has definite stages: birth, early growth and development, maturity, old age, decline and death. This organic view explains and justifies the needs of a civilization to grow and expand. Expansion takes place through war, conquest, acquisition of territory, trade and commerce, religious conversion. Many specialists have studied the rise and fall of the ancient civilizations of Egypt, Mesopotamia, Persia, Greece, Rome, China, the Middle Ages, etc. One of the most famous is the English historian Edward Gibbon and his famous book on *The Decline and Fall of the Roman Empire*, published in 1776, the same year that the American empire was just beginning.

Other important studies of civilizations include the German scholar Oswald Spengler'e *Decline of the West*, (*Der Untergang des Abendlandes*) 1918, and the Englishman Arnold Toynbee's *A Study of History*, 1934-61. These two writers are especially focused on an organic view of all the high cultures of human history. Spengler divides history into eight such groups (Babylonian, Egyptian, Chinese, Indian, Mexican (Mayan/Aztec), Classical (Greek/Roman), Arabian, Western or "European-American"). Toynbee makes finer distinctions and divides the world's cultures into 21 well-defined groups. Toynbee and Spengler theorized that all civilizations pass through several distinct stages: genesis, growth, time of troubles, universal state, and disintegration.

Both historians write of the origins of each group, its growth and expansion, high point, decay, and possible fall. Spengler regards the decline and fall as inevitable, whereas Toynbee sees the possibility of rebirth in some cases. Both books appeared after the end of the first World War, the "Great War", the "War to End all Wars", and became best sellers. Readers of these two books concerning the cyclical development of civilization naturally want to know at what point in the inexorable cycle of birth, growth, and decay we are at present.

Gibbon, Spengler, and Toynbee are merely the best known among the many historians, philosophers, and cultural critics who have thought long and hard about the broad questions of civilization. Some students of history look for the key to downfall and decay in the very success of the civilization itself. Gibbon, for example. felt that the decline of Rome was the natural and inevitable effect of its immoderate greatness and power, and that prosperity ripened the principle of decay by causing the ruling classes to become complacent. Rome's cultural elite of warriors and statesmen became a culture parasite of wealthy, self-indulgent men. Other critics have also suggested that no great civilization is ever conquered from without, but always collapses from within.

Jared Diamond recently published a book with the interesting title, *Collapse: How Societies Choose to Fail or Succeed (2005)*. He expounds the idea that cultures actually choose to collapse by the deliberate choices they routinely make but disregard the consequences of those chloices. He gives five major reasons for the collapse of the forty-one cultures he studied:

Environmental damage, such as deforestation and soil erosion

Climate change

Dependence upon long-distance trade for needed resources

Increasing levels of internal and external violence, such as war or invasion

Societal responses to internal and environmental problems

His book causes one to think of our own current rush to exhaust the world's supply of fossil fuels and to thereby destroy our atmosphere by disregarding the impact of our daily choices.

War and aggression

War, or the battle of one human group against another, must have developed very early on in the course of human history. One group has something another group wants and tries to take it from them: food, land, women, animals, resources, etc. The fundamental law of 'might makes right' is invoked, and the fighting begins. Once people are killed, deeper and more primitive instincts take over and powerful emotions are called into play. Once war begins, it takes on a life of its own and seems to be one of the constants of human civilization. A leader who can keep the peace by protecting his group so powerfully that no one dares attack them, deserves all the more obedience and allegiance of his people. He will be able to use more and more of the community's resources for his political and military ambitions, and few people will dare question his authority. The history and development of war and the weapons of war must surely be one of the deep and powerful strains in human development. New weapons such as today's drone airplanes flown remotely by pilots on the other side of the planet become increasingly powerful and deadly, but our basic understanding of killing fellow humans seems to remain rather simple and primitive.

The causes of war are many and complex. Psychological theories maintain that violence is an integral part of human nature and must manifest itself from time to time. Other theories are related to the territorial instincts of animals and inherent competition. Another theory states that if an essentially unbalanced but terribly persuasive person bent on war comes to power in the government, he is able to lead his country into war; the examples given are usually Napoleon, Hitler and Stalin. Another theory says that war takes place when people are able to transfer their grievances into bias and hatred against other ethnic and racial groups, religions, nations and ideologies. While such theories may have some explanatory value about why wars occur, they do not explain much about when or how they occur. Nor do they explain the existence of certain human cultures completely devoid of war.

Some theorists go so far as to say that peace does not really exist. Periods that are seen as peaceful are actually periods of preparation for a later war or exist only when war is suppressed by a state of such great power that no one is willing to go to war with it, such as the *Pax Romana* or *Pax Britannica*. A demographic theory explains that when a population—especially of young men without jobs and training—outgrows the local resources and land, war and aggression are likely to ensue. This is the famous Malthusian theory that war is caused by expanding populations and limited resources. Malthus (1766–1834) believed that populations always increase until they are limited by war, disease, or famine.

Still another theory says that insults to national pride can stir the populace to react, especially if the country is more powerful than the insulting nation. Another school of thought argues that war can be seen as an outgrowth of economic competition in a chaotic and competitive international system. In this view, wars begin as a pursuit of new markets, of natural resources, and of wealth. Many people, for example, think of the American war in Iraq simply as a struggle to control the vital natural resource of oil. There are many other theories of why nations go to war, and specific examples can be found for each. The upshot seems to be that the causes of war are many and diverse, and are determined by the specific economic and political conditions in each of the countries involved.

War is a question of the survival or death of a society and is therefore fundamental. Tremendous resources go into a war and great advances are often made in terms of weapons, tactics, technology, communication, etc. when a society is struggling for its very existence. In larger, more complex societies, however, it is usually only the poorer common members of the group who suffer most and are killed in greatest numbers. The leaders and their cohorts learn how to survive and to make peace with their enemies.

War and History

The historian Will Durant concludes his 11-volume *Story of Civilization* with a thin 12th volume entitled *The Lessons of History (1968)*. Here are his main points concerning history and war, each of which could serve as the basis of a long discussion:

**War is one of the constants of history and has not diminished with civilization or democracy. In the last 3421 years of recorded history, only 268 have seen no war. Long interludes of widespread peace are unnatural and exceptional.

**Man is a competitive animal, and his state is like himself. War is the ultimate form of competition, and natural selection now operates on an international plane.

**War, or competition, is the father of all things: ideas, inventions, institutions, and states. Peace is an unstable equilibrium which can be preserved only by acknowledged supremacy or equal power.

**The causes of war are the same as the causes of competition among individuals: acquisitiveness, pugnacity, pride, the desire for food, land, materials, fuels, mastery. Individuals will submit to morals and law, but the national state, if it is strong enough, acknowledges no substantial restraints.

**Nationalism gives added force in diplomacy and war. The state encourages nationalism as a supplement to its army and navy. Catchwords bring hatred to a lethal point against other states.

**One war can now destroy the labor of centuries in building cities, creating art, and developing habits of civilization; it also promotes science and technology.

**Rulers smile at the philosopher's dislike of war and say that the Ten Commandment must be silent when self-preservation is at stake.

**States will unite in basic cooperation only when they are attacked from without by a common enemy.

**Peace will come only when we defy history and dare apply the Golden Rule to nations; when we agree to discuss, negotiate, compromise, change, stress our commonalities rather than our differences, and respect and understand one another.

The future of civilization

In recent years a number of theorists and activists from many fields have tried to grasp the very large outlines of our modern world and determine where we are going, provided, of course, that we do not first kill ourselves off. These include Alvin and Heidi Toffler (*Future Shock,* 1970, *The Third Wave,* 1980, *Powershift,* 1990, *War and Anti-War,* 1995), John Naisbitt (*Megatrends 2000: The New Directions for the 1990s,* 1982), and Marshall McLuhan, who introduced the concept of the global village (*The Gutenberg Galaxy,* 1962). Vice President Al Gore has been influential in creating the World Wide Web and calling attention to the dangers of global warming. A new academic discipline called 'futuristics' has been introduced in some universities, and many concerned people have grappled with the question of mankind's future. What it will look like, and what do we want it to look like. An important book entitled *Operation Manual for Spaceships Earth* was written in 1969 by Buckminster Fuller, the inventor of the geodesic dome, in which he suggested that we humans are literally all in the same boat together, crew members on a fantastic spaceship but with limited resources. As individuals, nations, and world cultures, it is imperative that we learn to get along with one another.

The power of the computer grows by leaps and bounds and promotes rapid, easy communication between crew members of our spaceship to discuss global problems. The concept of globalization has become a reality in the thinking of a great many people. Megatrends are powerful, global trends that are changing perhaps the majority of societies on a worldwide scale. Here are some of them: poverty eradication, population control, globalization of trade and commerce, massive international travel and communication, global warming, space travel and international cooperation, explosion of computer power and technology, increased powers of consumers and number of choices available to them (Toffler even uses the term "overchoice"), the emergence of English as the world language to facilitate communication between people of all nations, the growth of the desire for democracy, the power of the worldwide internet,

Conclusion

Living in Los Angeles, surely one of the most technologically advanced cities in the world, and driving my car downtown, I am often struck by the ease with which I and countless other drivers do complicated tasks and interact with thousands of complete strangers by simply driving in traffic. We have all become so civilized and tuned into one another that we don't even notice how profoundly we have been conditioned by the sheer fact of living in a group of several million people. Like deep sea fish living at the bottom of tons of pressure caused by the weight of water, we are also living under tons of similar pressure caused by several thousand of years of civilization and its intangible cultural aspects. These include a common language used by 300 million Americans plus an equal number of other people abroad as a native or second language, an engrained respect and courtesy for other drivers which we have absorbed from our general cultural training, the ability of all drivers to read and interpret numerous symbolic signs and signals, common-sense adherence to the rules of the road, a willingness to cooperate, a tolerance for occasional irregularities, necessary control of our emotions in traffic, a general agreement to keep our vehicles in good condition, and many others.

What holds true for Los Angeles is essentially applicable to all American cities, and, by and large, to most of the other world cities that I am acquainted with. Countless millions of individuals driving their personal automobile is a world-wide phenomenon which enables every driver in every country to understand and empathize with other drivers everywhere. Having your engine stall in traffic or missing your exit are trivial examples of internationally valid experiences which tie the world's drivers together. These and a thousand others also illustrate something essential about the nature of modern man, everywhere. Driving is a complex task which has to be learned and practiced if one wants to drive in the heavy traffic of the world's cities, but hundreds of millions of people have mastered this modern necessary skill and are, I think, in some fundamental sense linked together. Like the cars themselves, the skills are essentially standardized and uniform, so that a driver from Rio de Janeiro can easily adapt to the streets of Moscow, Tokyo, or San Francisco. I believe this uniformity of cars, drivers, traffic problems, etc. helps modern humans in an essential manner to draw together in understanding and accepting one another.

Much the same could be said about a great many other technological areas of modern life where millions of us are doing the same sort of things: using the computer and internet, telephones and televisions, bus and subways systems, national and international airlines and airports, vacation resorts, etc. In contrast to the many different civilizations of the past, it strikes me that there is only one fundamental world civilization today, but with many local flavors and colorings. In numerous ways we are moving more and more towards the *One World* which the American presidential candidate Wendell Willkie advocated and wrote about in the 1940s. If we can continue in the same way a bit longer and avoid getting too angry at one another, we may save ourselves and our civilization yet. This is a task worthy of intelligent modern man.

Chapter 5.
Myths and religions

Introduction

In the course of his evolution, man has taken a number of paths in his attempt to understand and in some sense come to terms with the world in which he lives. I see four different but related approaches: the mythological, religious, philosophical, and finally the scientific. All four involve the emotional as well as the intellectual aspects of his nature. The general thrust is from the unreflected and emotional to the very conscious and intellectual, with the mythological path being heavily emotional and the scientific approach being almost completely intellectual. I think this process most likely began with fear as perhaps the major element. In his effort to simply stay alive man was confronted by forces and powers beyond his control and comprehension: violent storms with flashing thunderbolts and terrifying sounds, vicious animals trying to devour him, terrifying lightning strikes causing trees to burst into flames, etc. Like a frightened child, he must at times have been simply scared out of his wits and overwhelmed with incomprehensible phenomena of all sorts. Such things eventually caused him to try to make sense of them as his mind developed from that of a primitive emotional animal to a reflective creature trying to bring some order into his experience.

His mind was already evolved enough to distinguish between his physical body and the shadowy mental activities such as dreams, ideas, and reflections going on somewhere inside of him, especially at night while sleeping. The mind-body distinction was crucial and allowed him to begin developing some more-or-less meaningful grasp of his world by imagining invisible spirits or forces everywhere in nature: powerful, threatening, but sometimes friendly. This was the beginning of animism—the worship of spirits—and the underlying source of all religions. Man, then as now, tried to make sense of his experience and in doing so developed four powerful sets of emotional and intellectual tools to help him: animism, religion, philosophy, science. The fundamental emotions of fear and dread in animism and religion slowly and gradually developed into wonder and fascination with the onset of philosophy and science.

Animism

Man's first tool for coming to grips with his world is "animism," a term derived from the Latin word *anima* meaning *breath, soul,* or *spirit*. The preoccupation with animism is probably man's oldest belief, and its origins most likely date back to the Paleolithic age. From its earliest beginnings, animism is a powerful belief that a soul or spirit exists in all things, even in inanimate objects. Everything has an indwelling spirit, including animals, trees, plants, rocks, mountains, rivers, stars. Each "anima" is powerful, spiritual, and can help or hurt man, including the souls of dead humans, the "ancestors".

The basis of animism is the belief that the spirit world consists of benevolent as well as malevolent forces or souls which are far stronger than the power of humans. The powers of the spirit world infuse everything and must be reckoned with. Special spirits are often believed to dwell in particular objects, things such as trees or places, an area of the forest, or a village. Sometimes the spirits move around, even following people if they move.

Animism can be defined simply as a belief in the existence of invisible spiritual beings. It dates back to the earliest humans and continues to exist today, making it the oldest form of religious belief on earth. The basis for animism is the acknowledgment that there is a spiritual as well as a physical realm which humans share with everything in the universe. The current widespread concept that humans are endowed with souls and that souls have a life apart from human bodies, before and after death, is central to animism, along with the idea that animals, plants, and celestial bodies also possess souls. Animistic gods are useful in explaining the creation of the earth and all its contents, including fire, wind, water, man, animals, and all other natural earthly things.

Loosely speaking, animism refers merely to a belief in souls. However, most people use it specifically to refer to the belief that all objects have souls, not just people. Animism plays a role in many so-called "primitive" practices and shamanic traditions. The concept of animism is also at the root of many world religions, and traces of animistic belief can be seen in other belief systems. Plato, for example, believed that the human soul existed prior to its finding a home in a specific body. The ancient Stoics held the view that each human soul is a spark from a universal soul or fire, and that the purpose of the individual person's life is to keep the spark alive and pure, and then return it to the universal fire at death. Christians and Muslims also believe in the concept of an eternal soul and in a guiding spiritual force which oversees the universe. Religions emphasizing animism are mostly ethnic or folk religions, such as the various forms of ancestor worship, shamanism, Shinto, and Hinduism.

Sir E.B. Taylor in his 1871 book *Primitive Culture*, used the term "animism" to mean simply "a belief in souls". He did not restrict the term "animism" to religions that attribute souls to non-human entities. With such a definition, virtually all religions can be considered animistic, including Christianity and Islam. According to Taylor, all religions rest on, or stem from, a belief in gods or supernatural beings, which in turn stems from a belief in souls. The stories or portrayal of these many spirits and powers we can refer to as myths.

Myths and mythologies

The important point here, of course, is that peoples and cultures differ profoundly in various ways. This is especially true when we turn to the specific myths and religions which each culture creates to explain its early origins and its view of life. It seems to me that myths are older and more deeply rooted in a people's psyche than religion. The early myths almost all relate to the creation of a people and of the world in which they live. This is clearly shown in the Bible where God creates the heavens and the earth and then creates the animals and people inhabiting the earth. A creation myth is basic to any religion, and a religion, it seems to me, is simply a set of myths which have been codified, institutionalized, and spread to the entire population. But more on that a bit later.

Myths are explanatory stories; the collection of a people's myths is its mythology. Such stories originate in man's native curiosity about himself, his fellow humans and creatures, the world in which he finds himself, etc. Since he does not intuitively know where all this came from, he invents powers and creative entities to explain them. He imagines many of these creative agents to be like himself, only more powerful and resourceful, and he calls them gods. These gods populate the world and take on many diverse shapes, seen most clearly perhaps in Greek mythology, where we have a god of the sea (Poseidon, Latin Neptune), a god of the sky (Zeus, Latin Jupiter or Jove), a god of wine (Dionysus, Latin Bacchus), a goddess of sexual attraction (Aphrodite, Latin Venus), etc. All these gods are simply super humans with very human traits and passions (jealousy, lust, anger) in addition to their divine powers. Often mythological figures are man-animal combinations: centaurs (half man, half horse), satyrs, (half man, half goat), mermaids (half human, half fish), etc. Sometimes especially powerful animals and very important humans are elevated over the decades and centuries and worshiped as gods. Their function is to help man explain phenomena to himself and others, especially the problematic early origins of things and people.

Out of man's inborn curiosity arise stories and explanations of all sorts, and these slowly become accepted by all members of the community as the standard answers to the perennial questions of origins and authority. These explanatory stories over time become sacrosanct, accepted by all, codified, formalized, and emerge as the religion of that people. These religious "truths" are then institutionalized, endowed with dignity and authority, passed down from generation to generation, and become a central part of the very essence of that culture.

Different groups of humans of course develop different explanatory stories for their time, place, and the conditions under which they live. Their stories go through a similar process and over time become different religions. The religion of a sea-faring people will naturally be different from that of people living in the desert or in the mountains surrounded by wild animals. As long as the members of the community believe in the explanations given by their religion, the religion stays alive and is passed on to the next generation. But for many reasons, a religion can lose its power and its believers. It then becomes a collection of interesting but rather quaint stories which we call a mythology. So a mythology is simply a former religion which no longer has any committed believers. There are many mythologies based on former religions, just as there are today many vibrant religions. Greek mythology is probably the best known example, but Germanic mythology with its stories of Siegfried, Thor, and Wotan, or Egyptian mythology with its tales of Isis, Osiris, and Horus are also well known. The religions have lost all their adherents, but the mythologies live on.

Here is Webster's definition of myth: "a traditional story of unknown authorship, ostensibly with a historical basis, but serving usually to explain some phenomenon of nature, the origin of man, or the customs, institutions, religious rites, etc. of a people: myths usually involve the exploits of gods and heroes."

Religion

Religion evolved or developed out of animism and myths. Religion is the second approach used by man to make sense of his life and world. The souls or spirits of animism take on a more personal, human form and become gods of various kinds with whom humans can more easily identify. This is perhaps most clearly seen in the ancient Greek religion where the personalized gods of the sea, sky, earth, forests, fertility, wine, etc. take on male or female form to become Poseidon, Zeus, Ceres, Dionysus, etc. and play an active part in the lives of men and women.

Religion in some form probably goes back to the very beginning of human consciousness. We can imagine early man slowly becoming aware of himself, his fellows, and the surrounding world full of powers and events completely beyond his ability to grasp or understand: the awesome external forces of nature and climate, the power and danger of animals, the miracles of birth and death, the internal forces of emotions and dreams, etc. We can imagine our ancestors slowly becoming aware of the very fact of their existence and their struggle to stay alive. As their language skills develop, they begin to ask questions of all sorts about the conditions and circumstances of their life. Some of them begin to give answers and make up explanations which satisfy the other members of the group. Thunder, lightning, earthquakes, climate, the changing of the seasons, powerful and dangerous animals, disasters, sickness, death, etc. are interpreted by creative and persuasive members of the tribe; anthropomorphic gods of all kinds with superhuman strength are invented to clarify things and events; tales of a pleasant afterlife with reunions of family members help alleviate the burden of death and uncertainty,

Most people, then and now, are in general too busy with the cares of daily life to dwell long on such abstract matters as the meaning and purpose of things: They ask simple questions and are generally satisfied with short, simple answers. Some creative, clever people early on discovered that individuals who can create more-or-less satisfying answers concerning life's mysteries easily gain power and respect from their fellows. This, in my view, is the basic origin of religions throughout the world: They satisfy basic human curiosity and form a strong social unit by bonding fellow believers together emotionally and intellectually. Religion is an amazingly strong social cement. Religious leaders become a very powerful influence in their society and discover that the average person will believe the most fantastic stories and myths if they are presented with an air of authority and conviction. The questions of where we came from, what we are supposed to do, how we are supposed to live, what happens when we die, whether we will ever see our loved ones again, etc. are answered by similar fables and myths in virtually every society around the world.

The religious method

The tribal religion, once it has been established, is strengthened and perpetuated by essentially the same methods everywhere: emotional indoctrination of the young, rewards and punishments here and in the afterlife, elevation of the religious leaders to a special level of awe and respect, banishment and even death to non-believers or people who question the authorities too closely, sacred books and rituals—often in a special or even secret holy language—and taboo topics such as seriously questioning the basic doctrines. These and similar approaches are to be found in religions and mythologies throughout the world. We can describe the religious approach or method as consisting of early indoctrination, emphasis on authority and tradition, appeal to the senses through art and ceremony, strong emotional elements, use of rewards and punishments, emphasis on the community over the individual, special superior status of the religious leaders, use of rituals and special events, taboo questions and topics which are not to be discussed.

Using such methods, religions of many different varieties have flourished in virtually every human society and often employ the most fantastic kinds of explanations to satisfy basic human curiosity. The most cursory look at Greek mythology easily provides us with ample examples of the wide-spread human tendency to give and essentially only want short answers to deeply felt questions. "Why did my ship sink during the storm?" "Because you have angered the sea god Poseidon." "Where did we and the world come from?" God or the gods created us all." The Catholic Church long explained natural events (e.g. the famous Lisbon earthquake on Sunday morning in 1755 killing over 10,000 people) as a consequence of man's sinful nature. The average person generally is busy with life and doesn't really want a lot more explanation and therefore generally takes without serious questioning the answers which his religious leaders give.

Acknowledging our ignorance

There is a great deal that we simply don't know about origins and things in the past, but as humans we have the ability and the need to make up explanatory stories of how things got to be as they are. We know, for example, that the universe is here, that we are here, that societies have come into being, and that human beings have spread into virtually every corner of the world. The details of how all these things happened are still to a great extent beyond our capacity to explain, but it seems to me that we have made very definite strides towards explaining the perennial questions which mankind persistently asks itself. All brief explanations are simplifications, of course, and practically everything is far more complex than it seems on the surface.

We find facts everywhere, and most of us are content simply to recognize the facts, accept them, and move on. But the greater joy is to wonder about what seems so clear and obvious, and to ask that devilish question: Why is that?

We know, for example, that over hundreds of thousands of years humans have spread throughout the world and that they live in smaller or larger groups which are held together by an invisible but powerful force called culture. We also know that each infant is unconsciously indoctrinated or enculturated from birth to accept the culture of his group as normal reality. Few people ever give more than a passing glance at the structure of their society and virtually never seriously question or investigate the basic elements of their culture. We can make a basic but helpful distinction here between provincialism and cosmopolitanism.

Provincialism and cosmopolitanism

Provincialism is the strong and virtually universally held conviction that the way of life which we grew up with in our 'province' is normal reality, pure and simple, and that people who hold other views are essentially misguided or simply wrong. I believe that we are all automatically and necessarily provincialists by birth and conditioning. That is to say that we grow up with a given language, a given family structure, a certain set of mores and social habits which everyone in our group essentially conforms to. This includes, of course, the generally accepted value system, the common cultural traditions, the basic assumptions about the make-up of the universe, concepts about religion and humanity, etc. All of this early, inconspicuous training is part and parcel of what forms our mentality as small children. Many—perhaps even most—people in all societies go through their entire life without ever seriously questioning or wondering about the world view into which they are born and raised. They accept without question the reality as they find it around them and in them.

Cosmopolitanism, on the other hand, is based on the awareness that all people are provincialists living in many separate provinces, but that objective reality is far larger than the view offered in any one province; it is also the belief that it is possible to expand our provincial view through travel, study, and exposure to other points of view. Cosmopolitanism includes the understanding that provincialism is legitimate and quite necessary, but also limited and confining. When we travel or interact with people from other cultures, i.e. from other provinces, so to speak, we see that they are just as dedicated to their view of reality as we are to ours. But the thrust of education and the basic process of maturity, it seems to me, is to move us away from provincialism toward a larger and more inclusive view of life which I am calling here cosmopolitanism, i.e. a more comprehensive view of ourselves, the world, and the problems we face.

A few examples will make clear this important distinction between provincialism and cosmopolitanism. A very simple illustration which many people have observed in Europe is the way we Americans use our knife and fork at table. When eating a steak, for example, we hold our knife in the right hand, the fork in the left, and cut one piece of meat; we then put the knife down, take the fork in the right hand, and eat the piece of meat. Then the whole process is repeated, to the surprise of Europeans, who find our table manners strange and unnerving. They eat the entire meal with knife in the right hand, fork in the left, and then they are finished, they place knife and fork on the plate. German men wear their wedding ring on the right hand, and make a slight bow when shaking hands. The French kiss on both cheeks; Italians use their hands a great deal while talking; Englishmen don't easily talk to strangers, etc. The examples are trivial, but the underlying distinction of basic differences is profound and pervades all that we do: what we eat, what we wear, how many wives we can have at one time, our treatment of women and children, the style of government, manner of executing criminals, etc.

Language is a particularly good and clear-cut example. All European languages, other than English, have two, three, or even four distinct ways of saying "you," because they add a distinction of intimacy and formality when they talk, and some even have a distinction between singular and plural. An intimate "you" is used for family members, children, close friends, servants, and animals; whereas a formal "you" is used for strangers, people in authority, and persons of a higher social class. French has two distinct words, "tu" and "vous;" German has three. "du," "ihr," (plural of "du,"), and "Sie;" Spanish has four, "tu," "vosotros," (plural of "tu"), "Usted," and "Ustedes," (plural of "Usted"). And when you speak one of those languages fluently, you must embrace their view of social reality. Imagine what would happen when a culture linguistically delineates its social classes by adding additional distinctions of age, gender, reverence, etc., as some languages do.

Religion is a great and powerful example of the provincial-cosmopolitan distinction. The kind of gods people worship and the number of gods worshiped is astounding. Vastly different are also the moral systems embraced, the rites and rituals of various religions, the religious calendars, the number of prophets and saints, the types of worship, etc., with each community generally believing that theirs is the best and most holy.

Problems with religion

We use the words "religion" and "religious" very easily and assume that we know what we and others are talking about. We identify people with the names of their religion and naively assume that all people within that group essentially believe the same thing. In today's very heavy political climate, words like "Jew," "Moslem," and "Christian" play a vital role in many discussions, and many observers of the world scene think we are on the brink of religious wars similar to the crusades of the Middle Ages. Some think that these wars have already started and are being waged in new and unusual ways.

Religions are of course intimately related to the history and culture of a people and vary about as much as do human groups themselves. It sometimes seems that a people's religion is simply their way of life in general, and it is often hard to differentiate their religion from their type of government, political structures, economy, art forms, educational system, etc. A person completely ignorant of the stories and myths of Christianity, for example, would have a very difficult time understanding European art, music, architecture, political and cultural history. A serious inquiry into religion takes us into the closely related fields of anthropology, psychology, philosophy, history, and the general study of mankind and civilization. One thing leads to the next, and everything seems to be related to everything else, and it is difficult to know where to start and stop in trying to discuss the topic of religion. In a sense it is similar to language, namely so commonplace that it is simply taken for granted, and we assume that it is all quite clear and self-evident. Nothing could be further from the truth, both in the case of language and of religion.

I have long been fascinated with both language and religion, and with the mysterious relationship between the two. This connection is clearly shown by a couple of examples from the Bible. In the very beginning of the creation story in Genesis, God speaks and things happen in the physical world of sky, water, and land; another is found later in the powerful but problematic statement that in the beginning was the word, and the word was with God, and the word was God. Still another example is to be found in the theory of poetry which asserts that the poet is God's co-creator of the universe in the sense that while God creates material things like animals and objects in the physical world, man creates an intellectual, linguistic world of words naming them and the relationships between them. We recall that Adam's first task in the garden of Eden was to give all the animals a name, and that whatever he called them, that was what they were. Only God can make an animal or a tree, but it is man who creates names like lion, tiger, willow, oak, and pine.

I find that most people actually know only little about their religion, but this doesn't particularly bother them. They essentially believe the parts that they want to believe, and that makes them feel comfortable. They go through the prescribed rituals and generally embrace the ethical code of their faith, provided that it doesn't deviate too far from what they really want to do. Jews eat ham, Moslems drink whiskey, and Baptists dance up a storm despite the admonitions of their respective religions. The human mind is amazingly capable of entertaining a large number of self-contradictions with ease and comfort, as long as they are not directly emphasized side by side. Religion is a confusing, perplexing, but fascinating topic, at least for me, and I trust you will find some of that fascination along with the almost unavoidable problems and perplexity in the following pages.

Most of us use the word "religion" in the same way we use the term "God": as though we knew what we are talking about! When we discuss these topics with one another, the situation becomes all the more complex because we naively assume that the other person is using these words in the same way as we are. We think that we are essentially agreeing with one another and making only modest variations or clarifications when we assert that every society has a religion, that everyone except avowed atheists believe in one supreme being, that all religions essentially agree with one another, that monotheism is a more advanced form of belief than polytheism, etc. What a nonsense and confusion we foist upon one another and upon ourselves!

When we add to this semantic problem our inherent native provincialism, plus our appalling ignorance of other cultures and other parts of the world, we find that we are trapped in an intellectual and emotional morass from which we can extricate ourselves only by some harsh, draconian measures. It seems to me that we must follow the example of the French philosopher and mathematician René Descartes in the early 1600s: doubt and reject everything, and start again from scratch. That is what I am trying to do in this essay. Despite his rigorous intellectual analysis, Descartes ended up with essentially the same world that he started out with, but he had at least a much clearer idea of what he was talking about. Something similar may happen to us in this discussion.

The ideas presented here, like the speculative ideas of any essay, are of course limited by the writer's own experience, study, and character. Each of us is trapped within the prison of his or her own personality, time, and circumstance. Even when we think we are most free of personal prejudices and most objective in our deliberations, the stripes of our prison uniforms shine through and manifest themselves in our pronouncements through our choice of materials, selection of examples, use of adjectives, turn of phrase, and a thousand other ways. But the importance of the topic seduces us again and again into perhaps making fools of ourselves by trying to do independent thinking about an age-old institution deeply rooted in the very nature of man.

In trying to achieve a critical stance towards the forces which formed our early youth, we may be trying in vain to jump over our own shadow.

Fairness

Out of a sense of fairness I would like first to state my strongly felt bias and prejudice that virtually all the dogmatic aspects of today's religions are fundamentally outdated and only their moral and ethical teachings are applicable to contemporary life. These venerable mythologies and ideologies were developed many centuries ago in vastly different cultures and circumstances, but they have by and large outlived their usefulness as a comprehensive and meaningful way of looking at and interpreting the complex modern world. This is particularly true of the so-called revealed religions which we have inherited from the Jews, Christians, and Muslims. They all started as tribal belief systems aimed at uniting a select group of humans into a coherent group for mutual support and protection. Some of them have tried to increase their appeal to a larger group of people, but all three remain essentially provincial and intolerant of the basic dogmatic aspects and beliefs of the other two. Unless we can come up with a broader, more tolerant, and more inclusive world-view applicable to the realistic conditions of the modern world, the hatred and bloodshed among provincialists following their essentially closed tribal religions seem certain to continue their age-old history of intolerance, animosity, and bloodshed.

I think the world needs a new, realistic, and universally valid belief system and that it is possible to create one. It is not only possible but urgently needed if we are ever to escape from the destructive paths and conditions into which the traditional religions have led us. The current crises between Palestinians and Israelis, Irish Catholics and Protestants, Hindus and Muslims, and the widespread clashes between Islam and Christianity, are only recent examples of what has been happening between cultures and social groups for thousands of years. This sort of destructive confrontation between world-views seems likely to continue and become all the more deadly unless some fundamental changes are made. Something new and different is needed and can be created, I believe, by men and women of good will the world over. I also believe that the majority of the basic elements of such a new world-view are already in place worldwide and that only a sufficient amount of attention is needed to make them better known and more effective.

What is religion?

But first we have to get as clear as possible on exactly what we are talking about, and as you will see, that's not as easy as we might think. The question is: What exactly is religion? A simple question, but with a complex answer. The answer given here is a little long and complicated, but without some clear concepts of what we are talking about, the discussion goes around and around in circles and gets nowhere. Confusion mounts, frustration increases to a boiling point, anger ensues, and then we are back in a caveman mentality where only strength and violence count.

An historian's view

Again, at the end of his monumental, eleven-volume *Story of Civilization,* Will Durant adds a short twelfth volume entitled *The Lessons of History.* His remarks on the role of religion throughout the course of the world's many civilizations deserve our attention. Durant sees religion functioning and apparently indispensable in every age and culture; it comforts unhappy, downtrodden, and suffering humanity with promises of supernatural rewards, something which harsher critics call "pie in the sky." His study of human history shows that as long as there is poverty there will be religion; supernatural hope offers the only alternative to sheer despair and class war. Religion helps discipline the young, confers meaning and dignity upon the lowest of the low, and has acted as a stabilizing moral influence in society through the centuries and millennia. Durant quotes with approval, however, the caustic remark of Napoleon that "Religion has kept the poor from murdering the rich." Durant also finds that the gods were the results of man's fear of hidden forces in the earth, rivers, oceans, trees, winds, and sky. Religions were born out of the need to propitiate these dangerous powers through offerings, sacrifices, and prayer. Priests used such fears and rituals to support morality and to enhance their own leadership role, and in this way religion became a vital force in the entire structure of society. The priests said to the Egyptians, Babylonians, Jews, Greeks, Romans, Christians, Muslims that the local code of morals and laws had been dictated by the gods and that the earthly rulers were appointed and protected by the gods. Rebellion against the king therefore meant rebellion against the divine powers which put him on the throne. Nearly every secular government, says Durant, has shared its lands and revenues with the priests. The competitive conflict between these two powers, however, the church and the state, has dominated much of human history.

Definition and origins

The origins of religion are many and varied, and it is all the more difficult to talk about origins until we know what a religion is and what we are actually discussing. Talking about a specific religion is easier, but that is not the thrust and focus of this essay. If we can agree to leave things rather open for the moment and take a piecemeal approach concerning both definitions and origins, I think the discussion will become clearer and more manageable. We can use "world-view," "ideology," "system of belief," or even "way of life" as a rough approximation of what we are talking about under the heading of religion. Some would even add "mythology" and "organized superstition" to the list.

Usually there are supernatural elements or gods in a religion, but not always. If we later ask what differentiates a religious world-view from a secular one, the answer may be "very little," as we can see from the following definitions. We should keep in mind, however, that for many religious fundamentalists—including myself as a teenager—their particular holy texts and doctrines can solve all problems, contain all the truth we need, and should be embraced by everyone. This sort of approach, of course, drastically limits objective discussions which may enlighten us.

Some definitions

To get us started, here are some definitions of religion taken directly from two standard collegiate dictionaries, *Webster's New World Dictionary of the American Language* and *Webster's New American Dictionary*. Notice the diversity and wide range of meaning in answer to the question: What is religion?

1. the service and worship of God or the supernatural

2. devotion to a religious faith

3. a personal set or institutionalized system of religious beliefs, attitudes, and practices

4. a cause, principle, or belief held to with faith and ardor

5. belief in a divine or supernatural power or powers to be obeyed and worshiped as the creator and ruler(s) of the universe

6. expression of such a belief in conduct and ritual

7. any specific system of belief, worship, conduct, etc., often involving a code of ethics and a philosophy (the Christian *religion*)

8. any system of beliefs, practices, ethical values, etc. resembling, suggestive of, or likened to such a system (humanism as a *religion*)

9. the state or way of life of a person in a monastic order or community

10. any object of conscientious regard or pursuit

Already here we see one of the major stumbling blocks in any discussion of religion: the presence or absence of a supernatural power. For many people, the concept "God" or "the gods" is at the very heart of religion; for others, any reference to divinity in a meaningful world-view is a superfluous and confusing factor best left aside.

Theories of religion's origins

Such a list of standard definitions shows us immediately what a complex topic we are dealing with and some of the difficulties we will encounter in our discussion. To add to the problem of definition, here are a few helpful ideas about the possible origin of religion from S.G.F. Brandon's splendid article, "Origins of Religion" in the *Dictionary of the History of Ideas*, (pp. 92-99):

1. Religion stems from revelations by the gods

2. Religion stems from fear and need to propitiate the forces of nature

3. Religion stems from the adoration or cult of great leaders or animals (Buddha, Clan of the Cave Bear)

4. Religion is only an allegorical personification of the sun and its annual career (birth, death, resurrection: Christ, Mithras, Osiris, Bacchus)

5. Religion stems from rituals about birth, marriage, death common to all cultures

6. Religion springs from man's intuition that there is something more powerful than himself, leaving man dependent and reliant upon this higher power

7. Religion springs from animism, the deified spirits of nature. Man perceives a spirit (*anima, pneuma*), a body-mind split, within himself, and populates the organic and inorganic world with similar spirits, some good, some bad. Animals, stars, trees, etc. all have souls or spirits in addition to their bodies.

8. Freud in his *Totem and Taboo* sees the origin of religion in the sexual instinct and the Oedipus Complex; the sons in the primeval horde honor but hate the Father, kill and eat him to gain his powers for themselves, and then have remorse.

9. Frazier's *Golden Bough* regards religion as a propitiation or conciliation of powers superior to man which control and direct the course of nature and of human life.

We might think that while it is indeed hard to say what religion in general is, it will much easier to say what a specific religion is or believes, but on closer examination this turns out to be an illusion as well. Among the major world religions, each one on closer examination splits into a variety of beliefs, some of which are so unusual and different from one another as to cause us to wonder if they could all be in fact members of the same belief system. Christianity, for example, has three major branches with fundamental differences between them: Roman Catholic, Eastern Orthodox, and Protestant. Each branch—especially Protestantism—is further split, and then again, and again, so much so that the very concept of Christianity itself seems to have little more in common than the general name. Each variety believes it adheres to the original faith more closely than all the other varieties. Judaism, Islam, Buddhism, Hinduism, etc. offer a similar spectacle, although probably none so pronounced as Protestantism.

Another perspective

One additional approach helpful in answering the question, "What is a religion?" can be found in Ninian Smart's excellent book, *The World's Religions*. He proposes a seven-point set of aspects or dimensions for getting at the nature of religion.

1. The practical and ritual dimension includes regular worship, preaching, patterns of behavior such as yoga in the Buddhist and Hindu traditions, stilling of the self, meditation, etc.

2. The experiential and emotional dimensions of great religious leaders such as Muhammad, Paul, the Buddha as well as the emotions and experiences of regular believers who know that ritual without feelings is cold, doctrines without awe and compassion are dry, and myths which do not move hearers are feeble. Music is so powerful in religion because it has mysterious powers to express and engender emotions.

3. The narrative or mythic dimension is the story side of religion and hands down the sacred tales and vital myths of creation, the end of time, etc. as well as stories of the great founders and leaders of each tradition: Moses, the Buddha, Jesus, Muhammad, prophets, saints, and heroes.

4. The doctrinal and philosophical dimension explains the nature of divinity and sets forth the dogma of the religion as rationally as possible for the educated members who seek some sort of intellectual basis for their faith.

5. The ethical and legal dimension explains the ethical laws, regulations, and demands of the religion which are binding on the community of followers. The ten commandments of Judaism, for example, are supplemented by over 600 additional rules, and the central ethical attitude in Christianity is an ethic of love.

6. The social and institutional dimension has to do with the religion as it is

actually manifested among the people, something which could be called the sociology of religion. What is the religious world-view as actually seen in the activity of its followers?

7. The material dimension means the buildings, works of art, and other material manifestations which tend to be sacred and highly important for believers. Sometimes these include holy rivers (Ganges, Jordan), mountains (Fuji, Mount of Olives), and even cities (Jerusalem, Benares).

Meaning of the word itself

The dictionary explains that the origin of the word "religion" is unclear but is apparently related to the Latin verb *religare,* which means to bind or tie together. It may also be related to an old Indo-Germanic root *leg,* meaning to collect. That, to me, makes a lot of sense, and in my mind a religion, any religion, is a kind of social cement which unites, ties, or binds members of a social group together. "To be one of us" means to believe like us and to see the world essentially the same way we do; we will let you be one of our group if you embrace our belief system and rituals which tie together and reinforce all the elements and members of the group. This idea of social cohesion and social definition greatly enhances the group's ability to survive in a harsh world and seems to be obviously one of the major functions of any religion. Religion is in general a community's way of life and has several essential parts.

Parts of religion

In order to get clear on what religion is, it may be helpful to think of the major elements or aspects of any given religion, the techniques it uses to bind people together. Otherwise we slip around in our discussion and never pin down anything clearly. I think we are going to have trouble finding a suitable delineation of the basic elements, however, because what seems to be the major parts of one or several religions may not be equally applicable to others; and I repeat that it is the universal nature of religion which interests me here. Many religions have a crucially important emphasis on a divine element, while others seem to have no gods at all and are simply a community's traditional way of life

It strikes me, however, that there are at least three basic elements in any religion: the dogma, an ethical code, and a set of rituals. Let us try to determine what each part is and how it functions.

Dogma

In general, a dogma is a set of opinions, beliefs, or judgments which one believes in; but in theology it means a doctrine formally and authoritatively affirmed by the leaders of the religious group. It is the intellectual underpinning, so to speak, of the belief system and is the leaders' attempt to explain in a more-or-less logical manner the rationale of man's place in the universe. Such an explanation is indeed hard to do, and virtually every religious dogma eventually has to rely on myths, miracles, revelations, sacred and often inscrutable holy writings, and ultimately on an appeal to blind faith on the part of the followers.

Generally speaking, religious dogma and heresy are not taken as seriously in modern times as formerly. Some few centuries ago, however, heretics, i.e. people who did not believe or accept the established dogma, could easily end up suffering severely, including being burned at the stake. Heretical attacks were considered not merely an affront to the church but an attack against the very structure of society itself, so closely were secular and religious interests intertwined. Such attitudes and conditions still exist today in some religious communities. This underlines my belief that the purpose of religion is to bind people together. The dogma is the overall established doctrine for accomplishing this cohesion and ultimately includes ethics, morality, and rituals. During the many centuries when kings ruled by "divine right," any attack against the secular powers was considered an attack against the church as well. It is hard for us today to realize how much power the church had in former times and how closely church and state were united in their control over the people. In many countries this still holds true today, particularly in the Muslim world.

What I am here calling dogma can also be called the doctrine, the theology, or the basic mythology. The basic myth or explanatory story in the Judeo-Christian-Muslim belief system, for example, includes the fiction of an all-powerful creator who made all the universe, including man and the other animals and life forms some time in the distant past. Man, of course, was a special creation around whom the succeeding story revolves, in particular the relation of man to the creator. This creator-god gave a set of commandments to man and stayed in close touch with him during the early part of the story and kept a close eye on him. Then this basic common dogma of the three so-called "revealed" religions begins to diverge: the Jews go off on their own tangent of the story, later the Christians add their special twists to the overall story, and finally the Muslims a few centuries later present their additional explanations of man's relation to this creator-god. In each case the narrative of God's revealing himself to mankind becomes all the more elaborate, dense, and opaque as time and generations of believers go by.

Perhaps the key ingredient in this tradition is man's rebellion against a jealous father-figure of God and his desire to think for himself. Man is created by this powerful God, given an ideal place to live, disobeys God's command to keep his hands off that apple tree, and is kicked out of the Garden of Eden. He now has to work for his living, and his wife Eve has to suffer as well. Adam and Eve have children who also have problems pleasing God, and after a while there are a great many people busy with their own lives and paying only little attention to God and his commandments. God repents for having created such a self-centered creature and kills them all with a great flood, saving only one good man, Noah and his family, in a big boat called an ark. Time passes, these people multiply and increase in sinfulness and lack of attention to God. Things get so bad that God has to send down his one son Jesus to be sacrificed for the sinfulness of man. This doesn't seem to help in any sort of permanent way, and a few centuries later God has to try one last time through Mohammed and the Koran to get mankind on the proper path of devotion and obedience to their maker and creator of the universe.

The early texts and variations of this myth are regarded as sacred, usually dictated directly by God himself to some special messenger in the revealed religions. Later, the explanations, commentaries, and stories of the leaders themselves become sacred and are regarded as integral parts of the holy tradition. Since the priests and scholars within each tradition often disagree with one another, the larger story can easily become confusing and frustrating for the serious follower. The final solution usually suggested is simply to rely on faith and the authorities who allegedly know far more about the subtleties of the dogma than any mere believer.

I call all these stories and dogmatic explanations "myths" because no one can fully explain them in a clear, rational way; many of them might strike an unbiased listener simply as unfounded superstitions. The doctrine of a religion must ultimately be accepted on faith without question, and faith turns out to be one of the fundamental elements of every religion I have studied. Educated believers in each tradition, however, want to explain their belief system to themselves and others in a more-or-less rational manner, but their explanations are meaningful essentially only to fellow-believers. It seems to me that in our own time many people try desperately to combine two extremes: the strictly logical and highly successful approach of science with the divine revelation approach which is acceptable only through faith. An outstanding example is the attempt to reconcile the scientific study of evolution with the Biblical myth of creation.

The function of such religious mythology or theology is to give the adherents of that religion simple answers to fundamental, universal human questions: where did we and the universe come from, what is the meaning of life, what are we supposed to be doing with our lives, why the vast inequalities among humans, what happens to us when we die, will we ever see our loved ones again, etc.? Not taking the questions themselves too seriously, most people today seem to be quite satisfied with the answers given by their religion and simply go on with the more important and pressing aspects of life: family, work, trying to be happy, helping family and friends. They generally spend little or no time worrying or even thinking about the essentially simplistic answers given by their religion to imponderable metaphysical and theological questions. Briefly put, the dogma of a religion is generally a creation story trying to explain how everything got started in the very beginning and lies at the basis of a religion. It is fortunately disregarded as not particularly important by the masses of believers and is relegated to comparative theologians and students of mythology.

Ethical code

The second and far more important part of religion is its ethical code. People are much more concerned with questions of good and bad, what they can and cannot do, and the reasons why. The ethical system of do's and don'ts which each religion offers is therefore of much more interest and relevance to the average believer than the dogmatic niceties. In addition to general moral guidelines and precepts, many religions lay out a detailed code of behavior concerning dress, food and drink, types of recreation, hair styles, whom to associate with and marry, and often a great many other aspects of life down to minute details. Other religions content themselves with broad statements of how to interact with other people inside and outside one's own group. These larger guidelines of helping others and trying to be a decent human being are common to most of the world's religions and revolve around the basic idea of treating other people the way you would like to be treated, often called the law of reciprocity. This commonality of general ethical principles is what causes us to believe that all religions are essentially the same. Ethically they tend to be quite similar, but in terms of fundamental dogma they are often worlds apart and burdened with irreconcilable differences.

An important distinction to be made in the ethical consideration of many religions is that between the in-group and the out-group. A person motivated by the ethical commands of his religion can be quite considerate and helpful to members of his own religious group and utterly ghastly toward fellow humans of another religious group. Understanding in-group and out-group distinction becomes absolutely essential when we consider current examples of Sunni Muslims slaughtering Shi'ite Muslims through suicide bombings, the atrocities of Catholic Christians against Protestant Christians, or the murderous rampages of poor African tribes against one another. This is a mechanism operating on an individual scale as well as on a larger social level, in the sense that we almost automatically treat people differently as soon as we recognize that they come from our group or from other backgrounds. Treating a fellow human as a fellow human—pure and simple, as individuals or as groups—is a difficult lesson we all must learn.

Many people have such a dark view of human nature as to feel that any moral code must be sanctioned by God, or it will collapse against the untamed nature of man. They believe that no code of admittedly human origin will carry sufficient authority to control the anti-social instincts of man, and that fear of divine retribution, in this life or the hereafter, is essential. For such people, a sacred code of religious morality and tradition is essential; others view man and his history in quite a different, more optimistic light. History offers ample examples and illustrations of both attitudes.

Rituals

The third fundamental aspect or building block of religion in this account is rituals. Rituals are observances, practices, ceremonies, and acts, usually solemn and serious, carried out in accordance with customary or set standards of procedure. They can be both simple and sophisticated, solemn and happy, religious and secular. Religious rituals vary greatly but are important in any religious tradition. Together with the dogma and ethical code they make up the three vital elements of virtually every religious belief system. Rituals are generally community activities which indoctrinate young members of the group and bind the older members more closely together. They include holidays (holy days), ceremonies, important rites centering on birth, puberty, marriage, and death, plus routine activities of meeting regularly with other members of the group in church services, preaching and teaching, singing and prayer activities, visiting sick and aged members, helping the poor of the group, etc.

Important religious rituals in the Western World include baptism and communion in the Christian tradition, circumcision and Passover among the Jews, and the daily calls to prayer among Muslims. Secular rituals range from solemn coronation and inauguration ceremonies to such things as granting of degrees at universities, mass popular opening and closing ceremonies during the Olympic Games, political rallies, singing the national anthem at the beginning of sports events, etc. In many societies rituals are for specific purposes: rain dances and incantations to call forth rain, tribal dances to entice animals to approach the hunters, war dances in preparation for conflict, etc. Other rituals are used to commemorate some significant event or leader, to bring about a desired goal, to request safety and protection, acknowledge rites of passages from childhood to adulthood, to celebrate harvest and seasonal change, installations of religious and political leaders into office, etc. Rituals are many and varied in all societies, but all seem to correspond to some deep-seated need in humans for community, continuity, tradition, and acknowledgment of the basic aspects and processes of life. In this sense, rituals perform a vital function in virtually all societies.

Rituals are important ways of impressing on the members, especially the younger ones, the idea that they form a special community distinct from outsiders. People who otherwise have little or nothing to do with the formal aspects of their religion will still meet with other members once or twice a year to celebrate certain important rituals. The need for membership in something larger than mere family or professional groups seems to be at the heart of the religious "instinct," and people who consider themselves essentially beyond or outside their early religious training often feel a strong urge to participate in some of the basic rituals of their community: Christmas and Easter church services, communion and baptism, Bar and Bat Mitzvah, Passover, Rosh Hashanah, No Ruz, Ramadan, etc. There are in addition, of course, purely personal and family ceremonies and celebrations such as birth, marriage, death, and initiation rites, although these also often have religious overtones. All these things, religious and secular, form a sort of "social cement" bonding and binding people together into distinct communities. National rituals such as parades, mass singing of the national song, speeches by the group leader, etc. play the same role in forming a cohesive national group.

Overview

Such considerations and definitions of dogmas, ethics, and rituals will be helpful when we discuss later in this essay a much-needed new world-view and how it is already emerging in many parts of the world, in particular among people for whom the traditional approach to religion is no longer appealing. It seems clear that a religion has at least three essential parts: a metaphysical/ mythological part which explains the physical world, a moral-ethical part which controls behavior of the believers, and a set of rituals which reinforce and cement all the elements together. The first and most problematic part is called the doctrine, dogma, or theology, and generally contains a story of creation, man's relation to the gods, myths of sin and salvation, ideas about time and eternity, man's relation to his fellows and other creatures of nature.

It also refers to a set of holy writings and leaders, a general code of behavior and rituals, often a calendar, and similar elements.

The leaders of the religion codify the dogma and explain it to the followers, but usually the mystical and metaphysical aspects are clothed in such nebulous and mysterious terms as to make many parts by and large incomprehensible to the critical, inquiring mind. To make the dogma palatable, the leaders rely on early indoctrination of the young, an emphasis on faith, an authoritarian air of confidence and security, numerous rituals and customs, a grab-bag of myths and miracles, plus a prohibition on taboo topics and questions such as: Where and how did the gods originate? What was there before the first acts of creation? How can we know for sure about the points of the dogma other than by faith? The dogma or theology of the religions I have studied leaves a great many unexplained and essentially inexplicable questions, especially in the "revealed" religions of Judaism, Christianity, and Islam, in which God revealed himself and his will to special messengers and prophets. The origins of the "man-made" religions (Hinduism, Buddhism, Taoism, Confucianism, Shintoism, Communism) are intellectually much easier to grasp, because they tend in general simply to deify great teachers, leaders, or the powers of nature.

Religion as a social cement

Today the doctrinal quagmire of religion seems perfectly acceptable for the vast majority of followers because they essentially disregard it and concern themselves only with the overriding function of any religious belief system, and this is to weld together—through myths, rituals, and moral teachings—disconnected individuals and family groups into a larger, coherent whole, thereby lending them increased stability, security, and power. This can be called the "social cement" aspect of religion and is, in my view, the central reason for its existence. The religion provides this cement through a meaningful ethical and social code of behavior which satisfies the followers and permits them to feel at ease with fellow believers and essentially better than or superior to non-believers. The moral and behavior code is usually strengthened by numerous customs and rituals such as special holidays and celebrations, initiation of the young (baptism, communion, circumcision), frequent group meetings (with preaching, music, prayer, confessions), and contributions of time and money by the followers to the religious leaders. Most religious fundamentalists tend to think they have found the best way of life and generally want to share it with other people. Judaism is a special case and is essentially restricted to members of the "tribe." After talking to many Jews, however, I have become thoroughly confused about who is included and excluded in the tribe and how "Jewishness" is determined. Islam and Christianity are the two greatest proselytizing belief systems that I am aware of, but they fade in importance when compared to the emerging world religion of secular humanism, which will be discussed later.

I believe the traditional religious dogmas and mythologies have been surpassed and are totally out of date in the present world of science and technology. They remain as interesting stories and psychological illustrations such as we learn in our study of Greek mythology. Much of the moral and ethical teachings of most religions are applicable, however, to our current condition and therefore retain many "believers," but the theological doctrines strike me as excessively provincial and completely out of step with the circumstances of modern life. I find that most people of the Jewish, Christian, and Moslem faiths essentially disregard all but the moral teachings and key ritual behaviors of their confessions, and this is why they can comfortably and honestly assert that they embrace their traditional religion.

Summary of religion

Searchers and seekers like me—and perhaps you—are a strange lot indeed. Living in a fourteen-billion-light-years-across universe, we try to wrap our minds around such a mind-boggling concept and to locate our position in time and space. We try to understand the creation of the universe and what role, if indeed any, we humans are supposed to be playing in the unfolding of this cosmic drama. In our ignorance and hubris we humans have been asking for millennia what relationship we have to the creative force behind it all. Man's religious leaders, in their similar ignorance and hubris, plus their desire for power and social control, claim to explain, often in amazing detail, the mind and nature of this creative power and man's intimate link with this creator. What foolish nonsense! On what basis can they possibly know any more or any better than the rest of us?

One thing has become increasingly clear to me in my perhaps equally foolish search for ultimates, and that is the crucial role of consciousness, the ability to even conceive of the vastness of the universe and our place in it. I think this widespread sense of awareness among many modern people is the closest thing we have had thus far to any "divine revelation." But consciousness, as I understand it, has not been revealed to man in one fell swoop; rather, it has developed in thousands upon thousands of people over the millennia. Thanks to our myth-makers, poets, philosophers, and scientists over the centuries, we are now at a point where we can speculate more-or-less clearly and rationally on the size, origin, and creative power behind the whole spectacle—even including our own role in it! To do so, however, we must become as free and unencumbered as possible. Given the unavoidable childhood indoctrination we have all had, this is obviously hard to do. The main motivation behind this long discussion on religion is to help free the mind so that we can embrace some new thoughts and approaches.

Serious searchers will try as best they can, I think, to start anew with a clean slate, a *tabula rasa*, and develop their own scheme of things. Weekend and occasional searchers will find many people along the way anxious to keep them on the "right" path; more independent investigators will be leery of all such help, even though they have to accept many unavoidable conditions and restrictions willy-nilly: our language, cultural background, time and place, the state of scientific knowledge, etc.

Finding one's own way is a perilous but exciting adventure: very attractive to some people, abhorrent to others. It's like a giant, complex game: engaging, thrilling, perhaps ultimately meaningless, but deeply rewarding to the players, some of whom seem to have no option but to play. Detached onlookers might find it as absurd and purposeless as hitting a ball back and forth over a net, moving chessmen on a board, or throwing darts at a target. I think serious seekers must keep this game analogy in mind if they are to avoid the fallacy of taking themselves too seriously and regarding their game as the only one in town. This essay is meant as my illustration of the game principle.

Having sketched out what I take to be the general nature and inherent limitations of traditional religions of the past, I turn now to apply some of the key ideas and concepts to a new world-view or secular religion which I think is rapidly emerging worldwide.

Secular humanism

There is increasing evidence that there is today only one world civilization, in contrast to the many distinct civilizations of the past. The cities of the world resemble each other more and more with skylines, freeways, airports; the businessmen of the world talk more and more the same language of supply and demand, investment returns, profits and losses, quarterly earnings; the armies and navies of the world fly the same planes, shoot the same rockets and missiles, use the same weapons; the students of the world have more and more in common with one another; scientists and technicians of the world resemble each other more and more. Downtown Seoul is almost indistinguishable from downtown Berlin or Rio de Janeiro. As national distinctions disappear, an increasingly homogeneous world-view—physical, mental, emotional, spiritual—emerges. It seems to me that large segments of informed humanity are moving simultaneously in essentially new directions and on a global level, relying on intelligence, information, good will, and common sense.

For many years I have been trying to understand what is happening to my native language, English, and my native culture, that of the United States. For a long time I concentrated just on the spread of English itself throughout the world and wondered what was causing this to happen. In talking to many international students and non-native speakers using English as a very important second language in their daily lives, I learned that the sheer usefulness of the language globally was perhaps the major single reason for their learning my language. However, I then learned that it is not only this pragmatic factor which powerfully attracts them but also the whole culture and background from which the language springs. Foreign students learn English not only to enhance their job possibilities but also to participate in an exciting new world culture.

English conquers the world

I then began to think of the spread of English as a linguistic tool of British/American imperialism. I thought the language was like the proverbial camel's nose under the edge of the Bedouin's tent on a cold winter night: First just the nose sneaks in, and then little by little the whole animal is inside the tent. Through study of the language, the vast culture made possible by that linguistic tool starts influencing the student. This proved to be a highly rewarding approach and generated many spirited discussions about the language as a vehicle of Western imperialism. But I was continually struggling with an interesting and surprising paradox of this explanation: English and its culture were conquering the world, but I found that the conquered people—using this analogy—wanted to be conquered! They were not being subdued against their will, but voluntarily and willingly! They were gladly taking part in their own conquest by flocking to the U.S. and the U.K. by the tens and hundreds of thousands! Barriers of various kinds had to be erected to keep them out!

What kind of conquest was this? If this was an overwhelming of the world by the English language and culture, then it was a new sort of conquering activity. People were being powerfully attracted by something, but what was it? Was it just the fact that the world had discovered a powerful new tool of communication, useful in a thousand way? Was it just the glitter and glamour of a wealthy, highly developed, materialistic society which was being shown around the world through Hollywood films and alluring TV broadcasts? For a while I thought this was probably the answer: Wealthy, successful materialism was being promoted by a very useful international language through a highly developed means of global communication, and it was all intimately associated with the world's only remaining superpower.

But over the long haul this explanation was not enough and did not leave me completely satisfied in my quest to explain what I saw happening virtually everywhere in the world. Then I hit upon an idea which made the most sense and was capable of explaining most of the phenomena which I observed: A comprehensive new way of looking at the world, a new ideology, an exciting new world-view, is rapidly emerging, and closely resembles a religion. Its primary base and highest stage of development thus far is found in the U.S., and the language of conversion and propagation is English. This new ideology, religion, world-view, or interpretation of life, can perhaps best be called "secular humanism."

This approach became particularly useful when I learned that a language usually spreads for three main reasons: 1. power, or military, political, and financial might; 2. knowledge base, or science and technology; 3. religious proselytizing. Things began to fall into place, and more and more ideas began to make better sense, especially when I considered that all three factors were powerfully at work in the spread of English and Western influence—chiefly American—around the world.

The elements and spread of secular humanism

Religions have traditionally been primarily concerned with man's relation to some divine power or being. They generally offer an interpretation of life which explains our origins, provides a code of ethics, and tells us what our human existence means, what our relationship to one another should be like, and what we should be doing with our life. In Christianity, for example, this has traditionally meant believing in God and following his commandments and his appointed leaders, trying to love and help one another, and preparing our souls to spend eternity in heaven while avoiding the torments of hell. Judaism, Islam and other religions have similar guidelines and goals.

I believe there is another powerful interpretation of life, widespread today to a greater or lesser degree in almost all societies of the world, which might be called secular or non-religious humanism. It tries to focus on having a good life here and now while largely disregarding all questions of divinity and existence after this present life on earth. Humanism is the belief that men and women like you and me are the most important creatures on earth and have ultimate priority. The Greek philosopher Protagoras said two and a half thousand years ago: "Man is the measure of all things!" By this he meant that humans, not the gods, decide what is right and wrong, good and bad. Humans, not the gods, decide what man's existence is all about and what humans should be doing. "Knowledge is power!" said the English philosopher Francis Bacon almost four centuries ago, and knowledge can free us from ignorance, superstition, and authoritarianism, however deeply entrenched they may be. Ignorance, on the other hand, means intellectual and emotional bondage. Aristotle is right: "All men by nature desire to know!" and present-day knowledge is growing by leaps and bounds in virtually every direction and is creating a new world. Some of the chief characteristics of modern secular humanism include the following ideals and goals:

**Emphasis on the power of scientific, pragmatic ideas in controlling the life of an individual or a nation; change your ideas and the world changes.

**Democracy, or self-determination, which is the belief that individuals and nations should be free and allowed to determine their own way of life.

**Free enterprise or the free market approach, which means that if you can make a better product or provide a better service, you should be allowed to do so and reap the rewards of your efforts. By following your own interests and abilities, you and the whole society will profit.

**The value and dignity of each individual human being, and his right to live his own life as he sees fit, provided he does not impinge on the equal rights of other people. This is the powerful idea of personal freedom.

**Capitalism, or the idea that if you have some money and would like to start your own business and take your chances in the world of free enterprise, you have every right to do so. You should have the freedom to make a profit from your initiative and become rich, in the same way as you have the right to lose all your money and go bankrupt. It's up to you. It's your decision.

**Liberalism, this means that society should be open and flexible enough to tolerate and even encourage people to try new things, new methods of living, new approaches to life. Live and let live, and all will benefit.

**Materialism means simply the recognition that the basic necessities of life: food, clothing, shelter, a minimum of security, jobs, money are important and should not be taken lightly or belittled. Material things may not be the ultimate values in life, but they are fundamental.

**Pragmatism means that beliefs are ultimately validated only by their usefulness and practical results. By their fruits we can know which ideas are meaningful and worthwhile, and which are not.

These are some of the key elements and goals of secular humanism; there are surely others which I have overlooked. This democratic, capitalistic, liberal, pragmatic, materialistic, free enterprise approach to life has thus far reached its highest level in America, and the ideal of the "self-made man" has been realized here probably more often than any other place on earth. I think this approach to life appeals to a great many people around the world despite its many problems and dramatic exaggerations. For this reason, people worldwide are willing to embrace many aspects of the American way of life, including the culture and language which go with it. How else can we explain the worldwide fascination—especially among young people—with the external trappings such as Hollywood films, McDonald's hamburgers, Coca Cola, Pizza Hut, Madonna and Michael Jackson, music rock groups, including the incorporation of innumerable words and phrases into the local language, such terms such as Rent-a-Car, self-service, sandwiches, drinks, shopping centers, jeans, OK, take it easy, and countless others?

Americanism

Speaking in very broad and general terms, if we call this humanistic approach "The American way of life", or even "Americanism," for lack of a better term, we can understand that one of the main reasons why the English language is gently "conquering," "over-running," or even "seducing" the world, is because people everywhere are embracing and welcoming what might be called a new approach to life, a secular religion based in America. A great many people find it attractive despite its many distasteful aspects, and they want to participate in it, for good or ill. In traveling abroad, I find people in the most unlikely places who have a relative, friend, or even direct family member either living in America or trying to get here, and there must be some powerful reasons behind this other than the purely materialistic ones.

A closer look

From what I have understood of it thus far, this new humanistic American world-view has the following characteristics, among others:

1. It is a secular—in contrast to religious—movement or explanation of the human condition. There are no gods or non-human creatures who create meaning and purpose. The Greek philosopher Protagoras is right: "Man is the measure of all things!", and it is humans who decide questions of the meaning and purpose of life. Francis Bacon is right: "Knowledge is power!" and can liberate us; and secular humanists believe that knowledge and power should be spread to as many people as possible through training and education. It is the belief that we humans are—or should be—in charge of our own destiny, and by learning to cooperate we can control our destiny.

2. It is materialistic in the sense of the old adage, *"Primum vivere, deinde philosophari."* First live, then philosophize. Secular humanism embraces the tough pragmatic saying, "First things first!" This means knowing

what the first things are and then putting them clearly in the position of primary importance. This does not mean that first things are the only things of importance, but it does mean that without food, clothing, shelter, and a minimum sense of security not much else will take place. Material necessities are the basis on which all of human culture and civilization are built. Materialism is not the end of living, but it is the indispensable beginning.

3. Secular humanism is "now-directed" and this-worldly, not "eternity-directed" and other-worldly. Today—the here and now—is the most real kind of reality that we humans are capable of knowing; now is eternity. Immortality—other than through children and reputation—is highly improbable and very suspicious. This present life is the only thing we are really sure of, and we should not squander it. People around the world work hard to create for themselves and their families the best life possible, and they should be encouraged to focus their efforts on the here and now. The material aspects of the good life are within the grasp of increasing numbers of individuals. People worldwide see many examples of ordinary fellow humans—especially here in America—who seem to have brought the physical aspects of heaven down to earth.

4. Self-determination is one of the keys of secular humanism. Thomas Jefferson is right: all men are created equal and have the right to life, liberty, and the pursuit of happiness as they see it. This includes the right of self-determination for the individual and for his social group, state, or nation. Humans have human rights. Ignorance and slavery are abhorrent, and total equality of opportunity for all, without regard for age, race, sex, political or sexual orientation, etc. is the goal towards which we should all strive.

5. Ideally, democracy means freedom and self-rule as long as it does not impinge upon the rights of others; democracy also means protecting the rights of minorities. Freedom includes freedom of thought, worship, movement, assembly, the press, occupation, marriage, sexual preference, etc. These ideas have not yet of course been fully realized —in America or anywhere else—but as ideas or ideals they are very powerful and seductive.

6. The free enterprise system of buying and selling brings benefits to everyone involved. Private property and capitalism allows people to become vitally involved with their own interests, to develop their own talents, and to reap the rewards of their labor. The old adage, "Build a better mousetrap and the world will beat a path to your door" is right. Everyone will benefit. Most countries and governments seem to be moving slowly toward this powerful idea. Many of today's more progressive companies are now even

introducing a profit-sharing plan among their employees for much the same reason: they know that self-interest generally accrues to the overall interest of the group.

7. Rights and responsibilities are the flip sides of the same coin. Every individual has certain human rights, but he also has specific responsibilities to cooperate and help make things work. These are often hard lessons to learn, but they are slowly being assimilated by increasing numbers of people worldwide.

8. The idea of progress means that things can be made better through work, openness, cooperation, tolerance, discussion, compromise, give-and-take. These are difficult but indispensable goals in a new world order. Experience and common sense teach us that the welfare of the individual is closely tied up with the welfare of the community, and that an appropriate balance must be developed between the two.

These are some of the basic tenets of secular humanism; other will probably have occurred to you while reading this. Each is complex and problematic, of course, but once people grasp the ideas, the genie is out of the bottle and difficult or impossible to put back in.

The new world religion

If religion can roughly be defined as an interpretation or explanation of the human condition, together with guidelines for living, then I think we can justly say that a new world religion is clearly emerging on a global scale and has thus far reached its clearest outline and most pronounced manifestation in the U.S., with numerous positive and negative aspects clearly showing. This dynamic world-view incorporates the ethical guidelines of all the major religions and is truly cosmopolitan in the sense of embracing all mankind without the typically restrictive mythological underpinnings of virtually every religion. As yet unnamed and largely overlooked, I believe this rapidly emerging and dynamic way of life will eventually be adopted by and adapted to the entire world, provided, of course, that followers of more provincial belief systems do not first kill off all of us..

To return briefly to the three or four basic elements of any religion—dogma, ethics, rituals, faith—let's see how these would apply to this new secular world-view.

Dogma

The "dogma" of secular humanism includes the "Big Bang," geological time, the evolution of life, the ascent of man, DNA, the scientific method, and many other absolutely fascinating things. This complex scientific tale would not have gained so many adherents had it not been for the unbelievable changes in the world made possible by the technology spawned by this new knowledge. Trips to the moon, heart transplants, genetic engineering, and a thousand other scientific "miracles" have forced people to take the theories of scientists rather seriously, and today most educated people prefer the scientific explanatory tale of life on earth over the traditional religious explanations.

The dogma of secular humanism is the scientific approach to reality. This includes not only a complex story of man's origins but also an equally complex story of man's nature. Rather than being given once and for all as in the divine story, man's nature in secular humanism is also evolving and developing, and we don't know what all it can and will become. According to this new dogma, human nature is not fixed but is a work in progress, and the explanatory tale of secular humanism facilitates that progress far better than any other explanation offered thus far to sensitive, intelligent people.

Ethics

The ethics and morality of secular humanism follow along the same general lines as the dogma. This is to say that humans are clever, intelligent, immensely adaptable creatures who know what their problems are, where the shoe pinches, and by and large how to fix things. Over countless generations, in all climates and cultures, they have delineated the basic difficulties of social living and come up with solutions in the form of general rules; these have been codified as secular or religious laws and developed into a set of do's and don't's, mostly don't's. These general rules of behavior are the stock in trade of religions, and this is the area where secular humanism and religious beliefs touch most closely. The ten commandments of the Bible, for example, capture much of this universal moral code.

In this broad sense, the ethics and moral code of secular humanism incorporate the best aspects of thousands of years of human interaction and can still appeal today to traditionally religious people of all stripes. It is above all the religious dogmas which keep people divided, provincial, and apart; ethically we are all so much alike that we have strikingly similar views on actual moral behavior. Most of us don't really care what our fellow humans are thinking and believing as long as they treat us and others decently. Let us hope that the mind of modern man has become too informed and liberated to be ever again confined by narrow, provincial beliefs.

Ethical codes tend to divide people into two basic categories: the in-group and the out-group. This distinction allows us to love and help the members of our own in-group but slaughter members of the out-group with gusto and a clear conscience. The distinguishing mark between the two groups can be skin color, race, nationality, language, religion, political belief, sexual preference, and a thousand others. We humans have no problem convincing ourselves that we in our group are different (and superior) to all other groups. The in-group of secular humanism includes without question or discussion all humans, regardless of condition, because it recognizes that we are essentially all alike. Humanists therefore do not recognize an in-group/out-group distinction among humans. They believe that we are all one species with many different forms and variations, like it or not. To make distinctions among humans is to label oneself as a provincial bigot.

Rituals

These are as diverse in secular humanism as humans themselves and can generally be embraced by everyone as long as they do not cause harm. Our willingness to accept and rejoice in one another's general rituals helps bind diverse humans together, and the power of rituals to form people into closely knit coherent groups is hard to over-estimate. National leaders have long used them to join essentially isolated individuals and smaller groups into a powerful, unified whole. The National Socialists of Germany in the 1930s, for example, developed rituals of political rallies, parades, flags, marching songs, mass demonstrations, salutes, etc. to a very high degree and welded the German people into a powerfully unified group. Every nation does something similar, of course, to create a strong sense of nationalism, but seldom to the same extent or with the same intensity and success.

Rituals to promote secular humanism are perhaps a bit harder to imagine and develop than the typical nationalistic techniques and influences found in virtually every country. One outstanding example does spring to mind, however, and that is the elaborate international rituals and ceremonies surrounding the Olympic Games every four years: carrying the Olympic Torch across nations and states, the dramatic lighting of the flame in the stadium, the colorful parade of the athletes with flags and music, raising the national banners of the three top champions in each event, plus the daily close TV coverage of the contestants in action. All these things have a powerful emotional and intellectual impact, and they can be used as teaching examples. I think everyone watching these impressive mass demonstrations honoring international sportsmanship and excellence can easily be led into thinking about the truly universal nature of all humans beings. It's hard to avoid.

The Olympic Games, the Nobel Prize ceremonies, the work of the United Nations, the annual international meetings of top political, scientific, and economic leaders, the International Monetary Fund, the World Bank, Doctors

Without Borders, Habitat For Humanity, the Red Cross, global aid and emergency help organizations, plus many other nationally and internationally active organizations demonstrate, I think, that many people are thinking in broad humanistic terms and are working for the good of humanity. With a bit of creative thinking and good will, additional groups and rituals stressing universally valid human matters and cultural cooperation can be developed and brought to the attention of the world community. Many high schools, colleges, and universities have international exchange programs to promote good will and understanding among students. Young people are especially open to idealistic causes and commitments, and the future belongs to the young.

Faith

The concept of faith is as much at work among secular humanists as among the most ardent believer in any traditional religion. My professional life as a college professor leads me to believe that there are hundreds of thousands of young students worldwide who, through their scientific and humanistic studies, are day by day strengthening their conviction that they and others like them can make the world a better place to live despite the countless problems facing us on many fronts. Their faith and belief in the human potential are powerful motivating forces. Many of these young people are deeply religious in the best and broadest sense of the word and will welcome the chance to embrace a truly universal world-view aimed at all humans. John Kennedy's Peace Corps was a dramatic demonstration of active good will and sacrifice on the part of average people.

In contrast to other major religions, secular humanism is a work in progress and has not been created at one specific time by one or a few leaders. On the contrary, it is vastly more democratic and has arisen out of the experience of tens of thousands of human souls and minds over a very long period of time, along with a great deal of trial and error. It stretches back at least as far as Protagoras and Aristotle, and it incorporates the ancient Chinese doctrine of the union of opposites as seen in the symbol of yin and yang. It teaches that life is a whole, but filled with tensions and the conflicting powers of light and darkness, as taught by the Zoroastrian religion of Ancient Persia. The ethics of secular humanism stresses the commonality of all humans by embracing the moral highlights of virtually every traditional religion: respect for our fellows, help, service, tolerance, compromise, generosity, sacrifice, understanding, sympathy, and a dozen other such concepts, but applicable to all humans.

All this can be summed up in the concept of love and reciprocity: treating others as you would like to be treated, or in the negative version of the same Golden Rule as taught by Confucius five centuries before Jesus: don't treat others such as you would not like to be treated. All these ideas have been taught before by various religions, but always with the tacit or stated stipulation that they only apply to members of my own tribe, my own in-group. Secular humanism is the belief that all humans are intimate members of my tribe: all men and women are my brothers and sisters, all children are my children. This is a hard doctrine and exists more as an ideal than as a reality, but it is a lofty goal to strive for and is becoming increasingly clear to large numbers of regular people. I believe more and more people—especially younger ones brought up in the current international information age of the internet, computers, travel and student exchanges—are developing a strong sense of faith in the basic goodness of their fellow humans. And it is such faith that will change the world.

Conclusion

Secular humanism, as I understand it, is still undergoing strenuous trials and tests in many of its elements; it's progress is fitful and it may never reach a fully completed stage. In fact, by its very nature it is almost certain to never stop evolving. Each individual and each larger social group will have to determine its own best and most productive combination of the key elements of secular humanism and add others of its own making. For example, the crucial and complex balance between material and spiritual values must be worked out continually by individuals and groups. The same holds true for the fundamental question of the rights of the individual and the rights of the community. Rights and responsibilities on the personal and community level have to be established clearly and forcefully. The utilitarians' social goal of "the greatest good for the greatest number" is a powerful general guideline and must be continually held in central focus and re-examined by each generation.

Is man primarily a materialistic or a spiritual being? Which values should have the upper hand and be dominant in life? Secular humanism seems at first glance to stress the materialistic side with the strong argument that humans must obviously be fed, clothed, and sheltered if they are to do anything else with their lives, and the more this can be done well for all people, the better off we all are. But what then? Spiritual, moral, religious, artistic, creative values and questions spring automatically into being and demand resolution. Finding answers and the appropriate balance is obviously a difficult task requiring intelligence, information, tolerance, cooperation, free and open inquiry, human dignity, etc., all of which are at the very heart of secular humanism.

Worldwide, men and women of intelligence and good will are working on such issues and are helping to bring about a new world order. Many different things point in that direction: global trade and commerce, international travel by increasingly larger numbers of people from all walks of life and all countries, inexpensive and highly developed international means of communication, rituals such as televised sports and cultural events like the Olympic Games and championship soccer games seen simultaneously around the world by hundreds of millions of people, films and television programs from all countries, etc. Such things lead me to believe that a dynamic new world-view/ religion/way-of-life/ideology is coming into being and will continue to tie us increasingly closer together. There is hope in many quarters that humanity will eventually save itself.

Chapter 6.
Philosophy

Introduction

After animism and religion, philosophy is the third tool developed by our ancestors to come to terms emotionally and intellectually with their world. It developed much later in man's evolution because it requires ample leisure time and independence from the normal concerns and problems of daily life. It presupposes a more-or-less secure position in life, intellectual and emotional independence, and a certain cast of mind to inquire consistently into big philosophical and existential issues, a turn of mind which not everyone has. The big problems and issues of philosophy, however, are the problems and questions of life, things concerning everyone: the meaning and purpose of life, values, morality, wonder, birth, death, questions of an afterlife, etc. Philosophers are people vitally interested in these universal human matters who also have—or take—the time and energy to inquire into them in a thorough-going manner over a long period of time.

Philosophers show up in every society and deal with much the same questions and problems everywhere. We in the Western world have invested a lot of time and interest in Western philosophy, generally starting with the Ancient Greeks, but we have not spent much effort in the thinkers and philosophical systems of the Orient and other parts of the world. For this reason, most Westerners have at least a nodding acquaintance with Socrates, Plato, Aristotle, Augustine, Thomas Aquinas, Kant, and Hegel, but only little or no knowledge of Confucius, Lao Tze, Mencius, or the Buddha. In the West there is generally a rather sharp division between philosophy and religion, whereas in other parts of the world a people's religion tends to be closely interwoven with their philosophy, forming a systematic way of life. This seems to me to be especially true in China and India, but this may be the case only because we are not as conversant with other, non-Western, traditions.

The Greeks

It is hard to over-estimate the importance and influence of the Ancient Greeks on the Western philosophical and cultural tradition. They were a remarkable people living at a crucial time for our civilization and they laid out in general terms many of the broad paths which we have followed over the past two thousand years. This is especially evident in the many words, concepts, and fields of activity that we have inherited from them, directly or indirectly, including the very idea of democracy, which they tried but didn't like all that much, because in Athens it turned into mob rule. Most of the names for forms of government come directly from them: aristocracy, plutocracy, monarchy, patriarchy. oligarchy, anarchy, theocracy, plutocracy. Modern branches of science abound with Greek names: astrology, biology, zoology, anthropology, paleontology, theology, etc., in large part because the Greeks were the first thinkers trying to understand the world in objective, non-mythical and non-religious terms. To do so they developed a new approach for inquiring into new branches of knowledge.

The philosophical method

In contrast to the emotional and authoritarian approach of religious leaders in spreading knowledge of their dogmas and indoctrinating their followers, the Greek philosophers developed an impersonal method of logical investigation and analysis of terms, open and free discussion, and assumed that the truth can best be approached by arguments and counter-arguments. Aristotle, for example, in trying to determine the best form of government, collected and analyzed the constitutions of some 57 city-states in order to learn how societies actually organize themselves. To be fair, however, I should point out that Aristotle's teacher, Plato, created his ideal form of government out of whole cloth just by thinking about it and writing out a very detailed dialogue or discussion between Socrates and his friends about the best way to organize society. His book is called *The Republic* and is one of the great classics in political theory. The philosophical method developed in Greece was a sort of early prototype of the powerful scientific method used today, but in general it lacked hypotheses and controlled experiments.

The word itself

The word *philosophy* comes from the Greek language and means literally "the love (*philo*) of wisdom (*sophia*)." In an extended sense it is the search for meaning and purpose in life; it is also used today in the sense of a person's way of looking at things in general. The word was coined by the philosopher/ mathematician Pythagoras in the 6th century BC; he actually formed a society of like-minded thinkers who lived together doing scientific and mathematical studies. One of their famous theorems is still taught today in geometry classes everywhere. Most of the earliest philosophers among the Greeks were doing what we today would call science. They were zoologists, mathematicians, medical doctors and astronomers, as well as being concerned students of ethics, politics, and metaphysics. 'Philosophy' meant the love of all wisdom and knowledge, and until the 19th century, many scholars in the Western tradition considered themselves either as "moral philosophers' (what we would call 'philosophers') or 'natural philosophers' (which we today call 'scientists').

The Greeks thought of philosophy as the love of wisdom, the joy of knowing about things, the thrill of understanding, and in the beginning all wisdom was contained in philosophy, as philosophy slowly detached itself from the emotional and personal view of life called religion. Religion and philosophy, then and now, deal with many of the same basic human questions and riddles, but with different methods. In religion the emphasis is primarily on an emotional and authoritarian approach, together with faith, whereas philosophy relies on logic, observation, independent thinking, discussion, and argumentation. It was the great merit of the Greeks to sharply differentiate the philosophical method from the religious approach in explaining human life and activities. Thunder and storms at sea, for example, were no longer explained in terms of Zeus and his thunderbolts or Poseidon and his anger, but rather in natural terms of winds, weather, and currents. This philosophical method led eventually to the scientific method which in modern times has so drastically changed man's view of himself and his world.

Philosophy is generally regarded as the mother of all the specific sciences, and among the Greeks many of the outstanding philosophers were also the leading scientists—or "knowers" (which is what the Latin word *sciencia* means)— of the time. From a broad point of view, the history of science is closely associated with the early history of philosophy, and we see many mathematicians, astronomers, biologists, medical men, etc. among the philosophers. Some men began to specialize in only one or two areas of knowledge and in this way gave birth to the more restricted philosophical discipline of mathematics, biology, medicine, astronomy, etc. Until a hundred or more years ago these specific sciences were known as "natural philosophy" and stood in contrast to "moral philosophy," meaning ethics and political thought.

Socrates

First, a few words about the patron saint and most famous of all philosophers, Socrates, the first philosophical martyr. He lived from 469—399 BC, and spent his entire life in Athens, except for brief periods spent in military campaigns. He was short, fat, bald, ugly, poor, but he was possessed by a love of truth and wisdom which has endeared him to countless generations of students of philosophy worldwide. He devoted his life to what he considered the most important thing on earth, searching for clarity of thought and good definitions of big terms such as love, friendship, justice, knowledge, wisdom. Being physically so unattractive, his prayer was always: "Oh, God, give me to be beautiful from within!" And according to all accounts, he was. He was declared by the Oracle at Delphi to be the wisest man in Greece. His disciples loved him, but his wife Xanthippe had some reservations about a husband who did nothing to support his family and left all such mundane matters as food and rent to her! She raised the children, took in washing, kept chickens, and sold eggs while he occupied himself at the market place talking with his students about the important task of discovering what it means to be a human being.

His Doctrine

1. Know thyself!
2. The unexamined life is not worth living.
3. The one thing I know for sure is that I know nothing! "I know that I know not."
4. No harm can come to a good man.
5. Virtue is knowledge and knowledge is virtue; ignorance is vice. We do bad things out of ignorance; a person always wants to do what is good for himself, but he doesn't always know what the good is.
6. I confuse others not because I am clear and want to confuse them, but because I am utterly confused myself.
7. He is called the Gadfly of Athens. His questions sting us into activity.

His method

Dialectics, discussion; question and answer, point—counterpoint, example—counter example. Define your terms. Stay open, flexible, learning.

Follow wherever the argument leads; no one knows the answers at the outset, not even the religious and political leaders. Don't be afraid to question the authorities.

In 399 B.C. Socrates was tried by a jury of over 500 Athenian citizens on charges of impiety and leading the youth astray; he was found guilty by a slim majority and condemned to die by drinking hemlock (a paralyzing juice made from the bark of the hemlock tree). His influence has been simply enormous, especially through his student Plato, who wrote many dialogues about him, and through Plato's student Aristotle. Like Jesus, Socrates himself wrote nothing, had a following of devoted disciples, led a simple life, and was concerned about his executioner. Like Jesus, his influence has been worldwide and durable.

Socrates starts moral and political philosophy off with the powerful example of a man who really believes what he is talking about and is willing to die for his beliefs. His death is probably more important than his specific doctrines. His most famous student was Plato, who spent 20 years listening to Socrates and wrote memorable philosophical dialogues in which Socrates is almost always the chief speaker and thinker. We know Socrates primarily through his student and admirer Plato. We don't know which ideas stem originally from Socrates and which from Plato, and it doesn't really matter. *Plato's Dialogues* is one of the great masterpieces of world literature.

Aristotle

Philosophy—along with logic, ethics, botany, astronomy, mathematics, geometry, medicine, biology, metaphysics, and a number of other sciences—is generally said to have started with the Greeks, especially Aristotle, probably one of the greatest human minds who ever lived. Aristotle lived from 384 to 322 B.C. He was the third of a series of great teacher-students. Socrates taught the philosopher/poet Plato for 20 years. After the martyrdom of Socrates, Plato left Athens and traveled for many years, then returned and founded the first university in the western world—the Academy—where he taught Aristotle for 20 years. After Plato's death, Aristotle founded the second university—the Lyceum—and taught the world for the following 2000 years. In the Middle Ages in Europe he was such an undisputed authority in virtually every branch of knowledge that he was simply referred to as The Philosopher. For some 2000 years, Aristotle's influence was so great that early modern thinkers like

Francis Bacon and René Descartes had to struggle to escape his influence and think independently for themselves.

"First philosophy" or metaphysics is what Aristotle called the attempt to tie together all the diverse branches of knowledge into one comprehensive whole. Today we have many branches of knowledge which have become so highly specialized that no physicist, for example, would say that he knows ALL of physics and no medical person would say she knows ALL that there is to know in the field of medicine. During an earlier, simpler era, however, it was possible for a philosopher like Aristotle or Plato to have read all the books that existed and actually know virtually all that was known in all fields of knowledge. In this way they were able to create the grand overviews of life and knowledge that are so lacking in modern life. It is this overview of life which the study of philosophy can help us with today.

Greek philosophy is usually divided into two parts: before and after Socrates. The pre-Socratic philosophers were primarily scientific minds interested in speculations about the natural world, mathematics, geometry, and astronomy. They wondered about and inquired into the basic elements out of which all things are made, the shape and size of the world, the natural forces behind phenomena, in contrast to earlier thinkers who relied on mysterious spirits and souls for explanations. With Socrates, however, came a fundamental shift to human questions of ethics, morality, and politics.

The importance of the Greeks

The influence of Greek thought has been so great in Europe and America that some commentators maintain that every serious thinker is either a Platonist (believing that universal concepts or ideas such as 'man,' 'justice,' 'friendship,' exists independently of specific examples) or an Aristotelian (believing that such ideal forms exist, but only as exemplified in real life), and these commentators go on to say that all later philosophy is essentially only a footnote on the thoughts of these two seminal Greek thinkers. In a sense, the Greek philosophers sketched out the major human areas and problems with which philosophy deals and laid out the basic rules of the game, so to speak. In terms of fundamental ethical, social, and political questions, it is hard to see any major advances that later thinkers have made over them, with the exception of modern science and the scientific method. They asked practically all the basic questions about human conduct, invented or coined the majority of the technical terms and vocabulary used to discuss those questions and problems, and, surprisingly enough, gave us almost all of the possible answers to these questions. As indicated earlier, their method of inquiry and discussion, with its stress on logic and a non-emotional approach, led eventually to the scientific method which has so drastically changed our modern world. If slave labor had not been so cheap in Ancient Greece, some say they the Greeks might have developed an industrial revolution of their own two thousand years earlier than the British in the mid eighteenth century.

The major branches of philosophy:

As it turns out, the Greek philosophers dealt with the key human questions: What can we know for sure? What shall we do? What is the best form of government? What is the role of feelings and emotion in life? What is ultimately worth doing? Is there an afterlife? What is the role of beauty and art in life? What is the best way of arriving at truth? Such questions have developed into the five traditional branches or fields of philosophy. They are briefly introduced here:

1. Logic—-the study of right thinking and rational argument. This is the attempt to understand the nature of correct thinking and to discover what is valid reasoning. How do we distinguish between valid and invalid arguments? There are three kinds of logic: two formal and one informal. The first two were invented by the Greeks; the third springs naturally and universally out of human nature.

Induction: formal logic: arguing from many examples to a general premise. This form leads to probability, not certainty, and is crucial to the scientific method developed later. The conclusions are open to later revision as new evidence appears.

Deduction: formal logic: arguing from a valid general premise (admitting no exceptions) to specific examples. This leads to undeniable certainty, but absolutely valid general principles are hard to find. The famous syllogism illustrating deduction goes like this:

Major premise:	All men are mortal.
Minor premise:	Socrates is a man.
Conclusion:	Therefore, Socrates is mortal.

Seduction: informal logic: using every trick in the book (emotion, authority, force, precedent, age, threat of violence, etc.) to convince other people that we are right and they are wrong. This is the kind of logic practically all of us use almost all of the time, with lots of strong feelings and bombast. Seduction leads to no logically valid conclusion at all.

Deduction and induction are two processes of reasoning that we need to understand if we are to avoid serious errors and fallacies in our thinking. They are terms used to describe methods by which we can move from evidence to valid conclusions based on the evidence. So logic is the systematic study of the rules for the correct use of the supporting reasons, rules we can use to distinguish good arguments from bad ones. Most of the great philosophers, from Aristotle to the present time, have been convinced that logic permeates all other branches of philosophy and science.

2. Ethics—-the study of right and wrong, good and bad, just and unjust, including the basis on which we make ethical and moral judgments. For example, does might make right? Is religion—with rewards and punishments—necessary as a basis for morality?

3. Aesthetics—-the study of art and beauty and their role in man's life, and by extension, the place of emotions in human conduct.

4. Epistemology—-the study of the origins, limits, and validity of knowledge. This is the somewhat confusing and esoteric branch of philosophy with the basic question: On what basis do we actually know what we think we know? Is our knowledge of God and immortality, for example, based on sense data, intuition, hearsay, authority, or is it innate and given to us at birth? What is the human mind capable of knowing? Everything? From what sources do we gain the knowledge on which we depend? Or must we be satisfied with opinions and guesses? Are we limited to knowing just the bare facts of sense experience, or are we able to go beyond what the senses reveal? Many questions, many distinctions, many problems. Some important distinctions:

Empirical knowledge: that which we gain directly through the five senses: red-blue, sweet-sour, loud-quiet, hot-cold, heavy-light, etc.

Intuitive knowledge: things which people say we are born with, apart from or prior to experience: e.g. the idea of God's existence; the difference between right and wrong. These are called innate or inborn ideas which some say we know from the beginning; they don't need to be proved or demonstrated, say their defenders. But is such knowledge really true and valid?

tabula rasa: the notion that the mind at birth is a blank slate at birth and is filled in with experiences and ideas that come through the five senses; e.g, a man born blind could never have the idea of color.

There are three central questions in the field of epistemology:

1. What are the sources of knowledge? Where does genuine knowledge come from and how do we know? This is the question of origins.

2. What is the nature of knowledge? Is there a real world outside the mind, and if so, can we know it? This is the question of appearance versus reality.

3. Is our knowledge valid? How do we distinguish truth from error, dreaming from waking. This is the question of testing the truth of ideas, or verification.

It should be clear that there is a necessary relation between metaphysics and epistemology. Our conception of reality depends on our understanding of what we know, and of what can be known. Conversely, our theory of knowledge depends of our understanding of ourselves in relation to the whole of reality.

5. Metaphysics—-the study of ultimate questions of purpose and existence. Metaphysics or "First Philosophy" traditionally has been concerned with the ultimate nature of things, or with a reality beyond that of immediate experience. Aristotle coined the word, *ta meta ta physika,* 'things after things physical.' Metaphysics attempts to offer a comprehensive view of all that exists, all of reality. It is concerned, for example, with such problems as the relation of mind to matter, the nature of change, the meaning of "freedom," the existence of God, and the belief in personal immortality. It is often very close to questions raised by religion.

Of course, in philosophy as in life, everything is related to everything else, and only for the sake of analysis and discussion can we really isolate things in nice neat packages. In discussing any topic, for example, we easily see how the arguments shift from one field to another and how difficult it is to concentrate on the main topic and stick to it.

The philosophy of...X..

Philosophy also deals with the systematic body of principles and assumptions underlying any particular field of experience. For example, there are philosophies of science, education, art, music, history, law, mathematics, sports, religion, etc. Any subject, pursued far enough, will begin to reveal within itself philosophical questions and problems. For example, the philosophy of language asks the simple questions: What is language? Is shrugging the shoulders or frowning a kind of language? Where does language come from? Why are there so many different languages? How does the baby acquire language? Do animals have language? How do we best learn a foreign language? What is the relation between spoken and written language? Does the language we speak determine the way we think?

The idea of progress

In some areas of human life progress is obviously made, but in others this is not so. Beginning students in medicine or physics, for example, do not have to start with the history and development of their discipline. Students of biology, math, engineering or chemistry start with the present state of their study and go from there; they may go back for novelty's sake or out of curiosity to see what Galileo or Copernicus or Euclid or Archimedes thought about certain problems, but this is usually of purely historical interest. So in some areas of knowledge—primarily the sciences—we can say that some progress has been made.

In many fundamental areas of human activity, however, we seem to go around and around in the same basic circles, and a good introduction to the discipline is often a quick survey of its history and development, or a detailed study of some of its great contributors. In fields like literature, music, art, philosophy, poetry, politics, government, and other vitally important human activities, it would be hard to say that progress has been made and that modern musicians or artists or thinkers or poets are more advanced than Beethoven, Mozart, Rembrandt, Plato, Aristotle, Van Gogh, Shakespeare, or Thomas Jefferson.

To a considerable extent, philosophy falls into this latter category, and one of the best ways of getting into the subject is to look at some of its great practitioners. For modern scientific minds this may be a little hard to do, because they will assume that significant progress has been made in the field of philosophy over the centuries; they will probably want to start with the latest and greatest ideas in that field rather than with some thinkers who have been dead for 2000 or more years.

Philosophy as the study of ideas

Historically, philosophy has played an important role in most of the world's cultures and societies because the problems of philosophy are the universal problems of life. There are probably as many different approaches to philosophy as there are philosophers. I like to think of philosophy in very broad terms as the study of ideas. The central idea in philosophy is the attempt to determine what a human being is and what he or she should be doing with their life.

What is an idea?

Ideas are the most powerful and most important things in the world, even though we don't always know quite what an idea is:

** pi (3.1416) is an idea—-it is the naming of the relationship of the diameter of a circle to its circumference. Many relationships exist which we don't name. Names, words, and relationships are vitally important.

** Freedom and self-determinism are ideas; they are powerful right now in the former Communist Block and in many other parts of the world.

** Equality is an idea—-blacks, women, homosexuals, handicapped, and many other people worldwide are discovering the power and importance of this concept.

** Education is an idea: to become informed, skilled, disciplined, interested and interesting, alert, excited about life. The purpose of education is not to earn a living; the purpose of education is to live a life.

** Fair play is an idea which is powerful in our daily dealing with one another. "That's not fair!" is a strong criticism which most of us acknowledge as being quite legitimate and effective.

** The four-minute mile barrier was an idea until 1958 when a young man named Roger Bannister changed the concept of four minutes into 240 seconds in his mind, and then by making very slight improvements in his record of 242 seconds broke a previously regarded iron barrier or limit of the human body.

** Self-definition is an idea; either define yourself and determine who you are, or the world will do it for you and tell you who and what you are and what you should be doing with your life.

** 'Spaceship Earth' is an idea put forth by Buckminster Fuller in 1966 in his book, *Operation Manual for Spaceship Earth*. We are all crew members on a spaceship with limited resources.

** 'The global village' is an important concept put forth by Marshall McLuhan about the same time in his book, *Understanding Media*.

Our minds are filled with thousands of largely unexamined ideas and concepts acquired during the course of a lifetime. These ideas are extremely powerful and form our mental and emotional view of ourselves and the world in which we live. Change one fundamental idea about yourself or the world and your reality can change.

The information glut

There is a great deal of information in the world today, an over-abundance of data in almost every field of endeavor, but usually with only little overview, little knowledge and understanding of what it all means. We are swamped with specific information but lack perspective and insight. The task of the philosopher is to transcend specialization and formulate a life-view based on the wide areas of human experience. This is one reason why philosophical questions tend to be so large and comprehensive.

Philosophers often irritate people and society with their questions and investigations; they ask about things which many of us don't want to discuss. They often call into question the so-called common sense ideas of society and tradition. Why is the grass green? Where do kings get the "Divine Right" by which they rule? Is democracy really the best way of life? Does God really exist? Heaven and hell? Do I really have an immortal soul? What was God doing before he created the world? Where did he come from? Who created him? How can there be a beginning or end in time and space?

Philosophers are professionals like doctors, lawyers, and baseball players. They get paid for being specialists in the area of ideas; they help us learn how to think, how to ask questions, how to present our ideas and to defend them, how to discuss, to disagree, to go beyond people and things to get to the ideas behind reality. Voltaire and Rousseau, leading up to and preparing the French Revolution, are great examples of the power of ideas and philosophers, as is Karl Marx and his creation of Communism.

Philosophy in ancient times was a life-and-death matter; it was the soul's search for wisdom, meaning, truth, and purpose in life. Philosophy is a process of reflecting upon and criticizing and inquiring into our most deeply held beliefs. The activity of philosophy belongs to all thinking people. We need philosophy to help us solve basic human questions, to become more human, to do those things which only humans can do.

Perhaps the overriding idea in philosophy is the question: What is a human being? Who are we? What are we? What makes us tick? What is of real importance in human life and what is only surface? Who am I and what is the meaning of my life? What should I do with my life? What is worth doing? These are questions that have confronted and often confounded thoughtful men and women for generations. We live, move, and have our being in an intangible, invisible world of ideas. Philosophy helps us become more clearly aware of that world and to find our way through the blooming, buzzing confusion of life and daily activity. The principal task of philosophy is to figure out what it means to be a human being. "Know thyself!" says Socrates, and we all nod in agreement. We usually think we know ourself, but on closer inspection it often turns out that actually we don't.

The task of philosophy

The problems of philosophy are the problems of life. Philosophers deal in depth with problems which have occurred to everyone at one time or another:

1. Does might make right?
2. How did the world begin? What is everything composed of?
3. What happens to people when they die? Is there an afterlife?
4. What should I do? What is worth doing?
5. What are we here for? How should we live? Why be ethical? Why not cheat or lie if I can get away with it and not get caught?

6. Is there a God? Will we be rewarded or punished after this life? How can we possibly know such things for sure? What if we are wrong?
7. Who makes up the rules of conduct and morality? Why should we obey them?
8. What is worth spending my one and only life on?
9. Why shouldn't I just eat, drink, and be merry, since nothing seems to make any difference in the long run?

Dealing with such questions is a necessary part of coming to terms with life. We must each find answers for ourselves. Each of us must answer these questions for herself or himself. Philosophy is a very personal discipline; you have got to do it for and by yourself. You must find your own answers to your problems. So why do we need philosophers?

Philosophers can be guides or coaches. They work at such questions longer and more systematically than the average person. They can stimulate our own thinking by being gadflies and encouraging us to think some new thoughts, to see life in a different way, or from a different perspective.

The origins of philosophy

Aristotle says in the opening line of his *Metaphysics*: "All humans by nature desire to know," just as it's the nature of acorns to become beautiful oak trees. Not all acorns become oaks, for many reasons, but they and only they have this potential. This means that we humans are thinking creatures and automatically, by nature, look for meaning and purpose in what happens to us in our life. Other philosophers say that man by nature has a "metaphysical instinct." Virtually everyone believes that there is more to life than the basic physical necessities and the fundamental activities of eating, sleeping, working, reproducing, and dying. But what is this "more" and how do we go about finding out about it? Philosophy begins in wonder and amazement about the natural world, plus the human desire to know. Philosophy begins with an inquiry into man's nature.

What is life and why am I here?

Why is there anything?

Where did all these things come from?

Is the universe friendly or unfriendly?

Does anything really make any difference?

How should I relate to my fellow humans.

The great German philosopher, Immanuel Kant (1724-1804), says that there are really only three philosophical questions:

1. What can I know?   epistemology
2. What should I do?   ethics

3. What can I hope for?   metaphysics

To get in a philosophical mood, sit alone for an hour or so under the stars. This is an almost sure-fire way of changing your perspective and your attitude toward things, at least for a while. Try it!

Religion, philosophy, science, mysticism

First, it may be helpful if I lay all my cards on the table—without apology—and give the big view of what I consider the relationship between religion, philosophy, science, and mysticism. I find all these vital activities closely related to one another and clearly centered ultimately on the basic question of what it means to be a human being living in a complex, often overwhelming world. They may represent various developmental stages through which the human mind has journeyed over thousands of years, and at the same time they are also moods or attitudes in which the individual mind sometimes finds itself. These moods, attitudes, and urges include an emotional and child-like wish for dependence on some ultimate authority as in religion, the beauty of clear rational thinking of philosophy, the precision and majesty of purely scientific theories and systems, plus the deep-seated desire to integrate all our knowledge and experience in mystical moments of emotional and intellectual unity with total reality. I believe that many people would like to feel whole, unified, totally integrated, and at home in the universe. I would call this goal a mystical union with reality.

The long-standing conflict between religious faith—based on emotion, authority, tradition, indoctrination—and the right of the individual to think for himself in a philosophical-scientific manner—based on reason, logic, observation, trial and error—has continued from the beginning up to the present day, and still leaves many of us in the modern world in a quandary, especially in relation to the fundamental questions of meaning and purpose in human life. The only resolution that I can find to this widespread dilemma of combining ancient religious interests with the overwhelmingly complex new world of science and technology is a new type of modern mystical approach based on religion, philosophy, and science.

Despite the danger and misunderstanding involved with using the terms *mystic* and *mysticism*, I call this new approach mundane or pragmatic mysticism. It combines the deeply emotional religious questions of meaning and purpose with the clear rational thinking of the philosophers and adds to them as much of the factual knowledge of modern science as I have been able to acquire and understand. The result is a very personal interpretation of the world as I experience it, and I think many people find themselves in a similar situation. The last chapter in this book will give a more detailed discussion of this kind of mysticism.

By studying the history of religion, philosophy, science, and mysticism, I have learned that my questions and concerns are similar to those of many other people, past and present. Just as they have had to come to terms with their time and circumstances, so also must I. Someone has suggested as a working definition of mysticism, "a direct experience with ultimate reality." I take this to mean that each of us in a sense is a mystic and has to determine for ourselves what "ultimate reality" is. My ultimate reality has these three thick layers: religion, philosophy, and science, and I am trying to experience it as productively and directly as I can by sharing it with you. I think this is what mystics over the centuries have done: share their experience of ultimate reality—however they define it—with their fellows.

Chapter 7.
Science and technology

The fourth and most powerful intellectual tool our ancestors developed to explain their world is science, an amazing discipline which has its roots somewhat in religion, but especially in philosophy. While animism, religion, and even philosophy have strong elements of emotion mixed with reason, science is essentially pure reason without emotions. I think most scientists today would say that there should be no emotional element at all in science or in the scientific method: nothing but pure logic and reason. In fact, I believe they would say that science has made such amazing progress precisely because it has eliminated emotion altogether from its repertoire of tools and beliefs, and that the powerful emotions of music, art, religion, and mysticism clearly belong elsewhere.

We live in such a highly developed age of science and technology that we are hardly aware of the long struggle our forefathers underwent to get us to this point. We take new scientific miracles today more or less for granted and naively assume that things will continue to get better and more sophisticated year by year. Educated people automatically expect complex things to be explained and justified by the scientific method of hypothesis, experimentation, logical proof with supporting documentation and demonstration. They also expect other informed, rational persons to be willing to listen to controversial questions, consider the arguments, weigh the facts, and eventually be persuaded by the evidence before them. But this was not always so in the past, and is often still not the case today. I recently heard a report, for example, that only about a third of Americans believe in evolution, despite the overwhelming evidence available in virtually every natural science museum.in the country. We cling tenaciously to our irrational, emotional beliefs and often simply believe what we want to believe. Our ancestors had a much harder time still, and a quick look at the development of science will deepen our admiration for those who, over the centuries, helped build our fabulous scientific and technological world of today. This brief survey will demonstrate again and again the struggle between emotion and reason, i.e. between the life of feelings—what we want to believe— and the life of rational thought and experience.

Meaning of "science" and "technology"

"Science" comes from the Latin *sciencia*, meaning "knowledge," but the word "scientist" ("knower") was coined only in the 19th century, and in English it has come to mean only scholars in the fields of natural science (physics, chemistry, etc.). Until then, people working in the sciences were called "natural philosophers" and those in the humanities were "moral philosophers." In German, for example, all "knowers" are still called scientists or knowers ("Wissenschaftler") from the German verb "wissen," (to know) and are divided into "Naturwissenschaftler" (natural scientist) and "Geisteswissenschaftler" (intellectual scientist). A linguist, for example, is called a "Sprachwissenschaftler," where the words 'Language,' and 'Knowing, Intellect' are prominent.

"Technology" comes from the Greek words *technikos* or *techne,* meaning "an art, doing, or making." There is a strong emphasis on practical and useful skills such as weaving, building, or joining together, so that a *tekton,* for example is a carpenter. It seems that "technology" means knowledge and information put to use, as we see in the words "technical' and "technique." If science means knowledge in the abstract, technology means knowledge as applied, or science put to work. The following discussion will emphasize knowledge primarily for sake of knowledge itself, but there will be ample examples of knowledge applied to the chores and problems of man. But since manpower (primarily slaves or serfs) was generally so cheap in the Ancient World, there was no great need to use the scientific knowledge of the times in practical ways, and most of the thinkers we encounter among the Greeks are interested primarily in knowledge for its own sake, for the pure joy of knowing and understanding. It seems to me that this distinction still holds essentially true today. Modern scientists in their capacity as pure researchers or creators of knowledge are not particularly concerned about its practical use or application, often to their chagrin, as seen in the case of the Manhattan Project and the development of the atomic bomb in the 1940s, where, after the destruction of Hiroshima and Nagasaki, many of the creators of the bomb were sorry they had worked on it.

Early beginnings: astronomy

Since many people kept watch over animals at night and spent a great deal of time living under the stars, ancient civilizations early on collected detailed astronomical information in a systematic manner through simple observation, combined with a well developed counting system. Though they had no knowledge, of course, of the actual physical structure of the heavenly bodies, many theoretical explanations were proposed. Since the sun, moon, and stars were usually regarded as divine creatures or gods, most of the early explanations were religious or mythological in nature. People noticed, for example, that the monthly waxing and waning cycle of the moon corresponded to women's menstrual cycle, so the moon was regarded as a feminine goddess and the sun as the masculine counterpart bringing life and warmth to all creatures.

In prehistoric times, advice and knowledge were passed along from generation to generation in a purely oral tradition. Then the development of writing enabled knowledge to be stored and communicated across generations with much greater accuracy and fidelity. Combined with the development of agriculture and a surplus of food, it became possible for early civilizations to develop an ever-increasing store of knowledge because more time and effort could be devoted to tasks other than mere survival. Some privileged young people could take time to learn to read and write, for example, and this fact tremendously advanced the spread and development of knowledge.

By 3500 B.C., people in Mesopotamia were making precise observations of the night sky and amassing thorough, important data, and the science of astronomy came into being. Notations of the motions of the stars, planets, and the moon were left on thousands of clay tablets created by these early observers. Even today, astronomical periods identified by Mesopotamian scientists are still widely used in Western calendars: the solar year, the lunar month, the seven-day week. Using these data, early scientists developed arithmetical methods to compute the changing length of daylight in the course of the year and to predict the appearances and disappearances of the moon and planets, plus eclipses of the sun and moon.

Arithmetic, mathematics, and geometry

The human needs that inspired mankind's first efforts at mathematics, arithmetic in particular, were counting, calculations, and measurements. From practical needs such as buying and selling, mathematics was born. One view is that the core of early mathematics is based upon two simple questions: How many? How much? In addition to the daily problems of the merchant and trader, for example, the worth of a herdsman cannot be calculated unless some basics of counting are known; an inheritance cannot be distributed unless certain facts about division (fractions) are known; a temple cannot be built unless certain facts about triangles, squares, and volumes are known.

The early story of numbers and counting turns out to be a complicated matter far more interesting and involved than one would first imagine. Suffice it to say that numbers and counting are clearly very old and closely related to man's explanations of the world. He learned to count and keep records very early on and probably used his fingers and toes from the beginning. The history of counting gives us several key numbers, such as 0, 5, 10, 12, 20, 60, 100, 360, each with its own interesting explanation. For example, the invention of 0 as a vital place holder in counting, 5 and 10 for the number of fingers, 12 for 10 fingers and 2 fists, 20 for fingers and toes, 30 days in a month, 60 because it is easily divisible by the first six numbers, 360 days in a year, etc.

The development of a yearly calendar is a vital and fascinating chapter in itself. These varied processes of counting and keeping track of things took place a long time ago in Ancient Egypt, Babylon, India, China, and in Mayan cultures in Central America as human groups began to interact more frequently, acquire possessions, trade, pass wealth and possessions down to their children, etc. Today we use the decimal system based on 10, the concept of dozen, 12 months in a year, 60 minutes in an hour, 360 degrees in a circle, etc. that were developed by our ancestors several millennia ago. Each of these ideas, and of course many, many more in mathematics and astronomy, has its own distinctive history.

Since there is no way of actually knowing for sure when and how counting and arithmetic began, we can only speculate and extrapolate from imagined situations. A shepherd has 20 sheep, for example, and keeps a tally on them by putting 20 marks on a stick; even if he does not know how to count in words, he can keep accurate track of his flock by equating one mark with each sheep as he puts them in the pen at night. Newborn lambs or wolf attacks necessarily intensifies and sharpens the shepherd's mathematical ability.

Counting in terms of one to ten seems to come very easily by looking at our ten fingers, or in terms of twenty by counting fingers and toes. We can easily imagine this explanation—which was probably the case in a great many instances—as being universally valid. The problem with this facile assumption, however, is the fact that a number of tribes today which never have occasion to count many things of any kind have only the numbers "one, two, three, many." This and similar considerations complicate our explanations about these matters which seems so deceptively obvious and clear at the outset. Almost everything turns out to be far more complex than it first seems.

Geometry

Geometry (Greek for 'land measuring') seems to go back—at least in name—to the yearly floods of the Nile river covering the land with a layer of mud and the need to re-establish the boundaries between the farmers' fields, but there is much evidence that also the Babylonians, the Hindu civilization, and the Chinese had much geometrical knowledge that is generally attributed to the Egyptians and the annual flooding of the Nile. Thanks to their knowledge of angles, triangles, areas, and volume, the priests of Egypt were able to relocate the stone markers in the flooded fields and reconstruct each farmer's original plot of land, much to the amazement of the illiterate and innumerate peasants. Using the same geometrical knowledge, the priests were able to construct almost 5000 years ago the great pyramids which still amaze modern visitors today.

The Greeks inherited a huge amount of geometry from the Egyptians and Babylonians and put it to good use in creating their own civilization and philosophy. They found the method of geometrical and logical demonstrations especially important in constructing their philosophical systems. Around 300 BC, the Greek mathematician Euclid, living in Alexandria, put this vast knowledge of geometry together in his *Elements,* a book which has become perhaps the most widely read book in the world and is still widely used today.

A brief Who's who? of Greek scientists

With the name of Euclid we can switch the discussion from the individual sciences to some of the outstanding Greek thinkers and their contributions. This brief catalog helps to remind us of some outstanding men who broke away from theological and mythological explanations of natural phenomena, created the beginnings of a purely scientific method, and thereby helped to create our modern world view.

Thales and the Milesians

The Greek interest in scientific speculation is first seen in the city of Miletus, in today's Turkey. Here the philosopher Thales (ca.624-ca.546 BC) acquired fame by correctly predicting a solar eclipse for the first time in 585 BC. None of his works survive, but his reputation among Greeks in the following centuries is that of a man who takes a reasonable or 'scientific' approach to the mysteries of the natural world.

In contrast to the Egyptians' emphasis on divine elements operating in nature, the Greek thinkers tried early on to give a non-supernatural explanation of natural events and forces. They wanted to know about the origin and make-up of the ordered cosmos in which they lived. Thales, one of the earliest known Greek thinkers, is often called the "father of science" because of his attempt to give natural explanations for phenomena such as lightning and earthquakes. He thought water was the original element out of which everything came, in part because all living things need water and because water can be a liquid, a gas, and a solid.

Science is sometimes said to have begun with Thales because he tried to regard natural phenomena as explicable in terms of matter interacting by natural laws, and not as the results of arbitrary acts by gods. He regarded earthquakes and lightning, for example, as natural occurrences and not as caused by the anger of Poseidon, god of the sea, or of Zeus, the sky god. His prediction of the solar eclipse is often regarded as the beginning of the scientific tradition in the Western World.

An essential part of the Milesians' success in developing a new picture of nature was that they engaged in open, rational, critical debate about each others' ideas. It was tacitly assumed that all their theories and explanations were in direct competition with one another, and all should be open to public scrutiny so that they could be debated, evaluated, and remembered. This is still the way scientists work today, and all contributions, even that of an Einstein, depend heavily on what has gone before.

The Milesians struggled a great deal with the puzzle of the origin of the universe, what was here at the beginning, and what things are made of. Thales suggested that in the beginning there was only one basic substance, water, so somehow everything was made of it. His student Anaximander (ca.610-ca.546 BC) imagined that initially there was a boundless chaos, and the universe grew from this as from a seed. Anaximenes (ca.585-ca.525 BC) had a more sophisticated approach, to modern eyes. His suggestion was that originally there was only air (really meaning a gas) and the liquids and solids we see around us were formed by condensation and rarefaction of this air. These theories mean that a simple initial state develops into more complex forms using physical processes which were already familiar. Of course, this leaves a lot to be explained, but this idea of process and development is similar to the modern view.

Anaximander

He suggested lightning was caused by clouds being split up by the wind, which in fact is not far from the truth. The main point in all these deliberations is that the gods are just not mentioned in analyzing natural phenomena. The Milesians' view is that nature is a dynamic entity evolving in accordance with some admittedly not fully understood laws, but nature is not being micromanaged by gods to vent their anger on hapless humanity. Anaximander is also credited with being the first man to attempt a map of the world, and he offers a bold explanation of the origin of the universe. His concept of the beginning of life is equally astonishing. He argues that humans cannot always have existed (our infants are far too helpless and defenseless). The first living creatures, he believes, develop in water through the action of heat.

Concerning the universe, Anaximander suggested that the earth was a cylinder, and the sun, moon, and stars were located on concentric rotating cylinders. This is the first recorded attempt at a mechanical model of the heavenly bodies. He further postulated that the stars themselves were rings of fire. Again, a very bold conjecture—all heavenly bodies had previously been regarded as living gods. He also considered the problem of the origin of life, which is of course more difficult to explain if you don't believe in gods. He suggested that the lower forms of life might have been generated by the action of sunlight on moist earth.

Greek philosophy in general is strongly associated with Athens, because of Socrates, Plato, and Aristotle, but the earlier philosopher/scientists are not connected with Athens and are usually referred to as the Pre-Socratics. So the beginnings of Greek science testifies rather more to the prior colonial spread of Greek culture around the Mediterranean: Ionia in Asia Minor, the islands of Cos, Samos, and Sicily, Croton in the boot of Italy, and Alexandria in Egypt, These are the places where the Pre-Socratic Greeks established the rational traditions of Western science.

Pythagoras: 6th century BC

Ancient mathematics has reached the modern world largely through the work of Greeks in the classical period, building on the Babylonian tradition. A leading figure among the early Greek mathematicians is Pythagoras (ca.582-500 BC) and his followers in Italy. He regarded mathematics as the key to understanding the universe.

He was a Greek philosopher/scientist who made important developments in mathematics, astronomy, and the theory of music. The theorem now known as the Pythagorean theorem was known to the Babylonians 1000 years earlier, but Pythagoras may have been the first to prove it. He was an interesting character who tried to combine science with some aspects of mysticism and religion. He believed in reincarnation and the transmigration of souls, for example, and, strangely enough, in the sinfulness of eating beans, apparently for hygienic or even mystical reasons.

Pythagoras founded in southern Italy a society of disciples in which men and women were treated equally—an unusual thing at the time—and all property was held in common. The Pythagoreans were vegetarians, had no personal possessions, and believed that "Friends have all things in common." Members of the society had to obey strict religious orders: It was forbidden, for example, to eat beans, to walk in a field where beans were growing, to touch a white cock, or to look into a mirror beside a light.

It was Pythagoras' ambition to reveal in his philosophy the validity and structure of a higher order, the basis of the divine order, in which souls return in a constant cycle of birth and death. This is how Pythagoras came to mathematics. It could be said that he saw the study of mathematics as a purifier of the soul, just as he considered music as purifying and elevating. He and his disciples connected music with mathematics and found that intervals between notes can be expressed in numerical terms. They discovered that the length of strings of a musical instrument correspond to these intervals and that they can be expressed in numbers. The ratio of the length of two strings with which two tones of an octave step are produced is 2:1.

Music was not the only field that Pythagoras considered worthy of study, in fact he saw numbers in everything. He was convinced that the divine principles of the universe, though imperceptible to the senses, can be expressed in terms of relationships of numbers. He therefore reasoned that the secrets of the cosmos are revealed by pure thought, through deduction and analytic reflection on the perceptible world. He believed that the movements of the heavenly bodies were in certain numerical relationship which caused them to make a "music of the spheres" audible only to very pure souls.

His great preoccupation with numbers eventually led to his famous saying that "All things are numbers." Pythagoras himself spoke of square numbers and cubic numbers, and we still use these terms, but he also spoke of oblong, triangular, and spherical numbers. He associated numbers with form, relating arithmetic to geometry. His greatest contribution, the proposition about right-angled triangles, sprang from this line of thought.

Pythagoras embodied inconsistencies of the mystical and rational world, which are woven into his personality and philosophy. In his mind, numbers, spirits, souls, gods and the mystical connections between them formed one large continuous picture. There are many stories about his unusual personality. It is said, for example, that once he was walking up a lane in Croton when he came upon a dog being ill-treated. Seeing this, he raised his voice: "Stop, don't hit it! It is a soul of a friend. I knew it when I heard its voice." Spirits, ghosts, souls, and transmigration were obviously things he believed in deeply. However, they make his philosophy difficult to grasp.

The Pythagoreans and astronomy: 5th century BC

Followers of Pythagoras in the 5th century were the first to produce an astronomical theory in which a circular earth revolves on its own axis as well as moving in an orbit. The theory derived in part from the need to locate the great fire which they believe fueled the universe. This theory introduced the concentric circles of heavenly bodies which became the false orthodoxy of the next 2000 years, as eventually enshrined by Ptolemy. The Pythagorean astronomers were too far ahead of their time in proposing their one central grain of truth—the revolving globe of the earth. But Copernicus later, while developing this idea, will acknowledge them as his earliest predecessors.

Empedocles

Empedocles (ca. 490–430 BC) lived in a Greek colony in Sicily. His philosophy is best known for being the origin of the theory of the four classical elements: earth, air, fire, water, out of which all things are made. He also proposed powers called Love and Strife (attraction and repulsion) which would act as forces to bring about the mixture and separation of the elements. These physical speculations were part of his history of the universe, which also dealt with the origin and development of life. Influenced by the Pythagoreans, he supported the doctrine of reincarnation. Empedocles is generally considered the last Greek philosopher to record his ideas in verse. Some of his work still survives today, more than in the case of any other Presocratic philosopher. His death (legend has it that he jumped into the active crater of Mount Etna to prove his immortality) was mythologized by ancient writers, and it has also been the subject of a number of literary treatments.

Empedocles introduced a theory which was accepted in Europe until the 17th century. He stated that all matter is made up, in differing proportions, of four elemental substances—earth, air, fire and water—and four elemental qualities—hot, cold, wet, and dry. This theory of the four elements became the standard dogma for the next two thousand years. Not until the arrival of *A Sceptical Chemist* (a book by Robert Boyle in 1661) is there a serious threat to this Greek theory of the elements.

Empedocles believed that according to the different proportions in which these four indestructible and unchangeable elements are combined with each other, the difference of the structure is produced. It is in the aggregation and segregation of elements that Empedocles, like the atomists, found the real process which corresponds to what is popularly termed growth, increase or decrease. He believed that nothing new comes or can come into being; the only change that can occur is a change in the juxtaposition and relationship of these four elements with one another

The four elements themselves, however, are simple, eternal, and unalterable: As change is the consequence of their mixture and separation, it was also necessary to suppose the existence of moving powers to bring about this mixing and unmixing. The four elements are brought into union and parted from each other by two divine powers, Love and Strife. Love explains the attraction of different forms of matter, and Strife accounts for their separation. If the elements themselves form the basic content of the universe, then Love and Strife explain their variation and harmony. Love and Strife are attractive and repulsive forces which we can easily see at work among people, but they really also pervade the whole universe, according to Empedocles.

An atomic theory: Leucippus and Democritus 460-370 BC

In the late 5th century BC, Democritus sets out an interesting theory of elemental physics. Notions of a similar kind had been hinted at by other Greek thinkers, but never so fully elaborated as by Democritus and his teacher Leucippus.

They state that all matter is composed of eternal, indivisible, indestructible and infinitely small substances which cling together in different combinations to form the objects perceptible to us. The Greek word for indivisible is *atomos*. This theory gives birth to the atom and is remarkably similar to many modern ideas. Democritus describes an extraordinary beginning to the universe. He explains that originally all atoms were whirling about in a chaotic manner, until collisions brought them together to form ever larger units—including eventually the world and all that is in it.

With the work of Leucippus and Democritus in northern Greece, ancient Greek philosophy reaches its zenith concerning the initial question of Thales about the true nature of primary matter, the one basic substance out of which everything is made. This radically new system culminates in the subtle concept of the atom, a concept arrived at through the sheer power of logical thinking about cutting a piece of wood or stone into ever smaller parts. For this reason, Leucippus and Democritus undoubtedly deserve the first price for the best guess in antiquity, as far as natural science is concerned. Unfortunately, their contemporaries did not share their views with the same enthusiasm, and the atomic theory of matter had to lie dormant for more than two millennia.

Leucippus is a shadowy figure; his exact dates are unknown, some even say he never existed, but it is likely that he was a contemporary of Empedocles (around 440 BC) and that he came either from Miletus or from Elea in Asia Minor. Democritus, who was a disciple of Leucippus, is a more certain figure. He was born 460 BC in Abdera in the north of Greece and died at the age of 90 years, after leaving an expansive work elaborating his philosophy, including the atomistic theory in great detail. Democritus wrote approximately 70 books and hence overshadows his master by far. Unfortunately, none of his writings remained intact, but a great deal of what he said has survived in Epicurus and other Greek authors.

The question of change and permanence was a central one for these early Greek philosopher/scientists: How can things be constantly changing and yet somehow remain the same? Heraclitus asserted that change is constant like a burning fire, and you cannot step into the same river twice, because nothing is permanent. His catchword is *panta re* (everything flows, is in flux). Parmenides, on the other hand, maintained that change and motion are illusory, and the only true statement of reality is that "It is!" Leucippus and Democritus endeavored to develop a theory that would be consistent with sense perception—(i.e. we do in fact see motion and change)—by virtue of logical coherence and could not be contested by the Parmenidean arguments that motion and change are unreal. Change, the atomists explained, is an observation that does not deceive the senses; change is real, it happens on account of the recombination of more rudimentary substances, atoms, which remain constant and indivisible. The atomists held that the true nature of things consists of an infinite number of extremely small particles called atoms. Democritus described atoms as being indestructible and completely full, i.e. containing no empty space. Because of their indestructibility, atoms are eternal.

According to the atomists, nature consists only of two things, namely atoms and the void that surrounds them. Leucippus and Democritus thought that there are many different kinds of atoms, each distinct in shape and size, and that all atoms move around in space. Democritus illustrated the movement of atoms with an observation he made in nature. He compared it to the movement of motes in a sunbeam when there is no wind, but he gave no explanation of why the atoms move. The moving atoms inevitably collide in space, which in some cases causes them to be deflected like billiard balls, and in other cases, when the shapes of two atoms match in a way that they can interlock, causes them to build clusters upon collision, thereby forming substances which make up the objects of our perception.

Leucippus and Democritus came closer to the truth than anyone else in the following millennium. They developed a fully mechanistic view of nature in which every material phenomenon is seen as a product of atom colliding, joining together, and creating new things. Democritus' theory had no place for the notion of purpose or the intervention of gods in the workings of the world.

It is no surprise that these views earned Democritus harsh criticism. At a time when Orphic beliefs and religious superstitions dominated the spiritual world, Democritus' atom theory seemed odd and atheistic. People clung to the belief that their fate was steered by the gods on Mount Olympus. They were highly uncomfortable with the idea that everything, including human existence, is a product of mere atom collisions. Contemporaries and successors objected that the atomistic theory would leave everything to chance. Plato, for example, does not mention Democritus at all in his works. It is said that he disliked his ideas so much that he wished to see all of his books burned, although it is controversial whether these were his own words.

After Leucippus and Democritus, philosophy made a major turn towards ethics and politics. The atomists were the last in the line of true nature philosophers whose primary subject was the composition and order of the physical universe. The Pre-socratic period ended with Democritus. Athens had become the political, cultural and spiritual center of Greece, preparing the ground for the philosophical giants, Socrates, Plato, and Aristotle, whose works outshone the atomists for many centuries. Yet, the atom theory remains one of the most amazing intellectual accomplishments of Antiquity.

Medical science

On the island of Cos, just a few miles from Miletus in Asia Minor, lived the first great doctor known to history, **Hippocrates** (ca.460-ca.370 BC), "the father of medicine." He and his followers adopted the rational Milesian point of view and applied it even to epilepsy, which was called the sacred disease. They looked for some objective explanation, such as infection, which could perhaps be treated. Their view was that men think epilepsy divine merely because they do not understand it, and that if they called everything divine that they did not understand, there would be no end of divine things! Hippocrates and his followers held that in nature all things are alike in that they can be traced to preceding causes.

The Hippocratic doctors criticized some philosophers for being too ready with postulates and hypotheses, and not putting enough effort into careful observation. These doctors insisted on careful, systematic observation in diagnosing disease, and a careful sorting out of what was relevant and what was merely coincidental. Of course, this approach turns out to be the right one in all sciences.

Hippocrates is credited with being the first physician to reject superstitions, legends, and beliefs that credited supernatural or divine forces with causing illness. He was credited by the disciples of Pythagoras with combining philosophy and medicine. He separated the discipline of medicine from religion, believing and arguing that disease was not a punishment inflicted by the gods but rather the product of environmental factors, diet, and living habits. Indeed, there is not a single mention of a mystical illness in the entirety of the Hippocratic corpus. His book *On Airs, Waters, and Places* is an early attempt to call attention to the importance of environmental factors in life. However, it comes as no surprise to learn that due to the generally low level of medical knowledge of the time, Hippocrates did work with many convictions that were based on what is now known to be incorrect anatomy and physiology.

The Hippocratic Oath and the four humors: 4th century BC

Hippocrates is regarded as the father of medicine partly because he is unlike his more theoretical contemporaries in paying close attention to the symptoms of disease, but also because a century or more after his death a group of medical works was gathered together under his name. This *Hippocratic Collection*, and in particular the Hippocratic Oath which is part of it, has remained the broad basis of medical principles up to our own day.

The Hippocratic collection teaches that human beings are composed of four substances or 'humors', just as inanimate matter is made up of four elements. The humors are blood, phlegm, black bile (*melancholia*) and yellow bile (*chole*). Too much of any one will give a person certain recognizable characteristics. He or she will be sanguine, phlegmatic, melancholy or choleric. Classical Greece produced a brilliant tradition of theorists, the dreamers of science. Attracted by the intellectual appeal of good theories, many of them were disinclined, however, to engage in the manual labor of the laboratory where those theories might be tested.

Electricity and magnetism: 5th century BC

Two natural phenomena, central to the study of physics, were observed and speculated upon by Greek natural scientists, probably in the 5th century BC, although Aristotle gives credit for the first observation of each to the shadowy figure of Thales. One such phenomenon is the strange property of amber. If rubbed with fur, it will attract feathers or bits of straw. Modern science, in its terms for the forces involved, acknowledges this Greek experiment with amber (*electron* in Greek). The behavior of the amber is caused by what we call electricity, resulting from the transfer of what are now known as electrons.

The other natural phenomenon also derives its scientific name from Greek experiments. It is lodestone, a naturally occurring mineral (formed of iron oxide), which will surprisingly attract small pieces of iron. The Greeks found this mineral in a region of Thessaly called Magnesia. They call it *lithos magnetis*, the 'stone of Magnesia'. Thus the magnet is identified and named, though like rubbed amber it will only be a source of interest and amusement for the next 1000 years and more — until a practical purpose is found for it in the form of the compass.

Aristotle and the birth of biology: 5th - 4th century BC

The Greek philosophers, voracious in their curiosity, looked with interest at the vast range of living creatures, from the humblest plant to man himself. A Greek name was coined by a German naturalist in the early 19th century for this study of all physical aspects of natural life—biology, from *bios* (life) and *logos* (word or discourse). It is a subject with clear subdivisions, such as botany, zoology or anatomy. But all are concerned with living organisms. Aristotle may be wrong about a number of things, but in general he gives a far more complete and well observed account of biology than any other Greek philosopher. He inaugurates scientific zoology in his reliance on careful observation. He is particularly acute in his study of marine life, having much to say on the habits of fishes, the development of the octopus family, and the nature of whales, dolphins, and porpoises. He is also a pioneer in attempting to develop a system of classification. Observing an unbroken chain of gradual developments, as the life of plants shades into that of animals, he acknowledges the complexity of the subject and seems almost to glimpse the pattern of evolution. Aristotle's notes on botany are lost, but many of his observations no doubt survive in the earliest known botanical text, nine books *On the History of Plants* written by Aristotle's favorite pupil, Theophrastus. Writing in about 300 BC, Theophrastus attempts to classify plants, as well as describing their structure, habits, and uses. His remarks are based on observations carried out in Greece, but he also includes information brought back from the new Hellenistic empire in the Middle East, Persia and India, resulting from the conquests of Alexander the Great.

The beginning of chemistry

The center of the Greek world shifts in the 3rd century BC to Alexandria. In this bustling commercial center, linked with long Egyptian traditions of skilled work in precious metals, people were interested in making practical use of Greek scientific theory. If Aristotle says that the difference in material substances is a matter of balance, then that balance might be changed. Copper, for example, could perhaps become gold. Among the practical scientists of Alexandria are men who can be seen as the first alchemists and the first experimental chemists. For centuries they had been practicing the embalming of royalty and important persons, so they had a long tradition of working with all kinds of chemicals. Their trade, as workers in precious metals, involved melting gold and silver, mixing alloys, changing the color of metals by mysterious processes. These were the activities of chemistry. The everyday items of a chemical laboratory—stills, furnaces, flasks—were all in use in Alexandria.

Euclid and Archimedes: 3rd century BC

Euclid taught in Alexandria during the reign of Ptolemy. No details of his life are known, but his brilliance as a teacher is demonstrated in the *Elements*, his thirteen books of geometrical theorems. Many of the theorems derive from Euclid's predecessors, but Euclid presents them with a clarity which ensures the success of his work. It becomes Europe's standard textbook in geometry, retaining that position until the 19th century. Euclid laid down the foundations of mathematical rigor and introduced the concepts of definition, axiom, theorem, and proof still in use today in his *Elements*, considered by some the most influential textbook ever written.

Archimedes was a student at Alexandria, possibly within the lifetime of Euclid. He returned to his native Syracuse, in Sicily, where he far exceeded his teachers in the originality of his geometrical researches. He is considered one of the greatest mathematicians of all time; he gave a remarkably accurate approximation of Pi, and is also known in physics for laying the foundations of hydrostatics and the explanation of the principle of the lever. The fame of Archimedes in history and legend derives largely from his practical inventions and discoveries, but he himself regarded these as trivial compared to his work in pure geometry. He was most proud of his calculations of surface area and of volume in spheres and cylinders. He left the wish that his tomb be marked by a device of a sphere within a cylinder.

Aristarchus of Rhodes: a heliocentric theory

On the Greek island of Samos, about 270 BC, Aristarchus was busy trying to work out the size of the sun and the moon and their distance from the earth. His only surviving work is on this topic, and his calculations are inevitably wide of the mark. But his studies brought him to a startling conclusion. Aristarchus believed that the earth is in orbit round the sun (quite contrary to what is plain for anyone to see). There was an attempt, which came to nothing, to have him prosecuted for impiety. His idea joined the many other strange notions which enliven the history of human thought until Copernicus mentioned him, in an early draft of his great book, as someone who had the right idea first.

Eratosthenes, the circumference of the earth: ca. 220 BC

Eratosthenes, a Greek mathematician, geographer, astronomer, and librarian of the Museum of Alexandria, heard that at noon in midsummer the sun shines straight down a certain well at Aswan, in the south of Egypt. On the same day of the year in Alexandria it casts a shadow 7.2 degrees from the vertical. Using his skill in geometry, he knew that if he could calculate the distance between Aswan and Alexandria, he could determine the circumference of the earth. The story goes that he hired a man to walk the distance and count his paces; using this information Eratosthenes calculated the circumference of the earth with remarkable accuracy. He also developed a system of latitude and longitude, and calculated the tilt of the earth's axis and the distance from the earth to the sun, and created a map of the world based on the available geographical knowledge of the era.

Hipparchus, a scientific astronomer: 2nd century BC

Hipparchus was born in Nicaea (now in Turkey), and probably died on the island of Rhodes. He is known to have been a working astronomer at least from 147 BC to 127 BC. Hipparchus is considered the greatest ancient astronomical observer and, by some, the greatest overall astronomer of antiquity. He was the first whose quantitative and accurate models for the motion of the sun and moon survive. For this he certainly made use of the observations and perhaps the mathematical techniques accumulated over centuries by the scientists in Babylonia. He developed trigonometry and constructed trigonometric tables, and he solved several problems of spherical trigonometry. With his solar and lunar theories and his trigonometry, he may have been the first to develop a reliable method to predict solar eclipses. His other reputed achievements include the compilation of the first comprehensive star catalog of the Western World, and possibly the invention of the astrolabe, an early form of the sextant. It would be three centuries before Ptolemy's synthesis of astronomy would supersede the work of Hipparchus; it is heavily dependent on Hipparchus in many areas.

An observatory was erected by Hipparchus on the island of Rhodes. Here, in 129 BC, he completes the first scientific star catalogue. He lists about 850 stars, placing each in terms of its celestial latitude and longitude and recording its relative brightness on a scale of six.

Hero and his boiler (ca. 10-70 AD)

Hero, a mathematician/engineer in Alexandria in about AD 65, enjoyed inventing mechanical gadgets, which he described in his work *Pneumatica*.

Whether he had the technology to make them we do not know, but his scientific principles are correct. He is considered the greatest experimenter of antiquity, and his work is representative of the Hellenistic scientific tradition. Among his most famous inventions were the first documented steam-powered device known as Hero's boiler. Another was a windmill operating an organ, marking one of the earliest instances in history of harnessing the wind. It is not known, however, if any of his devices were capable of useful work. A syringe described by Hero controlled the delivery of air or liquids. The first vending machine was also one of his constructions; when a coin was introduced via a slot on the top of the machine, a set amount of Holy Water was dispensed. This was included in his list of inventions in his book, "Mechanics and Optics".

It is almost certain that Hero taught at the Museum, which included the famous Library of Alexandria, because most of his writings appear as lecture notes for courses in mathematics, mechanics, physics, and pneumatics. Although the field was not formalized until the 20th century, it is thought that the work of Hero, his "programmable" automated devices in particular, represents some of the first formal research into cybernetics.

The influential errors of Ptolemy: 2nd century AD

Ptolemy was the most influential of Greek astronomers and geographers of his time. He propounded the geocentric theory that prevailed for 1400 years. The *Almagest* is the earliest of Ptolemy's works and gives in detail the mathematical theory of the motions of the sun, moon, and planets. He made his most original contribution by presenting details for the motions of each of the planets around the earth. The *Almagest* was not superseded until a century after Copernicus presented his heliocentric theory in the *De revolutionibus* of 1543. Ptolemy, working in Alexandria in the 2nd century AD, is one of the great synthesizers of history. In several important fields (cosmology, astronomy, geography) he brings together in encyclopedic form an account of the received wisdom of his time.

Ptolemy first of all justifies his description of the universe based on the earth-centered system described by Aristotle. It is a view of the world based on a fixed earth around which the sphere of the fixed stars rotates every day, carrying with it the spheres of the sun, moon, and planets. Ptolemy used geometric models to predict the positions of the sun, moon, and planets, using combinations of circular motion known as epicycles. Having set up this model, Ptolemy then goes on to describe the mathematics which he needs in the rest of the work.

We know very little of Ptolemy's life. There is no evidence that Ptolemy was ever anywhere other than Alexandria. He made astronomical observations from Alexandria in Egypt during the years AD 127-41. In fact, the first observation which we can date exactly was made by Ptolemy on March 26, 127, while the last was made on February 2, 141.

Galen and medicine 129-200 AD

Galen was a prominent Roman physician and philosopher of Greek origin, and probably the most accomplished medical researcher of the Roman period. His theories dominated and influenced Western medical science for well over a millennium. His account of medical anatomy was based on monkeys and pigs, as human dissection was not permitted in his time, but his anatomy was unsurpassed until the printed description and illustrations of human dissections by Vesalius in 1543.

He was born in the ancient Greek city of Pergamon, now Turkey, which was part of the Roman Empire, attended the great medical school of Alexandria, then, aged 28, he returned to Pergamon as physician to the gladiators. During the four years there he learned the importance of diet, fitness, hygiene and preventive measures, as well as the treatment of fractures and severe trauma resulting from the gladiatorial contests. He went to Rome in August 162, aged 33, in the reign of the Emperor Marcus Aurelius. At the imperial court he became personal physician to Marcus Aurelius and his son Commodus.

Galen's works covered a wide range of topics, from anatomy, physiology, and medicine to logic and philosophy, both summarizing what was known and adding his own observations. His account of the activities of the heart, arteries, and veins endured until William Harvey in 1628 established that the blood circulates throughout the body with the heart acting as a pump. Galen performed many audacious operations—including brain and eye surgeries—that were not tried again for almost two millennia. His knowledge of muscles enabled him to warn his patients of the likely outcome of certain operations—a wise precaution recommended in Galen's advice to doctors. But it is Galen's dissection of apes and pigs which give him the detailed information for his medical tracts on the organs of the body. Nearly 100 of these tracts survived. They become the basis of Galen's great reputation in medieval medicine, unchallenged until the anatomical work of Vesalius.

The Greek legacy

By the time Ptolemy and Galen were putting into lasting form the fruits of Greek science in two important fields, astronomy and medicine, Rome had long displaced Greece as the dominant power in the Mediterranean and

Middle East. Comparing the relative scientific record of these two ancient civilizations illustrates one of the amazing contrasts in history. From Miletus in the 6th century BC to Alexandria in the 2nd century AD, the Greeks produce a glittering stream of scientific experiments and speculations. In Rome's equivalently long period of wealth and power, there is political and military genius in abundance but not a scientist to be seen. After the official establishment of Christianity in the Byzantine empire, in the 4th century, the Greeks themselves become more interested in theological than in scientific speculation. And with the fall of classical civilization to German tribes in the west and to Arabs in the east, it seemed at first that the Greek scientific legacy might be lost in the widespread destruction of the 5th to 7th centuries.

But the Arab conquerors, establishing their own civilization in previously Byzantine lands, developed a keen interest in the old Greek texts. In Arab translation, many Greek manuscripts of philosophy and science found their way through Spain to Western Europe, and were ready, by about 1200, to begin contributing to a renewed interest in intellectual and scientific theory. When the texts began to circulate among the learned men in medieval monasteries, it soon became clear how broad a basis had been provided by the Greeks. In fields capable of proof by theorem, such as geometry and mathematics, answers were available in surviving texts of Euclid and Archimedes. In areas where accurate observation was required, Aristotle's work in natural history offered models for the appropriate method. And in two subjects of absorbing interest, astronomy and medicine, Ptolemy and Galen would stimulate Copernicus and Vesalius to fruitful disagreement and fundamental scientific advancements.

Greek highlights

To summarize: After Thales and two centuries of scientific inquiry into the nature of the physical world, Plato and his student Aristotle produced the first systematic discussions of natural philosophy, which did much to shape later investigations of nature. Their development of inductive and deductive reasoning was of particular importance and usefulness to later scientific inquiry. Along with his teacher, Socrates, and his student, Aristotle, Plato helped to lay the foundations of Western philosophy and science for some two thousand years. Aristotle later established the second university, the Lyceum, also in Athens, and became the predominant authority in numerous fields for many centuries to come.

Aristotle is especially important for providing us with a survey of previous thinkers, almost all of whose works have been lost. He was also important for his work in logic, and is said to have invented the very idea of individual sciences, in the sense of delineating a specific field of study, defining its boundaries, outlining its major questions and issues, and creating much of the terminology for discussing its questions. He also emphasized the need for undertaking empirical research and collecting related data. When his student Alexander the Great went off to conquer all the known world, for example, Aristotle's graduate students went along with the army to collect specimen of plants and animals for the Lyceum's museum. Aristotle remained the leading authority in most fields of inquiry for the following two thousand years, and early modern thinkers such as René Descartes and Francis Bacon in the 17th century had to struggle greatly to liberate philosophical and scientific thought from his dominant influence.

The important legacy of the Ancient Greeks included substantial advances in many branches of factual knowledge, especially in anatomy, zoology, botany, mineralogy, geography, mathematics, astronomy, as well as in philosophy, logic, politics, and ethics. Thus, clear unbroken lines of influence lead from them to medieval Muslim philosophers and scientists in the Middle Ages, then to the European Renaissance and Enlightenment, and later to the secular sciences of the modern day. Neither reason nor inquiry began, of course, with the Greeks, but the Socratic method did, i.e. asking key questions, clearly defining the central terms, emphasizing the logical structure of the argument, and following the discussion to wherever it might lead. It seems to me that it is hard to over-emphasize the importance of the early Greeks in the history and development of science.

Other contributions

It was the great merit of the Muslim civilization that its scientists and thinkers were able not only to make significant contributions to science, mathematics, medicine, philosophy, and jurisprudence, but also to preserve this important Greek heritage for centuries when Europe was in medieval chaos, and then to pass it on to the Western World during the many centuries of Islamic occupation of Spain. The two great names here are the Persian physician, scientist, philosopher, and scholar Avicenna in the 11th century and the Arabian philosopher and polymath Averroes in Islamic Spain in the 13th century.

In Ancient India, the science of linguistics and phonetics developed greatly with the 4th century BC grammarian Panini. Sanskrit was the classical literary language of the Indian Hindus, and Panini's primary motivation was to ensure the correct Sanskrit pronunciation of Vedic hymns and religious texts. Ancient India was also an early leader in metallurgy; stainless steel was developed there by the year 1000, and their workshops forged the most famous sabers in the world. Indian mathematicians explained the use of zero as both a placeholder and a decimal digit, which, along with the Hindu-Arabic numeral system, is now used universally throughout the world.

In Ancient China, one of the earliest inventions was the abacus, along with four other great Chinese inventions and important technological advances: the compass, gunpowder, paper making, and printing, all of which became known in Europe by the end of the Middle Ages. The compass, gunpowder, and printing helped greatly to change the world. Chinese thinkers also worked on a theory of land formation, or geomorphology; a theory of gradual climate change in regions over time; plus work on the clepsydra or water clock, cast iron, blast furnaces, dry docks, and other pragmatic devices. Jesuit missionaries to China in the 16th and 17th centuries learned to appreciate the scientific and technological achievements of this ancient culture and made them known in Europe.

Early beginnings of change

Despite isolated brilliant thinkers and early scientific minds, the masses of people remained for centuries on end illiterate and captives of a local religious mentality, being indoctrinated to follow the authorities and to believe what they were told about the make-up of this world and the world beyond. Then a number of things began to happen which would eventually expand and jolt the mind-set of virtually everyone. The crusades of the 11th, 12th, and 13th centuries caused great numbers of provincial Europeans to come into direct contact with other countries, cultures, and belief systems. The fall of the Christian capital of Constantinople to the Ottoman Turks in 1453 caused many scholars to flee to the Western universities in Italy and France. Due in part to them, a rebirth of interest in Ancient Greek and Roman art and literature caused a great awakening or renaissance in European minds. Then the voyages of discovery by the Spanish, English, and Dutch in the 15th and 16th centuries expanded greatly the view of the world. Johannes Gutenberg's development of movable type and the printing press about 1440 made knowledge available to vast numbers of people, which, in turn, led to the growth of trade, cities, and universities and greatly increased the numbers of literate people and the spread of information everywhere. A recent cover of *Time Magazine* considered Gutenberg the most important man of the last thousand years. Martin Luther's reformation in 1517 and Nicolaus Copernicus's heliocentric thesis in 1543 gave shocks which eventually permeated the entire society. John Watts' invention of the steam engine in 1765 brought a powerful new source of energy and liberated human minds and muscles for other enterprises. The tempo of change steadily increased and spread into more and more aspects of man's life until the masses of common people began to protest and rebel against the restraining forces of church and state and ignorance that had kept them in bondage for centuries.

Controlling man's mind

Perhaps the greatest contest was over the basic question of who was to control man's mind: the traditional authorities or man himself? This debate continues to this very day, as seen in the on-going discussions of evolution, abortion, homosexuality, women's rights, etc. The traditional authorities for countless centuries have been the state and the church, and usually the two have worked in close collusion for the sake of controlling the masses of people. This is perhaps best illustrated in the history of France, where these two powers have closely cooperated virtually from the beginning of French society, to such as extent that sometimes it is difficult to know which of the two had the upper hand and made the final decisions. In terms of the people, however, there was over time less and less doubt about who should control the destiny of the common man. Independent thinkers like Martin Luther in Germany and John Calvin in Switzerland began to inquire into the very foundations of society by daring to question the religious authorities who had held power so long that people believed things had simply always been the way they experienced them. Then came the Enlightenment and free thinkers like Voltaire, Rousseau, and the Encyclopedists in France who began to question loudly and publicly the authority of both church and state with its insidious doctrine of rule by divine right, i.e. the belief that God himself had put the king on the throne. Until then, any attack on the doctrines of the church was seen automatically as an attack as well on the secular powers.

The daring but successful experiment of the American colonies to free themselves from England and establish a new form of democratic government in 1776 was followed soon afterwards by the French Revolution in 1789, with the overthrow and beheading of their king. The political and intellectual ferment of the 18th century has steadily increased until the present time, and today practically all authority has been called into question in virtually every field of human activity.

New sources of energy

The result of these recent centuries of liberation and development has been an explosion of information in almost every field of human knowledge and the creation of new branches of scientific investigation and activity which no one other than visionaries and science fiction writers could have even imagined before. One such fundamental field is the creation of new sources of energy. Until James Watt and his steam engine around 1750, virtually all work in all societies throughout history had always been done by human or animal muscle power; the steam engine was the first of many new sources of power to free man and simply revolutionized the amount and kind of work that humans could do. With the creation of the internal combustion engine 150 years later and the development of electricity, great new fields of human endeavor were made possible. Then came atomic power 50 years later, and at the present time solar, wind, tidal, and geothermal powers are being harnessed, thereby creating new potentials in many new directions. The crucial questions deal with the positive or negative uses of new power sources.

These new sources of abundant energy have made possible three other situations which are changing the fundamental structure of modern society worldwide: the development of the computer, the explosion of telecommunications, and inexpensive international transportation for great masses of people, all made possible by modern science and a scientific approach to reality. Creative minds can now be in constant communication worldwide, stimulating one another and generating new approaches and possible solutions to practically all of man's problems and aspirations. And great numbers of ordinary people are able now to travel to the four corners of the globe and experience first hand the fact that humans worldwide are pretty much the same everywhere, with the same hopes, fears, and ambitions. This gives us hope for the future.

Summing up

Two and a half millennia of scientific investigation and technological innovation have created a world so vastly different and expanded from what had gone on before that it is impossible to summarize the changes. To characterize the fundamental innovations in man's life since the beginning of the the Industrial Revolution two and a half centuries ago strikes me as almost equally impossible. The pace of change in the last hundred years has been so rapid that in the contemporary world changes come so fast that we hardly know at night what kind of world we will wake up to the next morning. I will try to give some brief indication of the dimensions of change by referring to only one mundane aspect, something very close to anyone living in Los Angeles: the car culture of America.

The United States has a population of 304 million people and 232 million registered cars; the population of California (the most heavily populated state in the US) has 37 million people and 28 million registered cars. This means that America is so rich and so prosperous that there are two cars for every three citizens. While nearly every big city in the world has to deal with traffic congestion, what makes Los Angeles unique is that it has not only one of the largest high-speed road networks in the world, but also the highest per-capita car population in the world. Due to its economic prosperity, the United States has become the country with the most registered vehicles, and California, being the country's most populous state with the biggest passion for cars, holds the greatest concentration of them all. This makes Los Angeles, America's second largest city, the world's most car-populated urban sprawl in the world.

There are more cars in California than there are people in any other state of the United States. The Los Angeles freeway system handles over twelve million cars on a daily basis. While L.A. holds the number one spot as America's most congested and polluted roadways, surprisingly enough, it does not hold the title of most chaotic car city due to its enormous freeway infrastructure that allows the residents of the Los Angeles area to carry on their daily migration of over 300 million miles. Living here is a very instructive experience for someone interested in understanding his place and role in the universe.

One last item: owning and operating a car is expensive. And a person who has a car almost certainly has also a telephone, television, a refrigerator, hot and cold running water, a decent dwelling, air conditioning, ample clothing, basic education, sufficient food, and a thousand other material possessions. And there are countless hundreds of millions of us in today's world. All this would surely make the heads of virtually all our ancestors spin with envy, amazement, and bewilderment. My point here is that America and all the other industrialized nations of the world have reached a point of material well-being and prosperity that would be simply unimaginable just a few generations ago, thanks primarily to science, technology, and the increasingly liberated minds and spirits of modern man.

As I drive my personal car through the well organized maze of highways and super-highways of this huge, sophisticated city and observe the literally endless numbers of other personal vehicles driven by fellow Angelenos, I often think to myself: Modern man has really brought most of the material aspects of heaven down to earth, and now it behooves us to tap into the vast spiritual, emotional, and intellectual treasures lying dormant in the human condition and awaiting discovery. Embracing such a task would honor the many creative minds who over the centuries have brought us to this elevated stage of development which we daily enjoy.

Chapter 8.
Art, music, literature

We humans are peculiar creatures consisting of emotions and intellect. I have long had trouble distinguishing clearly between what is emotional (i.e. full of feelings, desires, urges, instincts) and what is intellectual (full of reasons, rational arguments, informed opinions, memories), because it seems to me that all these aspects of the mind easily flow over into one another. Almost nothing in the mind strikes me as pure and without mixture. However, for the sake of discussion and in the pursuit of clarity, we can draw some arbitrary lines and make more-or-less clear distinctions between works or actions based on intellect and those based on emotion. I would call man's making a better cutting tool an essentially intellectual action and his making a song an emotional activity. In this essay I want to call those works and creations based primarily on emotions or the desire to elicit an emotional response, 'works of art,' and I will use the word 'art' to mean any and all such works. The spectrum ranges from the wood carvings of Tilman Riemenschneider around 1500 in Germany, to an illiterate peasant boy playing a tune on his hand-made flute anywhere in the past, to the prehistoric female statue called the Venus of Willendorf, and to the famous Mona Lisa painting by DaVinci in the Renaissance. It seems to me these actions are all primarily based on and appeal to the emotional side of man's nature. Their primary aim or function is to create and promote pleasure and beauty in man's life, with the possible exception of the Venus of Willendorf, whose major purpose or function was perhaps in connection with pregnancy and childbirth.

The origin of art

The very concept of the 'birth' or 'origin' of art may seem inappropriate, since humans by nature are artists (i.e. doers, makers, artisans, technicians) and the history of art begins in a sense with that of humanity. In their artistic impulses and achievements, humans express their vitality and their ability to establish a beneficial and positive relationship with their environment. They humanize their own brute nature with the help of art, and their behavior as artists has played a key role in the evolution of the human species. Evidence from a huge analysis of prehistoric rock art and cave paintings, engravings, and Venus figurines, shows that, from their origins, humans have also been *Homo aestheticus*. We humans, from our very early beginnings on, have wanted more than sheer existence; we also want beauty and pleasure.

Almost everyone agrees that art is difficult to define. It is one of the most unusual aspects of human behavior and a key feature distinguishing humans from other species. But even that assertion is uncertain and questionable, since some critics classify play as a kind of art and maintain that many animals also play. Art appeals clearly to our senses in general, and specific art forms appeal to specific senses: music and poetry to the ear, dance and painting to the eye, sculpture to the eye plus the sense of touch, literature to all the internalized senses, plus some ill-defined but vital function called the imagination. Each of these general art forms is then broken down into more specialized categories: dance into classical and modern; literature into poetry, drama, novel, short stories, sagas; painting into representational and non-representational; music into jazz, classical, folk music; etc. The intellectual and imaginative aspects of the mind are always heavily involved in creating, interpreting, relating, and enjoying any work of art.

Art is distinguished from other human activities by being in large part unprompted by necessity or biological drive. The work of art seems to exist in and of itself, without need of external justification or explanation. Art, like perhaps most games, is an end in itself and does not need further justification or explanation. Art brings pleasure to humans, and that is perhaps explanation enough. Trying to explain how and why it brings pleasure would take us far afield and could probably never be fully explained or resolved. Man could perhaps exist without art, but any higher level of human existence seems always to involve art in one form or another.

The word itself

The word 'art' goes back to an old Indo-European base *ar* which has the meaning of joining or fitting together; the Greek counterpart *techne* has the meaning of doing, weaving, or making. The closely related English words 'artisan' and 'artificial' (from 'art') plus 'technician' and 'technique' (from 'techne') help us see that skills and craftsmanship, a highly developed sense of doing and making, are closely intertwined in the meaning of art. The German word for art is *Kunst* from the verb *können*, meaning the ability to do or make something, and an artist is a Künstler, a person with skill and ability. I would imagine that similar distinctions are made in the Chinese, Japanese, or Russian words for art and artists.

A meaningful distinction can also be made between works of nature and works of art. Works of nature come into being due to their inner make-up and the intrinsic laws of nature, whereas works of art come into being due to the intervening hand, mind, and activity of man. Trees and wood, for example, are works or products of nature resulting from seeds and the laws of chemistry and botany, but a house or a cabinet are works of art in the fundamental sense of a doing, making, or creating by man. The sights and sounds of a thunderstorm are works or creations of nature and result from the workings of natural laws, but a symphony or a fireworks display are artistic works of man and his intelligence. The intervening, creative hand and mind of man are, in my view, the fundamental characteristic of any work of art.

The question of beauty deepens the concept of art but makes the discussion more complex. There are, for example, surely beautiful trees, beautiful sunsets and landscapes, and beautiful human bodies, but are they works of nature or works of art? Although they involve the critical eye of man to consider them beautiful, they do not involve the intervening hand and skills of man to create them and are, therefore, in my view, works of nature. The closing lines in Joyce Kilmer's famous poem, *Trees*, hits the nail squarely on the head: "Poems (i.e. works of art) are made by fools like me, but only God can make a tree."

An additional distinction can be illustrated with an ancient, vital artifact of early man: pottery. The need for containers for food and water led our forefathers to make simple containers out of clay and dry them in the sun. Such a clay crock is a work of art in the broad general sense of making and creating discussed above, but this utilitarian utensil becomes a more narrowly defined work of art when the potter starts decorating it with a simple pattern of dots or lines in order to make it more attractive or pleasing to himself and others. The decorated jug elicits pleasant feelings, and it is these inchoate feelings which make the one jug more of a "real" work of art than the unadorned one. The supposedly simpler needs and emotions of our ancestors tens of thousands of years ago have in the interim become highly articulated and sophisticated in today's world by art critics and art consumers. Comparing and contrasting a delicate china tea cup or a porcelain vase in a museum with a utilitarian water jug from prehistoric times in the same museum can help us think through and become clearer on these often confusing concepts of art.

In this brief essay I want to outline some of the major categories of art, mention some ideas about their early beginnings, the role they play in man's life, and finally try to define what art in general is and its placement in man's development. The purpose again of the whole discussion is to develop my—and perhaps your—sensitivity to one of the most interesting chapters in human evolution.

Prehistoric art

Creating, enjoying, and appreciating works of art seem to be ancient human behaviors. One of the chief obstacles in following the developments in man's art history, however, is finding artifacts which can serve as factual evidence for making assertions. To be preserved, art objects must be made of durable materials. This is the same problem that we encountered earlier in discussing the origins of life: the need for literally *hard* evidence. In terms of prehistoric artistic artifacts, this means carvings or scratchings in stone, ivory, or clay; paintings made with durable colors; significant piles or formations of stone called megaliths; pottery shards; etc. It is thought, for example, that our ancestors may have decorated their bodies with red and black materials perhaps one hundred thousand years ago, but given the softness of human flesh, how could we know such things for sure? Even the preserved artifacts are usually found in isolation and without a larger context; they must then be dated and interpreted in the light of other evidence.

Homo sapiens demonstrated a mature artistic style in Paleolithic cave paintings and sculptures which have survived some thirty two thousand years. Virtually all cultures in all times have practiced various forms of these ancient artistic behaviors of carving and painting, and these forms are still with us today. Elements of art are found today in our dress, furniture, buildings, monuments, entertainment, rituals, etc. In a broad sense, art seems to be a vital part of the human condition, and to persist in all societies. Key questions, but hard to answer, include: Why do people make art? What is its function? How did it originate? Why do we enjoy art?

In studying the earliest art forms and trying to determine their age, one of the most difficult problems is to substantiate claims, much the same as we saw in previous discussions of tools, language, etc. It is again the problem of finding evidence or fossils which have withstood the ravages of time, weather, and climate. It is not surprising, therefore, to learn that the oldest art fossils consist of very durable materials. These include sculptures in the form of stone or ivory figurines, designs or cross hatching scratched on stone or clay, plus shell beads, pottery shards, megalith constructions. Virtually every ancient culture demonstrates some early forms of art, some dating 40,000 or more years ago. It is thought, however, that all the unequivocal evidence of artistic expression was created by *homo sapiens* (i.e. humans like us), although there is a controversial flint object with a striking likeness to a human face which may have been created by another *homo* species, Neanderthal man in the Loire Valley of France some 35,000 years ago. This is a clear illustration of the problems of dating and authentication.

Earliest works of art

Among the oldest and surely most interesting preserved works of prehistoric art are small statues of women called "Venus" figures; the oldest is claimed by the discoverer to date back to between 500,000 and 300,000 years ago. Called the "Venus of Tam-Tan,' it is about two and a half inches long, clearly resembles a human figure, and was discovered by a German archaeologist in Morocco in 1999, but like a similar "Venus of Berekhat Ram" found by a Jewish archaeologist in Israel in 1981, it is not altogether clear whether these two small stone figurines are deliberate works of man or fortuitous works of nature, chance, and weather. A far more convincing example is the famous "Venus of Willendorf, a four and a half inch female statue discovered in 1908 in Austria and dating back about 24,000 years. There are many other stone age figures, mostly obese females with huge hips and breasts, but only rarely a male figure. They are all small statues, a few inches tall at the most, carved in ivory or stone, and sometimes etched in a stone wall.

Other prehistoric artifacts dating 30,000 to 70,000 years ago include engravings with grid or cross-hatch patterns, shell beads, painted pebbles, bracelets, ivory carvings, plus cave paintings in South Africa, Spain, and the famous Lascaux cave paintings in southwestern France. There are several theories about the purpose of these works of art, but they all show man's increasing awareness of himself and his environment. Prehistoric art seems to have been an important human behavior helping people in their lives. Body painting may have been of help in hunting animals; dance and song were perhaps helpful in propitiating the gods; pictures of animals on the walls of caves may have helped draw them near; carving of female statues was probably useful in aiding childbirth or becoming pregnant. Viewing art as a human behavior molded by evolutionary forces offers a useful point of departure in trying to answer some fundamental questions about art and human nature. Asking ourselves, for example, why we enjoy art today can provide clues about the universality and persistence of artistic forms among our early ancestors.

Works of art trigger emotional responses, but explaining how this happens is far more difficult than merely asserting that art and the emotions are closely related. This is a vast, complex topic and beyond the scope of this essay, in part because emotional responses can be so varied and subjective. Rembrandt and Jackson Pollack are both artists working with colors on canvas, for example, but the emotional responses which they elicit can be so diverse that one might wonder how they can both be called artists. Much the same holds true for the music of Beethoven and Arnold Schoenberg, or the sculpture of a Michelangelo and a Henry Moore, and many others. Works which some critics consider masterpieces are for others trivial exercises, or worse. Hence the century old admonition and bit of wisdom, *De gustibus non disputandum*, "About taste there can be no dispute." There is surely a certain wisdom in this saying, but it doesn't really explain much or help us have a deeper grasp of what art actually is or how it works on the mind and emotions.

Major forms and categories of art

The following discussion of the various forms or categories of art does not pretend to be comprehensive or given in much detail. Its purpose is merely to make us more aware of the breadth and variation in man's artistic activities. Most libraries have volumes of art books demonstrating and documenting this diversity in virtually every country and culture in the world over the centuries and millennia of man's tenure on earth. Many cultures have art forms which are practically unknown among other peoples. One would hardly imagine, for example, that origami (paper cutting and folding) could have developed into such a highly technical art as it has in Japan, or that marching band performances could have reached such a high level of skill and artistry as they have in the United States. Unusual uses of the word 'art' include flag throwing in Switzerland, canoe carving in Oceania, pottery creation and decoration in many societies, tattoo decoration of the body in numerous cultures, the geometric art and calligraphy of Islamic culture which does not allow iconic art or music other than that of the human voice. Mathematicians speak of the beauty and elegance of a solution, and the mimetic art of Marcel Marceau is in a special class. These and other examples of artistic endeavor almost force us to think of art in a broad, inclusive manner. Some critics maintain that art is simply anything the artist does, a view which easily reaches what many people would call meaningless extremes. All art forms, however, seem to bear witness to some fundamental human urge and need to engender and express emotion through special and sometimes problematic creative forms in many aspects of life.

Most people would probably agree, however, that music, dance, song, painting, sculpture, drama, and oral literature (story-telling) are obvious works of art, and that these art forms are old and deeply rooted in human history. I am using the word 'art' in this essay to mean many different kinds of doing, making, performing, creating. Art is so intimately tied up with man's nature that it is difficult to make a general classification of all the specific arts. Here are some of the major distinctions and subdivisions in use today, but it immediately becomes evident that they easily flow over into one another and are hard to delineate clearly. They are listed here simply to demonstrate the spread and diversity of what passes under the rubric 'art.'

The fine arts

The fine arts include decorative art, architecture, some crafts like weaving and basket making, calligraphy, design, drawing, graphic arts and print making, photography, origami. Most fine art creations are developed primarily for purely aesthetic purposes rather than for utility. But some, like architecture or a beautifully designed automobile, for example, are also used on a daily basis and have more than a purely aesthetic function. For instance, India's famous Taj Mahal is both a shrine and a splendid example of Muslim architecture drawing admirers from around the world, and the Empire State Building in New York City is a dramatic example of modern architecture as well as being the headquarters and offices of countless business enterprises. The fine arts are therefore obviously related to the practical arts (crafts), and in many cases the distinction is hard to draw. In modern society, most things of utility are expected to also have an esthetically pleasing appearance: cars, furniture, dishes, clothing, etc. Students primarily interested in art in colleges and universities usually earn a Bachelor's or Master's degree in Fine Arts (BFA or MFA).

The performing arts

The performing arts use the artist's own body, face, or presence as the primary medium. Performing arts include acrobatics, mime, dance, theater, opera, music, juggling, film, the martial arts, the marching arts such as brass bands. Stand-up comics, surfers, sky-divers, and other artistic sports could probably also fit the definition of performing artists. While watching other sports such as soccer, basketball, most of the Olympic games, etc., one is tempted to say that often the elegance, skill, and grace of the athletes would qualify many of these sports as a kind of performing art. The skier coming off the high jump platform and sailing hundreds of feet through the air before gracefully landing far below comes to mind as an example of skill and beauty,

Plastic arts

The plastic arts use materials such as clay, stone, metal or paint which can be molded or transformed to create some object, usually three-dimensional. Such artistic endeavors include architecture, sculpture, ceramics, collage, mosaics, metal working, and printmaking, but the term 'plastic arts' is also used loosely to include painting and film-making. Most of the works found in museums would fall in the category of the plastic arts.

Music

Music has been called the language of the soul and is said to amplify human emotions. Music expresses something which words cannot. It is an ancient art form whose medium is clearly sound, made by the human voice and a wide variety of external instruments: percussion, stringed, wind, rasps, rattles, bells, cymbals, plus music's greatest prop: rhythm. This rhythmic aspect was probably first done by clapping of the hands or stomping of the feet. Some sort of primitive drum used to keep the rhythm is thought to be the oldest musical instrument, although none has been preserved. The widespread interest in music is seen in the fact that India has one of the oldest musical traditions in the world, and the earliest and largest collection of prehistoric musical instruments was found in China and dates back to between 7000 and 6600 BC. The word itself comes from the Greek *mousike,* meaning 'the art of the Muses.' In many cultures, music is an important aspect of a people's daily way of life.

Some of the oldest preserved artifacts related to art are musical instruments, the flute in particular. German scientists have unearthed the oldest-known musical instrument fashioned by human hands. It's a delicate flute, eight and a half inches long with four holes, made from the wing bone of a vulture and dates to at least 35,000 years ago—just after the first *homo sapiens* entered Europe. An older, alleged flute segment, made from the femur bone of a young bear, was found in a Neanderthal site in Germany and is estimated to be between 43,000 and 82,000 years old. Six well-crafted bone flutes have recently been discovered in China and are considered to be 7000 to 9000 years old. They were all made from the wing bones of cranes and have between five and eight holes.

Music may be the oldest, most universal, and most popular of all art forms, although its origins are perhaps impossible to investigate. Of all works of art, music is probably the one most closely and directly linked to the emotions. Although the specific musical forms may vary greatly from one culture to the other, music seems to be a human universal, and the use of songs between mothers and infants, for example, can be found the world over. Lullabies and crooning are used in all cultures to calm and soothe infants to sleep. Today's movie makers exploit the unusual ability of music to influence emotions in virtually every film with background music powerfully setting the desirable mood and intensity, usually with the viewers hardly being conscious of being emotionally manipulated through sound. This intimate link between music and emotion makes music perhaps the most powerful art of all.

The close connection between music and emotions is also suggested in the animal world with vocalizations of sometimes amazingly high complexity and musicality. Numerous musical manifestations have evolved with several species of birds and mammals: songbirds, parrots, hummingbirds, whales, and seals. It is thought that the purpose of such sound displays is usually in reference to a delineation of territory or things relating to courtship and mating. Darwin theorized, for example, that human music perhaps had its origin in the sounds of man's half-human progenitors during the season of courtship, similar to the male gorilla pounding on his chest, but this has proven to be inadequate and untenable.

Dance

The earliest history of dance, like that of music, is also a mystery. Both seem to begin as partners in the service of community rituals drawing members of the group together. Since dance does not leave behind clearly identifiable physical artifacts, it is not possible to determine when and how dance became part of human culture. We easily suspect, however, that it has very likely been an important part of ceremony and ritual since man's earliest beginnings. One of its earliest functions was probably the acting out of hunting scenes and religious myths. Together with a rhythmic drumming and chanting, dancers could act out the evocation of spirits or the drama of the kill in a powerful, emotional performance before a tribal gathering.

Dance as a form of personal expression seems obviously to come from the joy of freedom of movement and perhaps as a method of non-verbal communication. People dance to relieve stress, to express social or spiritual values, and to attract attention. Choreography is the art of making dances. Dances vary so much from culture to culture that it is difficult to define dance other than movement of the body. It is hard to say what classical ballet, ballroom dancing, the repetitious jumping up and down of African natives, the slow movements of Chinese opera, the Polynesian hula, and the jitterbug have in common? The floor exercises of women's gymnastics, synchronized swimming, and figure skating are additional examples showing the difficulty of defining dance other than deliberate bodily movement. Much depends on social, cultural, aesthetic, artistic, and moral constraints, but various forms of dance can be found in virtually every human grouping in the world.

The literary arts

Literature means literally an 'acquaintance with letters,' something which the majority of people have historically only recently acquired, although they have enjoyed legends and epics recited by wandering artists for centuries and millennia, plus comedy and drama performances since at least the ancient Greeks. Today the literary arts include fiction and non-fiction prose, drama, poetry, epics, legends, myths, ballads, and folk tales, which in general are now usually directed towards a reading audience. Drama, comedy, lyrical and epic poetry are the early literary art forms and were aimed in general at a largely illiterate audience. They reach back into civilization's early beginnings, whereas things like the novel and short story had to wait for a literate public.

Literature is aimed at the inner stage of the mind and awakens the creative imagination of the listener. This makes the work far more personal and powerful than the objective words or scenes themselves as presented to the audience. In the case of both literature and music. the creative imagination plays an unusually powerful role, more so, I think, than in any other art form. I believe this is so because all the memories and personal experiences of the listener can be brought into play actively and intensely in recreating an inner drama. It is a common experience that we find the book far more rewarding than the filmed version, and this is because the book only sketches out the people and situations of the story and leaves the filling-in of details to the reader's imagination. Our creative imagination gladly uses the raw material presented by the text or music to create its own highly personal story or emotional situation. Michelangelo's *David*, Da Vinci's *Mona Lisa*, Rodin's *The Thinker*, or Hollywood's *Gone with the Wind,* on the other hand, present us with more or less completed works of art with only limited room for the creative imagination to make its own personal contribution.

Creative writing

Creative writing is considered to be any writing that goes outside the bounds of normal professional, journalistic, academic, and technical forms of literature. It includes novels, short stories, epics, poems. plus stories for television and movies. Generally speaking, creative writing is any sort of original composition and is a more contemporary and process-oriented name for what has traditionally been called 'literature.'

Creative writing is a peculiar form of art in that it uses everyday language to create scenes and stories which take place exclusively in the reader's or listener's mind. In pre-literate societies, wandering bards or story tellers journeyed from place to place reciting long epics of heroes and great deeds of the past, often accompanying themselves on a simple musical instrument. In this sense, literature is, in my view, a special form of mental or intellectual art entertaining and educating the listeners.

Theater

Theater is an ancient art form and probably goes back in its simplest form to hunters acting out in front of an audience in prehistoric times the chase and killing of prey. By using combinations of speech, gesture, music, dance, sound and spectacle, the actors were able to have a powerful effect on the spectators, and theater was soon allied to religion and politics in the sense of persuading and moving the populace in certain directions. In addition to the standard narrative dialogue style, theater also takes such forms as opera, ballet, mime, kabuki, classical Indian dance, Chinese opera, and mummers' plays.

The history and development of Greek theater shows clearly the forms assumed later by European and Western theater: Tragedy could deal only with the high-born and their stories of tragic flaws leading to their downfall, whereas the lives and experiences of common people were relegated to comedy. This was a reflection of what people thought of themselves for over two thousand years. The life and experience of a commoner did not become a suitable theme for tragic representation on stage or in novels until about two hundred years ago.

Drama in medieval Europe grew out of the Passion play at Easter which was originally a simple waving of the priest's hand during the mass and announcing to the two Marys that Christ was not in the tomb but had arisen. This simple scene was first done in the church in Latin, but soon music was added, the vernacular was used, then additional words and gestures, more characters, and finally the whole spectacle became so loud and exuberant that it had to be performed outside on the steps of the church. Devilish clowns, dance, secular music, costumes, and additional texts and scenes turned the early Passion play into lively dramatic performances.

Trying to define art in general

If the definition of dance or music is so complex, what shall we say about a definition of all the arts in general? Perhaps the wisest approach is simply to say that art—like language, friendship, happiness, health, love, life, and many similar examples—is what everyone knows it to be, and let it go at that. But that is hard to do, and we want to understand on a deeper level.

There are today many theories of art, often confusing and contradictory, so that is why I like to use the root meaning of the word and simple examples to illustrate it. Some theorists say that the work of art is anything the artist creates; others say everything is a work of art; still others maintain that art critics determine what art is and what good and bad art is; and yet others say that the public determines good and bad art by the price they are willing to pay; and so on. Almost everyone agrees, however, that there has to be an artist and that some degree of emotion is involved. Defining art is admittedly a subjective, involved, and problematic enterprise with no easy answers. A striking sunset or a beautiful tree causing an emotional reaction in the beholder might be a work of art if we consider God or nature as the artist, but this is obviously stretching the point considerably.

To a great extent art, music, and literature consist of man's emotional responses to sights, sounds, and stories; philosophy, science, and technology are based primarily on man's intellectual capacities. These two sides or aspects of man's nature are probably as old as man himself and underline his dual nature of being an intellectual as well as an emotional creature. Monkeys, dogs, cats, and other mammals seem to demonstrate to some extent these two sides of their nature as well, but man is distinctly set apart from them by his highly developed ability to verbalize his reactions and to demonstrate them in many diverse ways. Poetry, for example, is said to be emotion recollected in tranquility, and this sort of juxtaposition of emotions and the intellect may be the best definition of art in general that we can find.

Summary of the discussion

Where does this rambling and fragmentary discussion of art and its many forms leave us, and what have we learned? I, for one, have learned that the more I delve into these questions of art, the more intertwined things become and the more difficult it is to make any definitive statements about what art is and is not, and precisely how one art form is delineated from another. Why is this? I think it is because art and human nature are so closely and intimately interrelated in time and in man's evolution. We humans are loaded with emotions and are by nature as well as by necessity doers and makers, i.e. artists in a broad sense. Works of art, concepts of beauty, enjoyment of the senses, the pleasures of the mind, and human nature all strike me as being inextricably related and intertwined with one another. They are perhaps incapable of being closely defined and clearly explained, and of course to recognize and enjoy great works of art we do not need exact definitions and elaborate lines of demarcation between the various art forms. Researchers find ancient flutes, paintings, Venus figurines, and many other artifacts from the deep past, for example. and try to piece together the story of man's artistic development, but the story is necessarily incomplete and will likely always remain so. This intense preoccupation with art simply enhances and deepens the inquiry of what it means to be a human being. Like philosophy, science, religion, economics, and other basic activities, art in its many forms affords us another instructive vantage point from which to experience and evaluate the phenomenon of being human.

It behooves us as inheritors of this complex human development, I believe, to imagine our ancestors as fellow creatures who, under the given circumstances of their time and place, were as intelligent, versatile, and sensitive in their own way as we are. On the basis of what modern science tells us about the development of early mankind, we can regard them as meeting their challenges and expressing their joys and pleasures with remarkable success. It seems to me that given what we know about the often harsh and trying conditions of their lives, they have done remarkably well with what they had, not only staying alive and flourishing, but spreading throughout the entire planet and leaving us with a magnificent artistic and intellectual heritage. I think we can indeed be very proud of them and their accomplishments in art and in life.

Chapter 9.
Psychology, developing awareness

The over-all purpose of this book is to help me—and perhaps others— become more clearly focused on this amazing experience of being human. I do this by outlining and reviewing man's many aspects and activities, plus recalling the overall story of humanity. Our total, inclusive history starts with the Big Bang, proceeds through the formation of the universe and the earth, the creation of life and human evolution, the origin and development of civilization, the unfolding of religion, philosophy, science, and technology, and arriving finally at the complex modern society of today. My ambition from the beginning has been to bring my experience as a representative example of humanity into sharp mental and psychological awareness. In this brief essay on psychology, I want to rapidly remind myself of how humans in general have become increasingly aware of the complexity and multiple functions of the mind. In this way I want to clearly focus on awareness, consciousness, and self-consciousness in preparation for the final chapter on what I call "mystical insights," the best and most profound insights I have had concerning the human condition. They are mystical in the sense of sometimes being elusive and difficult to explain.

Many modern theorists regard the three-pound human brain as perhaps the most amazing piece of matter in the entire universe. The mind is the activity or functioning of that highly evolved human organ. The mind is what the brain does, and self-awareness is probably the most developed activity of that piece of physical matter which everyone has in his skull. Becoming aware, and especially self-aware, consists of many stages and has taken humanity a long time to develop. This most highly developed consciousness or sense of self-awareness is what interests me most. It is like the frosting on the cake. For many people it is probably not really essential to normal life, but I believe it is mankind's crowning glory and perhaps man's greatest accomplishment. This chapter is my attempt to briefly review how we got there.

Humans have been trying to understand the mind and one another probably since the beginning of time. Usually we think we know "what makes us tick" (which usually turns out to be an illusion), but the far more urgent task at hand is to understand our fellow humans, how to anticipate what they are going to do next, and how they will react to us. Understanding our fellows and ourselves is of vital importance, from the individual and personal level to the broadest and most inclusive levels of society. At the present time, for example, our governmental leaders are trying to determine what the Iranians and North Koreans have in mind concerning nuclear energy and atomic bombs. Historically, religious and political leaders in all cultures have attempted to understand and manipulate the human mind since time immemorial, whereas poets and philosophers have tended to focus primarily on the more subtle subjective aspects of the mind.

In a broad sense, we are all amateur psychologists trying to muddle our way through the complex human relations which preoccupy us consciously and subconsciously most of our waking hours. We are such social creatures by nature that I think we live primarily in a human context rather than in an objective context of external things or a purely internal world of our own making.

How could it be otherwise? The first six or eight or ten years of our existence are so socially oriented that we become indelibly imprinted for life. The language, culture, and world view of our group flow into us with our mother's milk, and without this intense socializing process we would perhaps not even be human. Without a great deal of human involvement and effort by others on our behalf for the first few years, we would surely not even survive. To be a human necessarily and fundamentally means to be a fellow human. It is therefore of vital importance to comprehend the human mind as much as we can. I believe this need is the origin and driving force behind the study of psychology, one of the oldest and most important human inquiries of all.

What is psychology?

The subject of psychology is a vast one with so many major theories, schools, important figures, etc. that it would require a thick book to deal—even superficially—with them all. What I want to do here is simply to mention briefly, in a roughly historical order, some of the major people, ideas, and problems in psychology which I have found to be especially meaningful.

'Psychology' comes from two Greeks words, *psyche* for 'mind' or 'soul' and *logos* for 'words about' or 'the study of.' The first use of the term 'psychology' is often attributed to a German philosopher in 1590, but it did not come into popular usage until almost three centuries later. Psychology was long called intellectual or mental philosophy, just as science was labeled natural philosophy in contrast to moral philosophy. In England, the term 'psychology' replaced 'mental philosophy' in the middle of the 19th century.

Professional psychologists today feel uncomfortable with such abstract concepts as 'mind' or 'soul' and prefer to regard psychology not as the study of some intangible 'soul,' "spirit,' 'mind,' or 'psyche' but as the study of human behavior. In this way they can set up objective experiments, make precise measurements, and quantify the results of specific, observable actions and reactions such as reflex times, learning and memory experiments, etc. They want to make psychology into an exact science using the scientific method, and generally they find the 'mind' too vague, too subjective, and too difficult to measure. The mind is often called 'the ghost in the machine.' But in their attempt to create an exact science, some essential aspects of the mind seem to slip through the cracks and get lost.

Religious views

Historically, one of the oldest and perhaps most problematic confusions was the distinction between the mind and the soul. In the Bible the mind easily becomes merged with a religious entity called the soul, a distinction which still remains quite important for many people today. Telling us that a person's actions are caused by a sinful or pious reasoning is not particularly helpful, but this has been a powerful method of explaining behavior for many people for a long time. Unusual or deviant behavior was often attributed to the soul's being 'possessed by devils' or by man's 'sinful nature.'

For centuries, people have talked about a soul inside each human and explained behavior in terms of this soul or entity which causes us to do good things and bad things. The vagueness and inscrutability of this concept have not prevented it from being adopted by countless millions of people as an explanation of our ideas, motivation, and behavior. This view goes back to the biblical story of God creating man and blowing the breath of life into him; 'breath' is along with 'mind', 'spirit,' and 'soul' one of the root meanings of the Greek *psyche*, since breathing is one of the key signs of life.

Universal interest in psychology

The ancient Egyptians, Greeks, Chinese, and Indians were also very keen on understanding human thought and behavior, as shown in some of their earliest writings. These early ideas about the human spirit were often embedded in religious texts or myths, but later writers like Plato and Aristotle wrote more focused discussions and theories of the mind and human behavior. The Greek theories influenced much of Christian and Islamic thinking on the subject. Several Greek and later Western philosophers developed theories of the mind or soul and discussed some of the broad issues and problems concerning human behavior. A brief survey of their ideas will give us some indication of the depth and scope of earlier thinking; it will also be helpful in understanding the evolution and complexity of critical self-awareness.

Plato (429-347 B.C.)

He divides the mind (psyche, soul) into three parts:
• 1. Reason — the thinking, reasoning, rational part of us; it is located in the head and brain; its task is to think, understand, plan. This part of the mind is immortal both before birth and after death and has seen or experienced the eternal forms or ideas of justice, beauty, friendship, etc. prior to being incorporated in a specific human body.

2. Will — this is the willing, striving, decision making part of our person; it is located in the heart and chest; its task is to carry out and implement the rational things decided by the mind.

3. Appetite — these are the emotions, desires, feelings; they are located in the stomach and in the sex areas of the body; their task is to provide us with sensual pleasure.

The good life for Plato is one in which these three parts of the human mind are in harmony with one another, in balance and equilibrium, each doing its own task and staying within its well-established limits, like the captain, officers, and crew on a well-run ship, avoiding arguments and mutiny. On the analogy of the mind, Plato also writes a theory of the state with three tiers of people: the philosopher-kings, the administrators and guardians, and the working people. After all citizens have been equally educated until age 20, the three specific groups start forming according to their basic inner character and propensities.

Aristotle

Aristotle (384-322 B.C.) and Immanuel Kant (1724-1804) agree that the mind is essentially the principle of organization. The mind is what the brain does: thinks, plans, emotes, organizes, remembers, etc.

For both of these thinkers, the mind is the highest capacity or function of the human soul; it is the active process which organizes and ties together all the sense and mental activities of human consciousness. It is like the melody of a musical instrument, and without the instrument there can be no melody. Aristotle says that if the eye were the body, vision would be its soul; if the ear were the body, hearing would be its soul. The soul is the organizing principle or specific function or purpose for which the physical object exists. Much the same holds true for the mind for both Aristotle and Immanuel Kant, a Greek and a German separated by 2000 years but having much the same ideas about the nature of the mind.

René Descartes (1596-1650)

This French philosopher and mathematician is usually considered to be the beginning of modern philosophy. His influence has been enormous, and today we still study Cartesian theories in algebra and geometry. For him, the mind is a thinking substance. For Descartes as for Plato, there are two different kinds of substance: one mental and one physical. This is called dualism, the dualism or split between mind and matter. As for Plato, mind for Descartes is characterized by rational thinking and self-awareness; matter, on the other hand, is characterized by extension, by the fact that it is tangible and fills space.

Descartes starts his philosophy with an attempt to find an absolutely solid basis on which to build his system of thought; he starts in systematic doubt and questions absolutely everything, including his own existence, the existence of the world, the existence of God, etc. From the beginning there is a tremendous emphasis on subjectivity and on certainty. Like the ancient Greek scientist Archimedes, he is looking for a place to stand in order to move the world. Archimedes wanted to do it with a lever; Descartes wants to do it with clear, precise, systematic thinking. He find his place to stand with his saying: I doubt, therefore I think; I think, therefore I am. It has come down to us in the Latin form that he published it in: *Cogito ergo sum* (I think, therefore I am) and is known as the Cartesian cogito.

The existence of one thing, his own doubting mind, is itself beyond all doubt; and from this one certainty he builds his entire, powerful philosophy. He unpacks the cogito and by deduction proves the existence of God, the world, and reality more or less as it comes to him through the senses.

John Locke (1632-1704)

This English philosopher is important for having explained how we come by our store of ideas through sensation and reflection. We directly receive data such as red, blue, hot, cold, etc. through sensations to our sense organs, and then through reflection (operations of our mental abilities) we come by the abstract ideas of color, temperature, etc. We never directly experience color, temperature, weight, etc, we sense only specific examples. Locke maintained that all our ideas are ultimately reducible to sense data which another part of the mind works on to create abstractions. This approach is called 'empiricism' and maintains that all our ideas and knowledge are essentially based on sense data; it denies that humans are born with innate ideas such as the existence of God, immortality of the soul, notions of good and evil, etc.

David Hume (1711-1776)

This Scottish philosopher is often called the ultimate empirical skeptic; he and the American psychological behaviorist B.F. Skinner (1904-1990) deny the very existence of the mind, because we can never sense it directly.

Hume says there is no mind as such, no discrete entity of which we can directly have empirical knowledge. For him, the mind is the sum total of experience, but there is no underlying permanent substance or substratum holding together or containing all the vast contents of experience. There is no personal identity or unity of the self or of the mind; there are only impressions and mental/emotional activity. Mind is only a convenient name for the sum total of all these experiences, just a vast collection of sensations, a stream of consciousness. But there is no clear impression of the stream itself, just of the contents.

Skinner also maintains that there is no mind as such; there is no discrete entity that can be scientifically observed and studied. The mind is simply the form of behavior, so let's study behavior which we can observe, measure, and understand empirically and just forget about the mind. It does us no good to posit such an inscrutable thing which no one can observe and study directly. The mind is like the movie screen at the cinema: We see only the continuous flow of images, but never the screen itself upon which they are projected. It is like an abstract, unobservable, unknowable ghost (much like the angels, demons, devils of religion) which just confuses everything. So let's just forget it, says Skinner, and get on with more meaningful things like clear-cut, observable behavior!

Early academic approaches to psychology
Wilhelm Wundt (1832-1920)

Psychology as a well-defined field of experimental study is commonly said to have begun in 1879 when Wilhelm Wundt founded at the University of Leipzig the first laboratory dedicated exclusively to psychology. He was a German medical doctor, psychologist, physiologist, and professor, known today as one of the founding figures of modern psychology. He is widely regarded as the "father of experimental psychology." By doing controlled experiments in his laboratory he was able to explore the nature of religious beliefs, identify mental disorders and abnormal behavior, and map damaged areas of the human brain. By doing this he was able to establish psychology as a separate science from other fields of study. He also founded in 1881 the first journal for psychological research. Students from all over the world, especially from the United States such as G. Stanley Hall, journeyed to Leipzig to learn experimental technique and to return to their home institutions imbued with the spirit of scientific psychology. Over the years until his retirement in 1917, Wundt served as the *de facto* parent of the "new" psychology.

William James (1842 - 1910)

A more exacting study of psychology was well on its way by the beginning of the 20th century and reached another high point with William James. He was a pioneering American psychologist, philosopher, and medical doctor. He studied in the US, France, and Germany and wrote influential books on the young science of psychology, educational psychology, the psychology of religious experience and mysticism, and the philosophy of pragmatism.

James studied medicine, physiology, and biology, and began to teach in those subjects, but he was drawn to the scientific study of the human mind at a time when psychology was constituting itself as a science. He introduced courses in scientific psychology at Harvard University where he spent his entire academic career. He taught his first experimental psychology course at Harvard in 1875.

He gained widespread recognition with his monumental *Principles of Psychology,* published in 1890. He is also famous for the James-Lange theory of emotions. This theory says that emotions follow actions rather than the common-sense belief that actions follow emotions. James uses the following example: We see a bear in the woods and start running, not out of fear but because we know that bears are dangerous. As we find ourselves running, we begin to get frightened. This is in contrast to the notion that we see the bear, get frightened, and run. That would be actions following emotions; the James-Lange theory turns it the other way around. Act scared or confident and you will start feeling it. This is an example of his pragmatic approach to understanding the mind.

Ivan Petrovich Pavlov (1849 - 1936)

He was a Russian physiologist. psychologist, and physician. He was awarded the Nobel Prize in Medicine in 1904 for research pertaining to the digestive system. Pavlov is widely known for first describing the phenomenon of classical conditioning. He rang a bell as he gave a dog food, and he dog began to salivate. After a few sessions of 'conditioning,' the dog began to salivate upon simply hearing the bell ring. The idea of conditioning or association of two unrelated ideas is a key concept in the training of the mind, especially among children and was popularized by the American behaviorist John B. Watson.

John Dewey (1859-1952) and Gilbert Ryle (1900-1976)

These two theorists maintain that the mind is the activity of solving problems. It is the way we function and act, the way we behave. The mind is the body in action. There is no internal director of our activities giving out commands and controlling our activities. Ryle says, "There is NO ghost in a machine!" Not one of us believes this, however, and we all think just the opposite, namely that there IS a ghost (a mind or soul) in the machine of our body which governs and controls our actions. Both Dewey and Ryle seem to agree with Aristotle and Kant that the mind is our principle of organization, and with Skinner that our mind is what we do, our behavior.

John B. Watson (1878-1958)

He is often referred to as the "father of behaviorism." His view that psychology was the science of observable behaviors has had a strong influence, and the behavioral perspective rose to dominate the field during the first half of the twentieth century.

Watson was one of the strongest advocates for behaviorism, suggesting that psychology should be objective and focus on the study of human behaviors rather than on vague abstractions like mind and spirit. He was so convinced of the power of conditioning that he asserted that if he had several normal healthy infants and the freedom to raise them as he wished, he could take any one of them at random and train him to become a doctor, lawyer, artist, beggar, or thief, regardless of the infant's race, talents, or abilities. Watson became a popular author on child-rearing and strongly sided with nurture in the "nature versus nurture" discussion. He later became an acclaimed contributor to the advertising industry where, by molding public opinion, he had a great influence and earned far more money than in academia.

Important distinctions and concepts
The mind and the brain

There is a sharp distinction between the mind and the brain. Medical people tell us that the brain is an organ located in the skull, weighs about three pounds, has billions of nerve cells and synapses, and has distinct areas which control the basic body activities like breathing and heart beat, plus centers controlling speech, bodily movements, hand-eye coordination, memory, emotions, etc. A great deal of scientific work has been done on the brain, whereas the study of the mind is in general left to the poets, philosophers, and a few psychiatrists and theorists who develop theories of how they think the mind works. No one really seems to know precisely what and where the mind is, but a good working definition says that the mind is what the brain does: see, hear, taste, learn, feel pleasure and pain, emote, think, remember, dream, plan, etc.

The area of behavior—what we do and why—is of course what most of us are really interested in and want to understand. We therefore subscribe to various theories of behavior in the hope of gaining some insight into what motivates people and explains their actions. Religious people embrace ideas of a divine soul which is led astray by the dark forces of evil, behaviorists believe in early conditioning with rewards and punishments, philosophers teach ideas about an inborn human nature which tries to develop and manifest itself under given social and physical conditions.

Freud: the conscious and unconscious mind

Due largely to the influence of Sigmund Freud (1856-1939) and his 1900 book, *The Interpretation of Dreams*, an important distinction in understanding human behavior has been made between the conscious and the unconscious mind. Until Freud, behavior and consciousness were thought to be matters of our rational, alert, and conscious mind. Poets and other creative people have long known, of course, that there are other powerful forces in our conscious decision-making processes and that rational explanations are often merely a cover story for the real reasons behind our decisions and behavior. Freud's clear distinction between the conscious and the unconscious or subconscious aspects of our mind has played a great role in modern theories about how our psyche works. Now we are all aware that there are powerful forces other than our rational, conscious mind which influence us in very significant ways. In addition to the libido or sexual drive, some of these other forces include overall health, cultural conditioning, energy level, intelligence, etc.

Like Plato, Freud has a tripartite view of the mind: the id, ego, and super-ego, plus several complexes (especially the Electra and the Oedipus complex), all of which have received a great deal of attention in novels, movies, and in popular discussions, especially in the US.

The mind-body relationship

This is an old, venerable problem going back to Plato and Descartes. If the mind and body are so fundamentally different from one another, one physical and one mental, how do they interact? How can they be interrelated and influence one another? How can they interact if they are basically different substances? All these problems rest on the assumption that there is a definite split between mind and body. There is really no good solution to the problem except for the behaviorists who say, "Forget the mind and study only behavior," but most of us cannot do this and strongly believe that we actually do have an independent mind, a 'ghost in the machine,' which controls the body. The modern science of psycho-somatic medicine is based on a mind-body distinction which goes back at least as far as the Bible where the Apostle Paul confesses that the spirit is willing but the flesh is weak.

The uses of psychology in modern life

In the last hundred or so years, psychology has left the philosophical arena of ideas and joined in the struggles of daily life, helping to solve some of the real problems people face. A number of important uses of psychology have developed to help an increasingly large and complex society. Examples include intelligence tests for placing students properly in academic situations, aptitude testing for industry and the military, psycho-analysis for people suffering from stress and inner confusion, constructively dealing with exceptionally gifted or retarded individuals, psychotherapy for persons with personal problems, etc. Many theories and schools of thought have developed and many psychologists strive to make their discipline into a more-or-less exact science. In all these endeavors, the idea of consciousness and self-awareness is enhanced and deepened.

Theories of intelligence and of learning

Soon after the development of experimental psychology in Leipzig, various kinds of applied psychology appeared. The American psychologist G. Stanley Hall brought scientific pedagogy to the United States from Germany in the early 1880s. John Dewey's theories of the relationship between education and democracy at the turn of the century were widely embraced, and for several decades Dewey at the Columbia University Teachers College reigned as the leading spokesman in the field of educational theory.

The concept of IQ, or "Intelligence Quotient" was first introduced in 1904 by the French psychologist Alfred Binet, who, together with a French physician, Theodore Simon, developed the Binet-Simon intelligence test at a boys' school by using increasingly difficult questions which measured attention, memory, and verbals skills. In 1916, the Stanford psychologist Lewis Terman released the "Stanford Revision of the Binet-Simon Scale", the "Stanford-Binet", for short. The use and development of the Stanford-Binet Intelligence Scales initiated the modern field of intelligence testing in America.

Soon the test was so popular that Robert Yerkes, president of the American Psychological Association, decided to use it in developing the Army Alpha and the Army Beta tests to classify recruits. Thus, a high-scoring recruit might earn an A-grade (high officer material), whereas a low-scoring recruit with an E-grade would be rejected for military service. Standardized intelligence and aptitude tests were administered to two million U. S. soldiers during WWI. Soon after, such tests were used in all branches of the U.S. armed forces and in many areas of civilian life, including academic and work settings.

The Stanford-Binet test continues to be widely used and reports intelligence as four separate scores: Verbal Reasoning, Abstract/Visual, Quantitative, and Short-term Memory. It covers the range from age 2.5 years old to young adult.

Modifying behavior

The formulation of behaviorism by John B. Watson was popularized by B.F. Skinner and adapted to changing or modifying behavior. Behaviorism proposed limiting psychological study solely to overt behavior, because only that could be quantified and easily measured. Behaviorists considered knowledge of the "mind" too metaphysical to achieve scientifically, but they felt that specific behavioral patterns, for example, could be altered and improved. The final decades of the 20th century saw the decline of behaviorism and the rise of an interdisciplinary approach to studying the human mind, known collectively as cognitive science. Cognitive science again considers the "mind" as a subject for investigation, using the tools of evolutionary psychology, linguistics, computer science, and neurobiology. This form of investigation has proposed that a wide understanding of the human mind is possible, and that such an understanding may be applied to other research domains, such as artificial intelligence.

Psychotherapy and helping others

In the wake of psychoanalysis and behaviorism, humanistic psychology emerged as a powerful new and important movement in psychology. Led by Carl Rogers and the slightly younger Abraham Maslow, who published *Motivation and Personality* in 1954, this approach centers on the conscious mind, free will, human dignity, and the capacity for self-actualization.

Additionally, Rogers is known for practicing "unconditional positive regard," which is defined as accepting a person "without negative judgment of ... [a person's] basic worth." A well-rounded life is the goal of both Rogers and Maslow, and they describe the lives of fully functioning individuals as rich, full and exciting, and suggest that such individuals experience joy and pain, love and heartbreak, fear and courage more intensely and meaningfully than the average person.

The mystery of consciousness

The area of psychology which interests me most is awareness or consciousness, by which I mean the fact that I am sitting here at my computer trying to clearly express myself to an unknown listener or reader who may be on the other side of the globe but who, through the mystery of language, education, and mental abilities on both our parts, can grasp what I am trying to share with him. I am alertly conscious of what I am doing, and I believe that he will understand me and can share in my attempt to understand the experience of being human, in large part because of my conviction and experience that human beings are remarkably alike. My mind and his mind can communicate with each other due to the mysterious process of language and due to the equally strong mystery of being human. My intense awareness can reverberate with another human mind even long after I am dead and gone, just as Aristotle's and Goethe's have with me. I call this 'rubbing of minds' the act of being aware, conscious, awake, and this process has its own validity even if there is no other mind at the moment reading these words. I believe this factor of primordial awareness is at the heart of the great mystery of being human and is perhaps the key force in religion, poetry, philosophy, and science.

Scientists today are trying to determine the physiological aspects of consciousness: i.e. which nerve centers are involved, what factors create it, in what parts of the brain intense awareness occurs, etc. My interest is on a more elementary, common-sense basis, and I do not feel especially served by the exacting or precise discussions which specialists present. Self-awareness for me is the concept that I exist as an individual, separate from all other people, and have my own private thoughts, my own inner world. It also includes the understanding that other people are similarly self-aware.

Perhaps no aspect of the mind is more familiar or more puzzling than our alert awareness and conscious experience of the self and the world around us. The problem of consciousness is arguably the central issue in current theorizing about the mind. Despite the lack of any agreed upon theory of consciousness, there is a widespread, if less than universal, consensus that an adequate account of mind requires a clear understanding of consciousness and its place in nature. We need to understand both what consciousness is and how it relates to the many other, non-conscious, aspects of reality. How and why have the forces of life produced a mind that is not only conscious of the world around it but also of the fact that it is very aware of itself asking such questions?

When the lines of demarcation become blurred and distinctions are hard to follow, the whole discussions slips into something which might be called a "mystical" interaction between two human minds. My best example of this is everyday verbal communication between two people. This is something so commonplace that we fail to grasp the mystical or miraculous action taking place in your brain when I utter the word, 'Eskimo" or 'bicycle' and you immediately see an Eskimo or bicycle in your mind's eye. Given enough time and interest, I could unload the entire contents of my mind into yours, and your mind can in some sense enter mine, provided, of course, we speak the same language. Otherwise, we just make verbal noises at one another.

Parapsychology

This is an important modern concept, popular today, which throws some additional light on the age-old problem of determining what the human mind is and how it works. Parapsychology deals with unusual aspects of the mind: beyond (Greek *para* means beyond) conventional psychology. It is controversial, of course, and many professional psychologists will have nothing to do with it and probably regard it essentially as nonsense. But parapsychology deals with special powers of the mind and causes us to think. Some examples:

1. Psycho-kinesis (both words from Greek meaning "mind" and "motion"). This is the power of the mind over matter: bending a metal rod, moving an object across the table, twisting a fork, etc. all without any physical contact. A man named Yuri Geller years ago caused great sensations with some of his tricks, most of which remain unexplained.

2. Telepathy (Greek *telos* = distant and *pathos* = feeling). This means non-verbal communication between minds. One person looks at the serial number of a one dollar bill, thinks the numbers to himself silently, and another person on the other side of the room repeats the numbers perfectly. I have seen this happen a number of times at large conventions between an expert (Kreskin) and a complete stranger. There is obviously something to it—at least in my opinion—even though no one knows much about it. Professor J.B. Rhyne at Duke University in the 1940's did some remarkable investigations into these matters and found that some people can consistently guess cards at a higher level than just mere chance.

3. Clairvoyance (from the French *clair* = clear and *voyance* = seeing). This means seeing objects beyond the range of normal vision. Police sometimes use

it to find kidnapped persons, and occasionally there is an amazing report in the papers and magazines about such unusual episodes.

4. UFO's or Unidentified Flying Objects, the Bermuda Triangle, etc. These have been the subject of many movies, special reports, and investigations. Most of the considerable amount of material remains unexplained, strongly believed by many people, and considered a hoax by others.

5. Stigmata—around Easter some religious people develop red spots in the palms of their hands, in the middle of their feet, and around their scalp. They are experiencing on some powerful level the passion of Christ, the crown of thorns, and the nails in the hands and feet. In some very devout people, the red spots start to actually bleed. It is pretty well documented that these things are for the most part genuine and not faked.

6. Voices, premonitions, visitations by angels or heavenly messengers—such as the heard voices and bright lights experienced by Saul of Tarsis (St. Paul on the road to Damascus), Joan of Arc, religious mystics of all sorts, as well as by many lesser people. How are these and similar things to be explained? There is simply a great deal we don't know about being a human being, and there is a great deal that we cannot explain. But experience and common sense tell us that we must keep an open, critical mind and be willing to be receptive to new information and experiences. Like Socrates said, "The one thing I know for sure is that I know really nothing for sure." We need to learn and find out.

7. The power of suggestion, especially under the relaxed state of intense concentration called hypnosis, is phenomenal. It is widely today used in medicine, dentistry, executive training, marketing, and other areas. The power of suggestion is especially important in sports, where records are often broken by athletes whose coaches have train them to use the power of vividly imagining perfect performances in their minds. Some amazing books have been written documenting unusual powers of the mind. My favorite is *Love, Medicine, and Miracles* by a Yale University oncologist and professor of medicine, Bernie Siegel. He has used hypnosis and powerful suggestions in his own practice with cancer patients and has had some amazing results. His innovations have of course brought him much sharp criticism from colleagues.

The result of this review

What is the upshot of this brief review of people, topics, and problems in the history and development of psychology? What does it teach me about the mystery of being human?

It teaches me that sensitive humans have been fascinated for centuries and millennia by the complex and multiple facets of the mind. They have developed many theories and different perspectives in their efforts to understand it. These range from religious myths to philosophical analysis to a scientific method disproving the mind's very existence altogether.

These many approaches illuminate various sides of our mental life but offer, at least for me, no general consensus on which to build and advance our understanding of what we are. We are left to our own devices, so to speak, to pick and choose parts of various theories according to our own predilections and personal life experiences. I think each of us has to work out for himself or herself an individual theory of mind, something which fits us individually. We can then modify and fine-tune our theories by comparing them with those of our friends.

In my own thinking I have incorporated much from the behaviorist's attempts to be clear and to stay away from vague, muddled-headed concepts such as the sinful nature of man and similar religious biases. Freud has taught me a lot about the powerful unconscious sides of my nature, things such as sex, violence, and intimidation. From Aristotle and Descartes I have learned the value of trying sincerely to embrace clear concepts and ideas, and to avoid murky thinking. The pragmatic approach of William James has helped me to switch tracks when a certain attack of a problem proves to be fruitless. My life-long pre-occupation with foreign languages has taught me to be constantly aware of the miraculous nature of human communication. From many poets, philosophers, and creative writers I have learned to view problems of the mind from multiple points of view but at the same time to stick with my own beliefs and convictions, and to state them as clearly and simply as possible.

My own view of the mind is that it is the epitome of life. The human mind is the most powerful, miraculous, and fascinating thing on earth and has almost unlimited possibilities for growth and development. It can grasp—at least in outline form—the Big Bang, the creation of the universe, the origin of the earth and all its life forms, the idea of evolution and the interrelated nature of all living things, time, space, causality, and almost anything else that our fellow humans can clearly present to us. Perhaps the mind's greatest accomplishment is its awareness of being able to do all these things. A clean, crisp awareness of being conscious and attempting to share this miracle of awareness with kindred minds is its own reward and recompense for all the effort involved in getting to this point. Being vibrantly alive now and knowing that this awareness will one day end puts a sharp edge on the whole venture.

Chapter 10.
Mystical insights

Coming to a conclusion

As I come to the end of this long personal account of me and the Big Bang, I try to sum up my efforts and insights with a number of pragmatic questions. The first is: So what? What does it all mean? Where does all this fumbling around with a survey of the universe and its contents leave me? Has it improved my life in any way? Have I learned anything of importance? Have I been able to share it with my reader? Am I or he or she any better off than we were?

I am confident that I am.

The two extremes

When I look again at my chart in the Introduction, the beginning and the end seem to be almost meaningless: the Big Bang at one end and my contemplation of it at the other. On the one hand, modern science presents something that we simply can only scarcely grasp: The idea that the entire mass and energy of the whole universe—all the galaxies, stars, planets, elements, everything—were compressed 14 billion years ago into something the size of a basketball, a grapefruit, or even smaller. Then this tiny something exploded, expanded, and cooled for the following few billion years and slowly formed the universe as we know it today. Then I, at the other end of the continuum, assert that in some equally strange and strained sense of the words the constitutive elements of me and my consciousness were there at the beginning and have gone through the whole evolutionary process. And the eight chapters in between try to maintain that I grasp, in some peculiar sense, how this whole phenomenon holds together.

Strange stuff, these two extremes. Both seem to be utterly absurd and linguistic nonsense, and yet it appears to be true in some way or another. The scientist tells us one thing, the struggling modern-day mystic another. How can we understand either?

Mysticism is essentially not a means of explaining man and the world such as animism, religion, philosophy, and science try to do. Mysticism, based on the insights and knowledge on these four approaches to the question of existence, tries not so much to explain but to experience. Knowledge in itself is not enough; something is lacking, and mysticism tries to fill that void. We know, for example, that humans are mortal, but something is lacking and only occasionally do we really feel what we know. My escape hatch from a feeling of being trapped in an impersonal, mechanistic universe—i.e. of being a meaningless piece of complex material floating around in an equally meaningless continuum of time, space, energy, and matter—is to be in agreement and at one with the Big Bang and all that it entails. I want to have a modern *unio mystica* or mystical union with 14 billion years of reality, to knowingly and willingly participate in it. The German philosopher Nietzsche calls it *amor fati*—to love what must be. My desire is to create meaning and purpose in an otherwise meaningless universe by aligning my energy and intelligence with the energy and intelligence of the cosmos. I want to be a part of it, and it to be a part of me.

Remarks on mysticism

My choice of ultimate values or priorities is consciousness, awareness, being alertly awake to the experience and mystery of being alive in an almost unbelievably complex, beautiful, and fascinating world of natural forces, a world which is full of amazing animals and life forms, including men and women with god-like intelligence and sensitivity. To consciously experience one's self and the surrounding world is for me the ultimate mystery and value: We are all living in the very midst of the greatest kind of miraculous experience possible. We need only to awake and become aware of it. Previous mystics, poets, artists, philosophers, scientists, and theologians have pointed out the path and direction in their own way; we can learn much from them, even if we don't actually follow their path.

Chapter 10. Mystical insights

Getting started: What is mysticism?

Mystics are a strange lot, and we must spend a little time saying something about what mysticism is, what mystics do, and how one decides who is and is not a mystic.

Mysticism is a state of mind, a desire to get as close as possible to reality, to some ultimate substance and value in life. In this sense mysticism is related to religion, philosophy, art, and even to science, although only few scientists would easily admit to being in any way "mystical." This quest for a feeling of closeness to reality seems to be as old as mankind itself and can be found in cultures throughout the world. Fortunately for us, a few sensitive seekers have had the time, leisure, and skill to put into words the story of their search and the results they have attained. Unfortunately for us, their reports are often presented in concepts, images, and terminology difficult to understand. The word "God," meaning some ultimate something, is perhaps the most common as well as the most difficult to comprehend and will plague us throughout our discussion.

And this leads us immediately into two of the central aspects of all mysticism: its very personal nature and the problem of communication. Today, for example, we all use the term "God" and assume that our listener understands with this word essentially the same thing we do. "Do you believe in God?" we ask each another, and when our listener says "Yes, of course!" we feel comfortable and assured that we understand one another. If she were to say "No, I don't believe at all in God! What do you mean by 'God'?," most of us would be hard pressed to explain our position. The more we try to explain ourselves, the more evident becomes the problem of adequate communication faced by all religious thinkers and mystics. In any serious discussion of such matters, it quickly becomes evident how personal and individual our position is concerning such ultimates as God and reality.

A large part of our problem with each mystic we study will consist in trying to get inside his mind, so to speak, and understand what his words meant to him. If he uses the word "God"—which most of them of course do—we easily become lulled into complacency and think we understand his meaning quite well. So we must be acutely aware of the inevitable problems of language and communication as we go along.

Problems of communication

Like all of us, mystics want to believe that their feelings and convictions are caused or prompted by some objective or external something, some situation, force, or entity quite distinct from themselves. To say clearly what that something is often causes them problems, and they usually rely on

188

available, pre-established concepts and names such as God, Reality, Nature, Existence, Being, etc. I call my motivating something the Big Bang and its consequences.

Explaining oneself and giving reasons for one's feelings is difficult under the best of conditions, and these difficulties are all the more pronounced in the nebulous area of mysticism. The result is that mystics and the various messages of mysticism are typically difficult to grasp. Perhaps only people who are intellectually open-minded or even predisposed to understanding esoteric pronouncements will be able to go beyond the surface level of important messages from fellow humans. The famous little book of the Chinese thinker Lao-Tzu, the *Tao Te Ching,* is a good example of what I am trying to make clear here. For 2500 years people have sensed its importance without being able to clearly interpret its meaning, and yet it is one of the cornerstones of Oriental thought. An illustration closer to home is the difficulty most of us experience in trying to explain to ourselves and others our love for wife and children. Explaining feelings, mystical or otherwise, is difficult, if not impossible, and yet we all try to do it. Feelings are one thing, explaining them is quite another.

Communication is the first big problem of mysticism; the second is its very personal nature. A friend asked me recently for whom I am writing and what kind of audience I have in mind, and I had to think long and hard to find the answer. Then it came to me: I am writing for myself. I am not writing to convince anyone of anything, nor to change their way of life, nor to sell them a book, nor to gain their admiration, nor to demonstrate what a clever fellow I am, nor any such thing. I am trying to get clear on my own thoughts, to see what I think about my life, and to try through words to get as close to some ultimate reality as I can. An ideal audience would consist of fellow seekers and searchers, each struggling in her or his own way to make sense of being here on this earth.

I find that feelings and words are intimately connected, and that words help me get in touch with reality. Learning and thinking and writing and knowing and sharing are approaches to feelings, and feelings are the end, the ultimate purpose, of action. And of all these activities, writing is the only one which is definite, clear, and permanent. Writing also has the dual characteristic of being very subjective and personal on the one hand, and yet quite objective as well on the other.

For the majority of us, religion by and large satisfies the very human desire to know, and generally we accept without question the religious interpretation of the world given by our culture and then get on with our lives. Philosophy, an outgrowth of this fundamental human desire to know, is not able to accept without question the answers given by religion and continues to investigate the nature of things, often at their own peril. Some thinkers long ago were not content with divine explanations and continued to ask and search for other, less mysterious answers. Then, in 585 B.C., the Greek philosopher Thales started a new chapter of human inquiry by correctly predicting a solar eclipse. He and his followers are usually considered to be the beginning of both philosophy and science in the Western World.

Thales, philosophy, and science

Thales and later philosophers created both philosophy and science by developing a new method of inquiry based on rational thinking and discussion rather than uncritical acceptance of tradition and the current authorities. The arguments and inquiries of these early thinkers were followed wherever they might lead. There were no taboo subjects, and all matters were subject to investigation, with reason, logic, and clarity serving as the only authorities. Discussion and inquiry were encouraged rather than discouraged. Geometry and mathematics were regarded as the great models of clear rational thinking and demonstration of proof. Modern science is the ultimate fulfillment of this venerable desire to know. In its purest form and with a little emotion, science can become almost mystical in the sense of deeply satisfying the very natural human desire to know.

The religious, faith-based method of emotion, authority, tradition, and early indoctrination stands in stark contrast to the scientific method based on reason, logic, experimentation, observation, trial and error. The former method locks a person into a secure, established world view, whereas the latter exposes him or her to doubt and uncertainty by giving them the right to think and decide for themselves. The disparity between these two methods has persisted from the earliest beginnings up to the present day; it leaves many of us in the modern world in a quandary, especially in relation to the fundamental questions of meaning and purpose in human life. The only resolution that I can find to this widespread dilemma of combining ancient religious problems with the overwhelmingly complex new world of science and technology is a new type of mystical approach based on religion, philosophy, and science.

Despite the dangers involved with using terms like 'mystical' and 'mysticism,' I call this new approach mundane or pragmatic mysticism. It combines the deeply emotional religious questions of meaning and purpose with the clear rational thinking of the philosophers and adds to them as much of the results of modern science as I have been able to acquire and understand. The result is a very personal interpretation of the world as I experience it, and I think many people probably find themselves in a similar situation. By studying the history of religion, philosophy, science, and mysticism, I have learned that my questions and concerns are very similar to those of many other people, past and present. Just as others have been compelled to come to terms with their times and circumstances, so also must I. And if I, then probably you as well.

Someone has suggested as a working definition of mysticism, "a direct experience with ultimate reality." I take this to mean that each searcher is in a sense a mystic and has to determine for herself or himself what "ultimate reality" is. My ultimate reality has these three thick layers: religion, philosophy, and science, and I am trying to experience reality as productively as I can by putting it as simply as possible into clear words and sharing it with others. I think this is what mystics, poets, philosophers, and scientists over the centuries have tried to do: share their experience of ultimate reality—however they define it—with their fellows.

Mystics and mysteries

We all know the words 'mystic' and 'mystical,' and we are pleasantly surprised to learn that they are related etymologically to 'mystery' and 'mysteriously', but most of us would find it difficult to say what a mystic is or give an explanation of a mystical experience. Images of Tibetan monks meditating in a monastery night and day, or an Indian guru sitting crossed-legged on the floor repeating the magic word OM, or people talking about leaving their body during a near-death experience, would come to mind for many of us, if asked to give an example of mystics or a mystical experience. Religious people would tend to think of great mystics in the Church who strive for a *unio mystica* or mystical union with God, or St. Francis of Assisi talking to the birds and animals of the forest, or the Blessed Virgin being visited by the Holy Ghost.

Mystic and mystical mean a lot of different things to different people; mystery and mysteriously are more commonly used in daily speech and relate to things or situations that are unclear or problematic, like UFOs, speaking in tongues (glossalalia), or the laying on of hands to heal sick members of the church. So we all have some acquaintance or knowledge of mystics and mysteries, even though our concepts and explanations may be vague and unclear.

Origins of mysticism in the Western World

The early Greek mystics were primarily fascinated by the reproductive power of plants and animals, plus the related questions of birth, growth, decay, death, and resurrection or rebirth. Part of the mystery was also the progression of the seasons and its relation to life and death: New life bursts forth in the spring, grows and develops during the summer, matures and reaches its high-point in the fall, then withers and dies in the winter, waiting somehow to be reborn the following spring. Mystics then and now inquire into the mysterious forces surrounding all of us: how tiny acorns become mighty oaks; how the sun goes down on one side of the world and comes up the next day on the other side; how a male and female adult create a new specimen of their own kind; where the person goes when his vital spirit has left his body; where all these people came from in the beginning; how things constantly change and yet in some sense remain the same? These and a thousand similar questions have stared mankind in the face from the beginning.

To our educated minds today, formed by the intense scientific research and technological development of the last three or four centuries, many of these questions no longer seem particularly mysterious, and we may smirk a bit at the naiveté of our ancestors, but we must be careful and try to put ourselves back into the more childlike mentality of a simpler time. Our great grandchildren will probably have to do something similar to understand us.

Out of the early attempts at understanding our world arose Greek philosophy and science, thinkers who were trying to understand the mysteries facing them. These men are what we might call "intellectual" mystics, since they were trying by and large to grasp and formulate intellectually the mysteries as they saw them. Their approach was in contrast to the emotional, authoritarian attempts of various religions to explain man and the universe. Plato and Aristotle might be called two early models of great intellectual mystics.

We find a mystical element in nearly all Greek philosophy. The Orphics of the 6th century B.C. maintained a mystical-speculative theory of religion. They held that the soul was divine in its origin and therefore naturally pure, and that the body was its tomb. The Pythagoreans, at about the same time, had much in common with the Orphics, and were responsible for the ethico-mystical doctrine of the transmigration of souls. Lead the life of a dog and you may come back as a dog in your next life. They held that the soul was immortal, that is, it has something of the Divine in it, and that the body was only its temporary prison. The end of man was to become like God. The poet Pindar, along with the philosophers Socrates, Plato, and Aristotle, felt that the soul was akin to the Divine and consequently immortal in some sense.

Plato had a profound influence on virtually all subsequent thought in the Western World by clearly distinguishing between a temporal, surface reality of appearance and a deeper, permanent world of unchanging forms. Individual men come and go, but Man is unchanging and not subject to restrictions of time, place, or local circumstances. The same holds true for abstract concepts of beauty, truth, justice, and it is with this permanent world of abstract ideas that the philosopher must concern himself. Plato held that the soul existed in a heavenly realm of Ideas before becoming incorporated in a specific body, and all knowledge here in this life is a sort of remembering of the soul's encounter in that realm of Ideas before being born. The soul is incorporeal, eternal, and the essence of the individual human being. God is the Idea of all Ideas, the Form of all Forms, and is that towards which the soul strives in an attempt to be reunited with its source.

Aristotle, although he was chiefly concerned with the scientific classification of the phenomenal world, had a considerable influence upon mysticism and succeeding mystics. God, which Aristotle called the "Unmoved Mover," was that which is absolutely real. The Unmoved Mover is a living, perfect, eternal, motionless energy which moves the world simply by being, like the lover is moved by the sheer existence of the beloved. The impulse of the soul is to be at one with the eternal being in the world, and the only way open from man to God is the way of pure contemplation, in which, according to Aristotle, beatitude or perfect happiness consists. By pure contemplation it is possible to pass beyond what is accidental and transitory, beyond the limitations of time and space, and at last to contemplate the absolute. Man possesses an "active reason" which is divine in origin, is indeed one with the divine reason, and in contemplation the soul is at one with that which it beholds. God is pure thought, a thinking on thinking, and man's ability to think makes it possible for him to participate in the divine. This idea of the power and importance of thinking permeates much of later thought in the West.

Stoicism, arising in the 5th century B.C., gave its adherents the concept that man could come into a close relation with God by fostering the divine element within themselves. In this way, men could come into contact with the divine mind of God. The Stoics believe that the human mind is like a spark from a divine fire, and that the purpose of life is to keep this divine spark alive and pure, and then return it to the universal fire at death. To the Stoics, as to other mystics, purity of heart and life was an indispensable condition of spiritual attainment. The inner spirit must free itself from everything individual, from emotion as well as from sensation, in order to become one with divine reason. Only by surrender of all that is personal and materialistic could the spirit of man make its way to, and become one with, the universal spirit.

But the school of classical philosophy which had the most far-reaching influence on mysticism was undoubtedly that of the Neo-Platonists, and among them the master-mind was Plotinus, a pagan thinker in the third century of the Christian era. He gathers up the threads of the older Greek philosophy, plus the ideas of Plato and Aristotle and the Stoics, and in his teaching we find a mystical doctrine of great power and spiritual insight. He was the most profound thinker not only of his own age but for many ages to come. At the heart of his doctrine is his belief in the essential unity of the universe; everything is an emanation from one central source, which Plotinus calls The One. There is in the universe a movement downward from The One towards man and a movement upward from man towards The One, whom the early Christians were pleased to call God. *Me and the Big Bang* seems to be a variation on the same theme; it is also an example of how people continue to think in very similar patterns.

Christian mysteries

With the advent of Christianity, the attempt to get close to the powerful and mysterious elements of life took a decidedly different turn. Interest in the external world became much less significant and was replaced by a completely different set of mysteries: God as creator of the universe; the triune nature of God as Father, Son, and Holy Ghost; the very real existence of heaven and hell; an eternity awaiting all humans; the story of original sin and salvation only through Jesus Christ; the Virgin Birth; the death and resurrection of Jesus; the Second Coming of Christ; etc. These mysteries were to exercise some of the most learned men and women for almost two millennia and continue today to be crucially important mysteries for many people. We can call this "religious" mysticism, and it has its counterpart in Judaism and Islam.

The clash between the intellectual mysticism starting with the Greeks and the religious mysticism of Christianity has been one of the central chapters in the history of Western Civilization. The conflict represents two different approaches as to what the basic mysteries are and how they can best be investigated. It involves the age-old conflict between faith and reason, between authority and independent thinking, and between the rights of the establishment to assert itself and the rights of the individual to do with his life and mind what he thinks best for himself.

A closer look

Mysticism is the personal attempt of an individual to get as close as possible to whatever he or she regards as ultimate reality or the most genuine kind of being. For the sake of simplicity and ease of discussion I will label this final or ultimate state of reality or profound being simply as "reality." This is perhaps confusing because we all tend to think we know pretty well what reality is and see nothing particularly mysterious or mystical about it. At the same time, however, many of us would probably want to distinguish between a normal "surface" reality and deeper levels of reality which impress us from time to time on special occasions.

In this discussion of mysticism, "reality" will be taken to mean the deepest—or highest—level or kind of ultimate being that we know or can imagine. "God" is a good shorthand term for this sort of ultimate; "nature," "mind," "creative urge," "intelligence" are other useful terms. Aristotle speaks of the "Unmoved Mover," Plotinus calls it "The One," Lao-Tzu refers to "The Way," and there are surely other useful designations to indicate whatever we can imagine as an ultimate or final something lying behind or deeper than normal surface, humdrum reality. My conviction is that virtually all of us have some inkling of a "higher," "deeper," "more real" kind of existence or force than what we experience on a day-to-day basis, even though we are generally quite vague and uncertain as to what we actually mean. It is a personal, subjective feeling, and this quiet feeling is at the heart of mysticism. It usually takes some practice or training in meditation to arbitrarily get to this point of profound insight, but sometimes life simply throws it at us, whether we want it or not. The cause can be a near-death experience, the sudden loss of a dear friend or family member, unusual experiences of all sorts. I think we all have deep levels of which we are scarcely cognizant.

The mystic is a person who is aware of something more important and more powerful than himself and intensely wants to align himself as closely as possible with that something. The devout Christian wanting to lose himself in the warm love of God the Father is a good example; the person sitting quietly in a forest or at the beach who wants to feel herself intimately identified with the power and flow of nature is another. Mysticism takes many forms; it is personal and individual. The true mystic is one who has sufficient courage, confidence, energy, and desire to go his own way and create his own mystical union or alignment with reality. This will exclude the majority of us, since most will be content to join a religious crowd and follow a prescribed set of beliefs without undue personal interest, inquiry, or doubt. And that's as it should be, since most people are preoccupied with more important things closer at hand: family, job, money, sex and personal relationships, and a thousand others. The mystical approach is neither better nor worse, it's just different and appeals to different people under different circumstances.

Kinds of mysticism

My own study leads me to believe that there are only a few basic kinds of mysticism and that most mystics can be grouped in perhaps four or five broad categories: nature mystics, religious mystics, intellectual or mind mystics, and social mystics. In trying to classify the various types of mystics, it might be helpful to use the image of climbers trying to scale a high mountain, with the top of the mountain representing the most intense and gratifying form of existence possible. The peak has various names: God, Allah, Brahman, Nature, the Unmoved Mover, Tao or the Way, the One, the Sacred Ultimate. All the climbers want to get as close to the top as possible in order to merge or be at one with whatever they consider to be the ultimate and highest. The four or five paths to the top might be briefly characterized as follows:

**Nature mystics seem to be the oldest group historically, but they are hard to differentiate from the religious mystics because the powerful forces of nature were deified early on and then worshiped as gods, as seen in the Greek gods of Mount Olympus. Probably every drunkard sees himself as worshiping Bacchus or Dionysius, and every whoremonger as a disciple of Aphrodite.

**Religious mystics are perhaps the most numerous and most widespread kind of mystics. They are what the popular mind most easily recognizes as "mystics." Their highest reality is generally a personal god with whom they want to be on the most intimate terms possible, either as parent-child or bridegroom-bride. Saint Francis of Assisi, St. Teresa of Avila, St. John of the Cross, Hildegard of Bingen, the American Thomas Merton, are examples.

**Intellectual mysticism counts few adherents but includes some of the most illustrious names in philosophy and science. Reality is experienced by these mystics as an expression of creative intelligence and can be best approached through knowledge and understanding: Plato, Aristotle, Plotinus, Spinoza, Isaac Newton.

**Social mystics see their fellow humans as the Sacred Ultimate; humanity itself is the top of the mountain, and social mystics want to lose and find themselves in service to their fellows: the Buddha and perhaps Gandhi and Mother Teresa are examples.

**Life mystics, art mystics, creation mystics, and perhaps other possibilities wait to be explored and explained.

The mystic path

How does one become a mystic? Some people say that no one chooses to become a mystic of his own volition; rather, he or she is pushed or propelled by some experience or situation into a new state of being, either dramatically at one occasion or slowly over a longer period of time. Sometimes there is a sudden, overwhelming experience such as that of Saul on the road to Damascus, where a blinding vision of Christ turns Saul of Tarsus on his way to persecute the early Christians into the Apostle Paul who carries the new religion into all the known world as the Apostle to the Gentiles. Even in such dramatic cases as that of St. Paul, St. Francis of Assisi, or Martin Luther on the way home in a thunderstorm, there has usually been a long build-up of inner conflict and struggle; then a conversion or illumination of some sort forces them into a new realm of experience. Sometimes the turning point comes quietly after a long period of study and meditation, as in the case of Gautama Siddhartha in India who gently turned into the Buddha or Enlightened One after years of fasting and introspection.

In many mystical traditions there is talk of a method or path to becoming a mystic, with definite steps or stages along the way which prepare one for the intense experience of enlightenment or union with God. In the Catholic tradition the mystic way is roughly divided into three stages: purgation, contemplation, union. The first stage is one of repenting and cleansing one's soul of distracting elements; the second stage consists of prayer, meditation, and single-minded focus on God; the third stage or union with God is a complete loss of self and the merger of the individual ego into God. This *unio mystica* or mystical union with God is described by Catholic mystics in several ways, the most common being that of the love union of the bride (the soul) with the bridegroom (Christ), or the lost child returning to the bosom of a loving father.

Ways of looking at the world

There are various ways of viewing the world. One way it to regard it as a more or less intelligible phenomenon spread out before us which we can examine in a detached and dispassionate manner. Its nature can be grasped by thought, discourse, investigation, analysis, and classification. This is the view held by most philosophers and scientists and is the one that educated people can readily embrace and accept.

Another view says that the world is not like that at all, that it is a "mystery," the secret of which can be only partially grasped by thought, analysis, and classification. This view holds that in order to penetrate into its inner essence and deepest secrets, we must not stand apart from it but become engaged in it by trying to feel and experience it, to become part of it. This other view says we must behold and contemplate the world in the same way we gaze at a picture, not to analyze its brushstrokes and painting techniques but to penetrate its meaning and significance. This kind of loving contemplation can become a tool of knowledge, another way of knowing things, but it heavily emphasizes and involves the mind of the viewer, with all the problems that that involves. This contemplative approach easily leads us into mysticism; watching children play or the sun set can become far more than the simple facts as they appear on the surface.

Expanding our awareness and knowledge

I think our awareness can be expanded by our experience in terms of both time and space. Let me explain the expansion of space first, since it is perhaps easier to grasp than the expansion of time. Until Copernicus, a sensitive person could have a pretty firm concept of space: the earth and the vast heavens circling around the stable home of humanity. Space was huge and could extend far out to the planets and fixed stars, but it was still manageable and comprehensible. But then Copernicus with his new theory put the earth up in the skies alongside the planets and stars. Trips to the moon have allowed astronauts even to photograph our earth floating around in a vast continuum of space, and the Hubble telescope has expanded our concept of space immeasurably with pictures of galaxies millions and billions of light years away. The upshot here is that our consciousness of the size and extension of space has grown exponentially in recent years.

Something similar has happened to our awareness of time. Bishop Ussher in England around 1650 wanted to know how old the earth is, so he read the most authoritative source available, the Bible, took notes, and calculated that the entire universe began on October 23rd in the year 4004 BC. The emerging science of geology in the 18th century soon destroyed that tidy bit of knowledge and began pushing back the age of the earth by tens of thousand and millions of years. Then Darwin's theory of evolution in the 19th century offered evidence of life on earth hundreds of millions of years ago. The sciences of astronomy, spectroscopy, and carbon dating in the 20th century shifted the entire counting system over into the billions of years for the age of the earth and the universe. The upshot here again is that our consciousness of time has grown exponentially in recent times.

The central point here is that our consciousness grows, expands, and becomes at ease with greatly expanded ideas of time and space which would have been unthinkable in past ages. As our consciousness develops, we become capable of incorporating stunning new ideas into our thinking and our world view. These vastly enlarged concepts of time and space eventually become standard parts of our general world view.

An explosion of awareness

Along with an explosion of knowledge in virtually all fields of endeavor comes also an explosion of awareness. We all know, for example, that the earth revolves daily on its own axis and annually around the sun. Knowing it intellectually is one thing, being aware of it is quite another, and this awareness aspect is what I find so interesting. Increasing factual knowledge is the task of the scientist, increasing our sense of awareness of this knowledge is the task of the thinker and mystic, for lack of a better word. Mystic and mysticism are perhaps unfortunate words because of their connotations in the popular mind with seances, telelocation of bodies, telepathy, telekinesis, communication with the dead, and other sorts of esoteric, otherworldly experiences.

What I mean by "mysticism" is a sharp, focused awareness of what scientists are telling us about the world and ourselves. Things such as the fact that this huge earthen platform on which we are located right now is actually revolving on its own axis at about 1000 miles an hour, that our earth is in fact a special sort of spaceship hurtling through space with a crew of some six and a half billion members, that the hair on our body clearly relates us to the 200 other primate species and all the other mammalian species as well. Mysticism, in my view, is the attempt to grasp this kind of knowledge experientially, that is, in more than a merely intellectual way. I often find this hard to do.

I like the words 'mystic' and 'mysticism' because they tie us into an old, venerable tradition of people trying to connect with some form of being on a higher plane than that of humdrum, daily reality. Most of them were related to some religion, but not all, and all of them were exploring higher levels of consciousness, which is my primary interest. I think most of us have had some moments when daily reality becomes in some sense more "real" and more intense than normal. Falling in love comes to mind is an example of what I mean by an altered state of mind. What I am working on is something similar, but based on scientific data and commonly acccepted factual knowledge. Look at "Me and this tree" as one of my attempts to articulate my "mystical" meaning. Poets and sensitive, creative people of all kinds try, I think, to do something similar and have done so for centuries.

Me and this tree

Just across from our balcony is a large California pine tree in which I have hung a couple of bird feeders, along with a hummingbird feeder which I placed just inside the balcony. I often sit on the deck, watch the birds come and go, and try to get in tune with the pace of life happening right there in front of me. Behind the tree are flower beds and a lawn with nice green grass. There is also a pesky squirrel that comes from time to time to feast on the seeds which I have set out for the birds. The tree, the birds, the flowers, the lawn, and that pesky squirrel are all manifestations of vibrant nature existing at varying paces of life right in front of me. Judging by their movements, the humming birds are living at probably the fastest tempo, followed by the birds at a more leisurely pace. Although we see no rapid movement among the flowers and grass, we know that they are also living entities, changing, developing, and aging in the course of a year or so. The pine tree shows no external changes at all over long periods of time, but we know that it too is a living creature which comes into being, reaches maturity, reproduces, and in time will die and go out of existence. I am attracted above all to that pesky squirrel because of his high degree of awareness, especially when I get my long pole and try to knock him away from the bird feeder. I look at him, he looks at me, and something seems to happen between us, two intensely alert creatures of nature. I try to spend some time every day observing and studying this scene.

I am also a living creature following the same organic pattern of life which these fellow creatures are following, each at our own pace and for our own duration: the flowers for a season or so, the lawn perhaps somewhat longer, and the birds and squirrels may continue for a year or more. The tree and I are much longer lived, the tree probably longer than me. Since the tree and I are slower developers and will live longer, I feel a special kinship with it. I think right now we are probably about the same age and are both glorying in our full maturity.

As I sit contemplating these things, I try to understand myself as a part of this flow of life; I try to feel myself into a sort of harmonious union with these other life forms. We are all creations or products of the universe and want to feel at one with it. I think that they probably feel more at home in the universe than I do, but I also want to feel at home and be at peace with the cosmos, like a child in the bosom of its family and not like some alien creature apart from and unattached to other life forms. The mystery and power of life are overwhelming, and I am clearly part and parcel of that mystery.

So I figure I should stick to the words "mystic" and "mysticism," at least until I find better words. Aristotle coined the word "metaphysics," meaning 'things after the physical things,' and perhaps I should call my undertaking "meta-science" or "meta-knowledge," meaning therewith this focused awareness or acute consciousness of the knowledge which our scientists are continually giving us in ever greater abundance.

The value of perspective

Again, the German poet Goethe said about two centuries ago, "He who cannot give an account of history for the last three thousand years is a poor fool and will have to live from day to day." (*Wer sich nicht von drei tausend Jahren Rechenschaft kann geben, ist ein armer Tor und muss von Tag zu Tage leben.*) He was probably thinking chiefly about the known course of human history, including the rise and fall of entire civilizations. For the modern person, those three millennia have expanded into billions of years and an almost incredibly involved and interesting story of the rise and fall of galaxies and species of life as well as cultures, religions, and nations. To understand the broad outline and to knowingly participate in the drama is its own reward and can make all of us rich beyond compare, but for this an overview and perspective are indispensable.

My experience, however, has been that by and large most of us are poor fools who try to piece things together in a haphazard way and make sense of them day by day. This is quite understandable since the majority of us are too busy fighting the daily battles of life and do not have the necessary time, energy, or interest to concern ourselves with these large and ultimately meaningless questions. In times of need, our local religious leader, preacher, guru, psychiatrist, or popular philosopher will gladly help us over any rough spots. I feel especially privileged to have spent virtually my entire life investigating my own questions: Who are we? What is this world where we find ourselves? What are we supposed to be doing? Does anything make any difference after all? and similar "useless" inquiries. And after a lifetime of spinning my wheels, so to speak, I am still convinced that this was the most meaningful and rewarding thing that I could have done with my life. What is true and valid for me, of course, may not be at all true for you or anyone else. As Joseph Campbell says in his many discussions on myths and the human situation, each of us must discover and then "follow our bliss."

I have duties and responsibilities toward my fellows, my society, and indeed toward the whole human context. But I think that we humans are all so much alike and are so intermeshed with one another that I can make my greatest and most meaningful contribution to other humans by striving hard to be the most sensitive, informed, energetic, and compassionate person I can be. And probably much the same holds true for you. I think virtually all the great thinkers and spiritual leaders essentially agree on this point. There are many different ways to get to the top of the mountain and to merge as closely as possible with some ultimate reality, just as there are many different names for this reality. I believe that most human beings are trying to climb the mountain in their own way and to discover the meaning of their life, even if largely unawares. Many great teachers have pointed us in the right direction and shown us some of the paths; our only task is to undertake and complete the journey as well as possible in our own time and in our own way. The journey itself is its own end and the essential meaning of life; lending a helping hand to others along the way is an additional reward.

Something should be said, at least briefly, about the motivating force behind my philosophy of life, and indeed behind my life. I am quite aware of some dynamic energy which sometimes leads me, but more often pushes me through my life's experiences. Sometimes I think it is simply a raw, amorphous, vital energy or force which takes many forms: sexual fascination, intellectual emotion, desire and ambition, an urge to create, a fear and repulsion towards boredom and apathy, a lust for life in all its forms and manifestations, the sheer joy of experiencing the flow of life in, through, and around me. It seems clear to me that there is obviously some motor or force which drives us all, and it drives us at a higher or lower pitch during various stages of our life. People call it by various names: life-force, *élan vital,* God, nature, reality, evolution, will, desire, love, libido, cosmic energy. I don't know what it is, but I see and feel it everywhere, from the tiny insect crawling across my page as I write in my backyard to the growth of a blade of grass to the movement of the planets and stars. We need not name this pervasive energy, but we do need to be aware that without it there would be nothing. Being aware of it, experiencing it, and trying to grasp it emotionally and intellectually are among the greatest joys and pleasures in my life.

The evolution of consciousness

My real interest is consciousness. By this I mean I want to be as alertly aware as possible of what's going on inside and outside of me. I start with the obvious fact that I am here and the universe is here, and that there is an intimate relationship between us. We are connected. I feel confident that, along with you and the rest of us, and everything else, I am a child or creation or natural product of the universe and consist of basic universal substances. I want to understand what that means and I want to understand as much as possible this fascinating universe in which we all exist. The earliest beginnings of consciousness began in some sense, I think, with the origin of the universe itself and has, like the whole cosmos, gone through a long, complex evolution. I think that the development of consciousness is closely tied up with development of the universe, although I really don't understand how or why. Let me state the absolute bottom line of my thinking straightaway. I believe that the universe itself is coming into consciousness, becoming aware of itself, through its creatures, like you and me. We are all involved in one gigantic, miraculous process of evolution. Wow! It will take a bit of doing to explain this, and that has been in large part the aim of this essay.

Modern science tells us that the universe is somewhere between 13 and 15 billion years old, give or take a few hundred million years, and I believe that consciousness or awareness of many kinds began its evolution—its coming into being—at the moment of the Big Bang. Not only the elements of my consciousness began then, of course, but also the consciousness and evolution of all life and all sentient being, plus the existence and evolution of the galaxies, stars, planets, moons, including time, space, energy, and matter. Everything that exists began its embryonic development at the same time.

So the Big Bang was a fruitful and significant moment for everything there is, and we have all come a long way in the meantime. The whole thing is an amazing, on—going, almost incomprehensible story, and I want to find my place in that story.

This long inquiry harks back again to the ancient Socratic notion, "Know thyself!" I start with the Big Bang as one extreme point in the story and end up with the notion of my being consciously here and now at the other extreme. I see everything as being related in one huge continuum, with a definite beginning but perhaps no end. The origin of everything we know—time, space, matter, energy, the cosmos—started with one mighty explosion, and at the other end of the spectrum I am sitting quietly at my computer trying to work out and articulate some of these complicated thoughts in order to understand them for myself and to share them with other searchers and seekers.

An oasis

While writing this book I am well aware of creating a kind of inner oasis for myself, and perhaps for others as well, for the difficult times which will eventually come in the lives of us all. Death awaits everyone, sooner or later, as we all know. Many of us will probably have occasion at one time or another to ask ourselves, "What was my life all about?" But to ask it at the last moment is cutting it very short, and there may not be time to hear the answer. The more curious among us will perhaps want to know what anyone's life, or even existence in general, was all about. And we will need some time for those answers.

In thinking about such questions in advance, I am trying to avoid a panic situation in which we have only minutes or hours to sum up our time on earth and determine its significance. I don't want death to catch me by surprise, so I build a rather elaborate answer in advance, not that my doing or anyone's doing will make the least bit of difference in the larger scheme of things. Panic-stricken people grasping at the last straws of life or calm philosophers embracing the inevitable will all die in the end. But I would prefer to die like Socrates, calmly questioning, experiencing, and accepting reality to the very end. Whether or not I can actually do that in the final hours is another question, but we will see what happens when the time comes. The idea of having an intellectual, emotional, and pre-arranged oasis to retreat to will be helpful, I think, at that moment. The very thought of having such an oasis brings calmness and acceptance of a day-to-day basis. It helps me now and will, perhaps, later at a more turbulent moment.

The value of wisdom

All this knowledge and thinking and striving for understanding gets us perhaps a little closer to wisdom, and wisdom is a precious thing. We all know intellectually that we must die, for example, but the more we understand the process of coming into being, of growing, developing, reproducing, maturing, and aging, the better able we are to accept death willingly as a natural complement of life. I believe that this is wisdom, and for the sake of this wisdom I will gladly embrace and freely accept death and extinction. I do not need an extension of my existence in some form of afterlife. I have had the full-blown human experience of living, loving, traveling, learning, reproducing, knowing, gaining and sharing wisdom with my fellow humans, and that is its own reward, and quite sufficient unto itself. To have had the time and leisure to study the Big Bang, the creation and development of the universe, the evolution of life and humans, the creation and unrolling of civilizations, the wonders of religion, philosophy, and science, is its own reward and justifies everything.

About the author

Richey Novak was born and raised in Texas. After sailing the oceans of the world for five years in the engine room of a US Navy light cruiser, he studied languages and philosophy in the US, France, Germany, and Mexico. He earned the B.A. and M.A. in philosophy from Columbia University and the Ph.D. in German from the Johns Hopkins University. He also received certificates in language and culture from the University of Paris, the University of Heidelberg, and the National Autonomous University of Mexico.

Dr. Novak taught German at Wilson College (a small Liberal Arts college in Pennsylvania) and at Duke University, where he received the distinguished professor award in 1975. He and his wife, Dr. Sigrid Scholtz Novak, then taught English at the Abadan Institute of Technology in Abadan, Iran, for four years until forced out of the country by the Iranian Revolution in 1979. They spent the following fifteen years teaching languages and humanities at McNeese State University in Lake Charles, Louisiana. They were then for two and a half years visiting professors of English at the State University of Ceará in Fortaleza, Brazil, before retiring. The couple now lives in Southern California and has two sons.

In addition to academic books and articles, Dr. Novak has published three books dealing with the broad questions of meaning and purpose in life: *The Mundane Mystic: An American Approach to Mysticism* (1st Books Library, 1999); *The Call of the Cosmos: An Introduction to Pragmatic Mysticism* (1st Books Library, 2002); *My Life Story: Physical and Metaphysical* (AuthorHouse, 2006).